The
Yellow
Finch,
a # Black
Bikini,
and a
Rat Called
Hernandez

A Memoir

WENDY FREDELL

RIVER GROVE
BOOKS

This book is a memoir reflecting the author's present recollections of experiences over time. Its story and its words are the author's alone. Some details and characteristics may be changed, some events may be compressed, and some dialogue may be recreated.

Published by River Grove Books
Austin, TX
www.rivergrovebooks.com

Distributed by River Grove Books

Design and composition by Greenleaf Book Group
Cover design by Greenleaf Book Group
Cover images used under license from ©Adobestock.com

Publisher's Cataloging-in-Publication data is available.

Print ISBN: 979-8-90052-015-5

eBook ISBN: 979-8-90052-016-2

First Edition

In memory of my husband, Lars Fredell, and my sailing mate, Lee Adamson

Contents

Prologue

"Darling—Lars must be so proud of you! You always look so beautiful, and your figure is perfect. You're so slim." Maud, my Swedish mother-in-law, says these uplifting things as I prepare for a business conference with my husband, Lars. She's our designated babysitter while we're away, and I know that once we're out the door, she will immediately immerse herself in making her delicious Swedish *pepparkakor.*

This is in the spring of 2002, in our house in Redding, Connecticut. I continue packing for our four-day trip to Amelia Island, in Florida, for a rendezvous with the crème de la crème of the Canadian beauty industry along with the top French perfume companies and fashion houses. I pack my off-the-rack clothes—not Chanel, Gucci, or Armani like the women attending the conference.

Every year I manage to pull it off and make Lars look good. I beam with pleasure when women in designer clothing ask, "Where did you get that? It's really nice!"

On our first evening at Amelia Island, beautifully dressed women gather around each other, wanting to be seen, wanting to be admired. I watch the dazzling crowd of men and women laugh and joke and flirt with each other. *I'm fine just as I am,* I remind myself. Admittedly, self-esteem has always been a struggle for me. Trying to hide this from the world around me, I find solace in repeating silent affirmations under my breath.

I stand beside my husband, watching him entertain a group of men and women who are laughing loudly. He loves being center stage. I clench my teeth as he holds a full glass of red wine in his left hand and gestures grandiosely like an orchestra conductor while talking. Used to dodging wine droplets, I move discreetly into the background to avoid another expensive dry-cleaning bill.

Lars loves to flirt. Usually I put up with it and even flirt a little myself, but tonight, I'm not in the mood to be ignored by him, so I scoot out the door and walk clumsily toward the elevator in my painful, pointy high heels. As soon as the door closes, I whip them off while thinking, *I'm finally free. Hallelujah!*

Hours later, feeling a little miffed, I stare at the ceiling in the dark wondering how to pay him back. Suddenly Lars lumbers through the door and then crashes into the side of my bed. His tux halfway off, he falls instantly into a deep sleep. Soon the snores start. I shake his arm gently while asking, "Would you please stop snoring?" This is met with grunts and even deeper, more intense snores.

So, wrapped up in three blankets, I move to the balcony overlooking the ocean seeking peace and quiet, but slumber is fragile here too. The loud, piercing cries of the seagulls and the rhythmic movement of the waves are lovely sounds, but sleep eludes me. My body is toasty except for my nose which is freezing. And Lars's powerful snorts have snaked their way through the sliding glass door to the balcony, further ruining any possibility of sleep.

Early the next morning, I try not to disturb Lars as I prepare for an ocean kayaking trip with my adventurous friend Sandi. After that we'll rent bikes and head to American Beach, the first Black beach in the US, which is just a mile south of our hotel. Shortly before we leave for Sanibel Island, I read an intriguing article in the *New York Times* about Amelia Island's most famous native, MaVynee Betsch, and I decide that I want to meet her in person. When I question a local tour guide about MaVynee, he exclaims, "She's so strange! Her nails are about three inches long, and they curl like claws. And her hair is waist-length. It's wrapped like a hose around her head then over her shoulder, then her chest, then the rest sits in a small purse at her waist. And she never bathes! She stinks! She's weird!"

I don't care. I want to meet this woman. From the locals, I learn that her millionaire great-grandfather Abraham started the first African American insurance company in the US and founded American Beach. Since his death, she has served as the protector of the beach, which the fancy resorts are rapidly encroaching on.

At American Beach, Sandi and I approach four elderly men sitting at a card table under a collapsing carport roof. "MaVynee might be at the grocery store," says a toothless man with skin pulled tightly over high cheekbones. "Someone usually drives her there on Thursdays. Her house is over there. Just knock on the door."

No one answers, so Sandi and I take pictures of each other in front of Maven's small trailer, which is covered with environmental and feminist stickers. On our route back to the highway, we pass tiny bungalows with small signs in front stating "The First African American Beach."

The following morning, Lars is out cold after another late night of flirting and partying, so I borrow his rental car keys and head out the door, forgetting to leave a note behind as to my whereabouts. I'm feeling a little miffed because he ignored me again most of the night. Unable to locate Sandi and her husband in the huge crowd, I spent the evening again introducing myself to people I'd never met. That only went so far. Their eyes glazed over when I attempted to connect beyond the basic questions such as "Where do you live? Do you have children? Do you work in Toronto? Ottawa? Montreal?"

I had hoped Lars would pull me into conversations with his business compatriots. It would have made it easier for me to interact.

I'm determined to meet MaVynee this time. I learned that she's a philanthropist and an active environmentalist. She's been written up in countless newspapers and magazines, including the *New York Times* and *National Geographic*, and was the subject of a documentary filmed for PBS. Earlier in her life, she was an opera singer and sang in *Madame Butterfly*, *Carmen*, and *Salome* in Germany.

I'm thrilled when she answers the door and then leads me to her porch, where we sit and chat over a cup of coffee. As MaVynee tells me all about her life, I glance at the buttons in her hair that say "Save the Rainforests," "Save the Honey Bees," and "Save the Butterflies." Not wanting to leave, I spend the entire afternoon with this soulful, enlightened being.

She pats me gently on the knee when I mention Lars's behavior the previous night. "Remember, Wendy, you are a goddess, and you are above this."

My heart lifts when I hear her say this. It is as if she just plugged me into something deeper. I leave MaVynee that day in an elevated state of mind. For quite some time, I've yearned for something more meaningful in my life, and I feel the beginnings of a strong shift inside.

Feeling guilty over not answering Lars's calls, I finally answer just as I'm waiting for a table at a small local restaurant. Sounding contrite and wanting to make up for ignoring me, he begs me to come back. On my return, after a long heartfelt hug, he promises to be more attentive when we're in social situations, especially when we're in a room full of people I hardly know. I realize he's not ignoring me on purpose. He gets carried away in the moment and forgets to include me. Now that I've made my point, I'm sure he'll be more thoughtful.

Soon after our return to Connecticut, I receive an exciting invitation to join Toronto's Wild Women Adventure Club. I'm absolutely thrilled because during this last business conference, Sandi introduced me to several women who love traveling together to exotic places. I've longed to find like-minded women to explore the world with. Perhaps my dreams of visiting Nepal and climbing Mount Kilimanjaro will finally come true.

Unfortunately, fate steps in the way of my dreams.

1

The Yellow Finch

You can die making love, playing tennis, shoveling snow, mowing the lawn—or walking through Arrivals at an airport, like my husband. That morning I dreamed that my family and I were standing around our bed where Lars lay with his eyes closed.

It is June 28, 2002. On that spectacular cloudless summer day in Redding, I am feeling energized and happy after my brisk hike in the woods. My usual walking partner, Lena, is away for the summer visiting her relatives in Sweden.

My son Alex just celebrated his eighteenth birthday five days before, and we are looking forward to seeing Lars, who is returning from a short business trip to Toronto. Our plan is to have dinner that evening at our favorite Italian restaurant in nearby Ridgefield.

Lars routinely travels to Toronto, Montreal, and Ottawa. He works for a prominent international company in New York and is the general manager for all of Canada. Alex and

I are accustomed to his travels, which sometimes include Africa, Western Europe, Asia, and the Caribbean.

This summer, Alex is working as a lifeguard at a local park while I work part-time at my friend Gregg's upscale flower shop in nearby Georgetown. I recently ran Fisk & Company for two weeks while Gregg vacationed in Provincetown, Massachusetts. Just before closing one day, two refrigerator-sized packages arrived from UPS and took up most of the available space in the tiny shop. I'm not sure how I ever managed to unpack them within inches of delicate vintage lamps and flower arrangements in porcelain antique cachepots perched precariously on rickety pedestals. It was a close call. Thankfully Gregg wasn't there to witness the near fiasco.

On summer weekends, our lifestyle is laid-back. Lars and I usually take walks together if the weather is decent. When Alex isn't busy, he will go with us to movies and restaurants in neighboring towns. My favorite restaurant is the Italian one in Ridgefield. Their eggplant parmigiana is the best I've ever had.

On other weekend afternoons, Lars and I share a bottle of wine on our deck overlooking the woods while we take turns minding the grill. If Alex isn't with friends or playing video games, he'll join us. During those tranquil moments, Murphy, my white American Cocker Spaniel, rests at my feet while we discuss the happenings of the past week plus Lars's upcoming business travels.

On that hot and humid summer day, I leave work a little early so that I can collect Murphy from Mr. Hitt, the groomer, before Lars arrives from Toronto. On my way there, I have a premonition that something is wrong—very, very wrong. Feeling off-center, I stammer a little as I talk to the groomer.

Shortly after picking up Murphy, I receive a call. "Are you Mrs. Fredell? This is Northwest Airlines. Your husband was taken to St. Agnes Hospital in White Plains, New York. Please phone the emergency room."

I think about Lars's half-full glass of water by the bathroom sink and his dark grey socks on the floor where he left them, reminders of his presence there only two days ago. But he isn't returning. Ever.

That very morning I had a dream about my family and friends standing around our bed, where Lars lay with his eyes closed.

For the past six weeks, a small yellow-bellied finch had perched on the ledge outside our bedroom window and appeared to be looking into our room. Since it always flew away when I tried to show it to my husband and Alex, I was the only one who saw it.

"Please give me the name of a friend I can call for you," the doctor at St. Agnes is asking after he delivers the bad news.

In my shocked state, no one comes to mind. *Oh my God, this isn't happening.* Then I think of Mia, who lives nearby. She and her husband arrive within minutes. At home, friends and neighbors quickly fill the front porch as the news of Lars's death spills out into the neighborhood. At the sound of Alex coming down our long gravel driveway in his blue Subaru, I run to intercept him.

Bewildered and scared, Alex asks as he steps out of his car, "Mom, why are all these people here? What's going on?"

It is like being in a dream—or rather, a nightmare. All the people on the front porch, Alex in his fearful state, me in shock, and Lars gone from our lives forever. Nothing prepared me for the sudden death of the man I'd fallen madly in love with in Sweden thirty-two years ago.

———

In 1968, I joined UC Berkeley hippies, draft dodgers, and Ingmar Bergman aficionados at the University of Stockholm. I almost canceled my year of study there after meeting Emillio Arenales Catalan from Guatemala, who introduced me to his father, the president of the General Assembly of the United Nations. After begging me to let him pick me up in Stockholm in his father's private plane, I said no. Someone else was now at the forefront of my mind.

We met on a blind date. Lars drove a secondhand canary-yellow Porsche with high mileage that had an annoying habit of breaking down on Stockholm's narrow bridges during rush hour. He was from a famous family with close connections to Carl XVI Gustaf, the King of Sweden, and Volvo. And his maternal grandfather was the tennis partner of the former King of Sweden at Wimbledon.

A year later, we married in my hometown of Anniston, Alabama, nestled in the foothills of the Appalachian Mountains. My parents' house was situated on a mountain overlooking the city on one side and Choccolocco Valley on the other.

Three weeks before our wedding, there was a glitch with Lars's application for a US visa, so my father called a family friend who was the current postmaster general in the Nixon administration. President Nixon gave his personal go-ahead for Lars to enter the US two days later. Meanwhile, an outrageous rumor spread around Anniston that he was a Swedish prince, and we laughed over our short-lived fame.

Did Lars have any inclination that something was wrong that day as he walked down the long, crowded Arrivals hallway carrying his well-worn brown leather briefcase filled with papers from a corporate business meeting in Canada? What were his last thoughts? It is heartbreaking that we weren't given the gift of saying goodbye. Even worse, we never had a chance to make up with each other. We'd had a disagreement the evening before, and he left without saying goodbye to me or Alex. The thought of it still stings.

A dynamic, brilliant, and creative man, Lars was a good provider and an anchor for me. He had wonderfully thick, softly greying blond hair, high Scandinavian cheekbones, a cleft chin, an upturned nose, and friendly blue eyes framed by thick, wiry, salt-and-pepper eyebrows.

When Lars entered a room, he was soon surrounded by people who were captivated by his colorful stories, his charming Swedish accent, and his charisma. Everyone enjoyed his frequent, possibly intentional, mispronunciations of English. A wide-angle lens was pronounced "wide angel lens," "vine" was the name for wine, and a wheelbarrow was "vheel barrow." In response to his often describing himself as a "wedgetarian," I explained that vegetarians don't eat meat, chicken, or fish. Lars would insist, "No. I'm a wedgetarian."

Resigned, I would retort with, "Whatever."

After ten years in Sweden and England, where Lars worked for an American cosmetic corporation, we moved to Connecticut with our two sons: Thomas, who was born in Sweden, and Markus, who was born in England. Lars finally realized his lifelong dream of living in America.

As we built our life together, I discovered that my husband had some annoying habits. He drove with one foot on the gas and the other foot on the brake, so anyone unfortunate enough to ride with him became carsick within a few minutes.

At social gatherings, he gestured like an Italian, showering red wine on anyone standing nearby. I always stepped away as soon as he started sweeping his hands dramatically into the air. And since he usually knocked over wine glasses during dinner parties, I sat as far away from him as possible.

He was a time machine. If you weren't in the car on schedule, he would start driving slowly down our long, rain-rutted gravel driveway. I would run after the car while clutching my purse and my heels, sweating profusely, and he would slow down just long enough for me to jump in.

Our house, which overlooked the forested hills of Connecticut, used to vibrate with the sound of Lars's enchanting music. My sons grew up to the sounds of Steely Dan, Jeff Beck, Mike Mainieri, Flim and The BBs, The Fabulous Thunderbirds, Moby, Dead Can Dance, and Supertramp. These are just a few of the many musicians he listened to on his world-class music equipment. According to music aficionados, Lars had one of the best music systems in the country. He was a well-known reviewer for *Fi*, *Ultimate Audio*, and a Swedish hi-fi publication.

Audiophiles take music to a whole new level. These people are interested in all the components that go into the making of a record plus how accurately the musical instruments are reproduced on vinyl. The object is to make the listener feel as if they're at an actual concert.

It's been estimated that only one percent of the population can be classified as audiophiles. These folks give their undivided attention to music over a hi-fi. Lars had an amazing listening ear and could even detect the subtle moments when a singer takes a quick breath.

The creation of a good listening room takes a lot of knowledge and expertise. My husband had various audio treatments such as acoustic panels to make the room more neutral which means having sound absorbed and bounced off in the right places. He also had discs made of mpingo wood from a company called Shun Mook. These are used to regulate resonance and dampen and eliminate bad vibrations. In the corners of his listening room were big towers to counteract undesirable sound vibrations. Lastly, he had a sensitive microphone with a measurement device connected to his laptop. He could position that microphone exactly where his head was and make micro-adjustments to his speakers to achieve the best effect.

I loved his music so much that while I stood at the kitchen sink washing the dinner dishes, my hips would start moving to the music's beat, and I would dance and sway across the slippery wooden kitchen floor. His music always had a way of transporting me into a different realm.

Soon after his death, a headline in *Stereophile Magazine* read, "Lars Fredell, the World's Greatest Audiophile, Dead at 58." His fame in the audiophile music world grew exponentially, mostly because *Stereophile*'s most beloved writer, Sam Tellig, who was Lars's best friend, wrote comical articles about his unusual use of the English language. Readers of the magazine believed he was just a figment of Sam's imagination.

"Are you *the* Lars that Sam Tellig writes about all the time?" a man at the annual Las Vegas Consumer Electronics Show once inquired. "I thought you were just a fictional character."

———

According to the doctor, Lars fell face-down onto Westchester Airport's long Arrivals hallway in the midst of travelers rushing about. At age fifty-eight, he appeared to be in good health except for some recent forgetfulness. He would head out to the hardware store and then, within a few minutes, come back looking for his wallet that he left on the kitchen counter.

Arriving at the hospital, I expect to see Lars. I ask the emergency room doctor, "Which room is my husband in?"

"Mrs. Fredell, I'm so sorry," the doctor replies. "Your husband has passed away. He died instantly of an aneurysm." In that moment, my life shatters into tiny fragments. Then Alex and I are led to a chapel where we are told to wait for a grief counselor. As we sit down on a wooden pew, my son, his brown eyes agog, asks, "Is Dad laid out here?"

Within minutes, a petite nun in a crisp grey habit joins us and explains that she was present during the last rites for my husband. She reassures me that he is saved. I'm not a Catholic, and neither was Lars, but her words are comforting, and I am profoundly touched that this took place before he passed.

In the unreal dark emptiness of it all, where everything seems to be moving in slow motion, Alex and I tearfully say our last goodbyes to Lars, who lies on an examination table in the middle of a small, dimly lit hospital room. After I sign several legal papers, a nurse hands me a large black garbage bag containing his dark grey pinstriped suit, his black leather shoes, a gold watch, a well-worn wallet containing several lottery tickets, and a brown briefcase. Lars deserves something better than a black garbage bag, which seems so incongruent with who he was.

That evening, my oldest son, Thomas, arrives from Boston along with his wife, Susan, who is nine months pregnant. Markus, three years younger than Thomas, shows up the following day from Boulder, Colorado. Lars's mother, Maud, arrives soon after in her friend's 1978 light blue Chevy Malibu that has grass stains from when she veered off the road. That same day, my brothers and sisters fly in from Alabama, Texas, and Mexico.

My house is in the process of being renovated.

Friends and neighbors carefully pick their way across the muddy, slippery, newly graded and reseeded front yard then hoist themselves onto the under-construction porch that has neither steps nor handrails. After they make their way into the living room—which is cluttered with a refrigerator, a stove, and other kitchen appliances—they perch on the two sheet-covered couches and three randomly placed chairs.

Maud, wanting to be helpful, says, "Dahlink, let's fry up some salmon skin! And some bacon! How about a nice batch of butter cookies?"

Where? In the living room? The stove is in the living room, I think.

A business associate of Lars drops off a tray of roasted Perdue chicken, which unfortunately becomes a mold factory in the downstairs refrigerator because I forget that it's there. Thankfully, my messy house is beautified by the constant stream of flowers from Lars's business contacts in the US and Canada.

Three days later, in my whacked-out state, I notice a faint, almost sweet odor coming from the rear of my station wagon. I am horrified to discover that I forgot Lars's clothes, which are still in the far back. That afternoon, a close friend reminds me that I have a funeral to plan. *A Funeral? What? I have to plan a funeral?*

The fourth day after my husband's death, my first granddaughter, Tori, is born two weeks early.

A few weeks later, my childhood friend Deidre from Vermont calls to insist that I come to a black-tie dinner party in Manchester. "I'm very concerned about you," she says.

"Thank you," I tell her. "But no, I can't. No! Absolutely not!"

Deidre is persuasive, so I give in while rationalizing that it might be good for me to get away for a few days with Markus, who decides to join me. My drive to Vermont, however, is blurred under a thick downpour of tears and rain. Several times, I pull over to call Deidre. "I'm turning around. This is crazy. I'm going home."

"Damnit! Just get yourself here. No backing out." She is insistent.

Four hours later, in a room she rented for me at a local inn, I soak in a tub of hot water and then put on my makeup and a long dark blue taffeta gown with a deep décolletage that Deidre brought for me.

After making my half-hearted entrance, she pulls me aside. "We need to get you a husband. *Fast!* I'm going to find someone for you tonight. You're fifty-four years old."

The two potential marriage candidates she picks for me are great guys. Fun, interesting, handsome—and gay. She means well, of course, and I appreciate her desire to find a husband for me.

I've known Deidre all my life. When school was out in the summers, I visited my grandparents in Scarsdale, New York. She lived directly across the street, and I was always thrilled when her family invited me for sleepovers. Five years older than me, Deidre was like an older sister, and I wanted to be just like her one day. Oddly enough, we both ended up living in Connecticut in our adulthood, where we renewed and now cherish our lifelong relationship. On our monthly lunch dates, she enjoys imitating the heavy Southern accent I had as a child. And she always claims I looked like Shirley Temple with my blond sausage curls.

When we meet again several weeks later, Deidre advises me to put my house on the market immediately. "Honey, buy yourself a set of business clothes and apply for a job in a corporation," she says. Knowing, however, that I'm not ready to make any major decisions, let alone apply for a job, I thank her for wanting to help.

————

The apparently endless conveyor belt of fried chicken, potato salad, and quiche continues to arrive. I rationalize that alcohol is the way to go because it will break down the cholesterol from all the fried chicken.

I tough it out during that desolate, lonely, depressing year with the welcome company of Markus and Alex. Thomas is having his own struggle with grief in a suburb outside of Boston with his wife, Susan, who lost her father the year before.

I live and relive the ongoing pain of Lars's sudden death from morning to night. I am in crisis mode. We all are. Bravely, I try to create a sense of normalcy while coping with ongoing financial disasters. Having no appetite, I force myself to eat regular meals. And Rachmaninoff, whose music plays constantly in the background, helps relieve some of the desperation I feel.

My older brother, Tommy, an Emmy Award–winning television writer, distracts me by asking me to help him write segments involving Sweden for the soap opera *Another World*. While working on the Swedish dialogue and other relevant information about the culture, I blissfully escape reality. At least for a while.

Upstairs there are piles of clothing everywhere and boxes

half-filled with miscellaneous items. A partially packed grey suitcase lies on the floor next to my bed while a myriad of unfinished renovation projects and unused plumbing parts taunt me. Dust covers everything, even my clothes in the closet. I am deeply angry at myself because I can't finish things. What I *really* want to do is to rent a pickup truck and haul everything to the dump. But I can't. I know I will regret getting rid of the things I so carefully collected over the years.

"I'm still standing," I affirm to myself daily as I try to deny the psychic pain. "It's all going to work out. Everything's going to be fine." Truthfully, I am terrified of being abandoned, not to mention the ensuing loneliness that comes with it. I had never lived without someone taking care of me. My parents, then my husband, had always been there to support me emotionally and financially.

One day, I cry all afternoon and into the evening. Jackie, our cleaning lady, approaches me in her turtle-tentatively-peeking-out-from-under-its-shell manner. In her halting English, she asks, "Are you okay?"

I look into her brown eyes big with worry and think, *how sweet of her to ask.* "I'm okay," I say hugging her.

A few days later, I find myself in the office of the middle-aged CPA recommended by Lars's company. The man has a bulbous head, a ruddy face from perhaps too much alcohol, and a pretentious upper-crust accent. I am fascinated by his lips. And his eyes. The inside line of the upper lip comes to a point in the center, giving him a bird-like appearance, and his eyes resemble the brown buttons on my jacket. After quickly spreading out a stack of financial papers onto his desk with great fanfare, he basically says I am screwed. Suddenly feeling wiggly, squirmy, and uncomfortable, I decide that this beak-faced man is a sadist who is out for my blood.

"Well, I've got to go," I say, suddenly standing up. "To be honest with you, I'd prefer to contact someone else. Thanks for your time."

Frank, Deidre's high-powered Greenwich estate lawyer, remarks after reviewing my file, "This is going to be the worst year of your life. You can't afford me but Ted, my assistant, will handle your case. I'll oversee his progress."

I watch as Ted pulls out my papers from a worn-out accordion file. "Fredell" is sloppily written across the top. *Wow*, I think. *He looks like Paul Simon in his heyday.* His dark hair is cut neatly into bangs, and he has deep, sexy brown eyes and a boyish persona. *Maybe I could take him home and take care of him.* Suddenly my inner parent chides, *Stop that! Behave yourself. Focus. Concentrate.*

Frank ended up handling my case, and eventually, the whole team of lawyers became involved in putting out all the fires following Lars's death. During one of our many group meetings, the financial expert in the group states, "This is the most complicated financial mess we've ever seen."

I begin to look forward to my weekly appointments at the law office, which I think of as a social outing and a way to leave hibernation mode for a few hours each week. My time at home is spent wading through an endless, depressing collection of legal papers strewn across the new grey granite countertops in the kitchen. The remainder of my time is spent trying to figure out what to do with years' worth of stuff.

Another social outing is probate court. Frank stated during my last visit, "Don't worry, Wendy. The probate court is here to protect mothers and their children." So I view the probate process as something positive, not humbling. Knowing the judge personally helps too.

I find a less expensive builder to finish the interior and exterior remodeling jobs. Wooden handrails are installed on the completed wrap-around porch, and Thomas and Susan paint them white while Tori sleeps in her stroller nearby. Alex plants miniature boxwoods along the front of the house while Markus paints the outside of the house light sage green. Joanne and Nancy, my two younger sisters, arrive from Alabama to help me repaint the four upstairs bed-rooms. Friends visit occasionally, tiptoeing gingerly across the muddy yard, and, not knowing what else to say, ask, "How are things progressing with the house?"

During that year of hell, not one of the neighbors asks how I am coping with the new unwelcome version of my life, nor how I am feeling. Life just moves on without me.

During the daytime, I take short breaks from dealing with the mountain of legal paperwork and all the hellish details related to the inevitable sale of my house. During these moments, I drift slowly through my house like a ghost, often slumping heavily into Lars's favorite armchair, where I stare blankly out the window at the ancient oak tree in the front yard. The life I once thought of as *normal* has now irrevo-cably shifted into something alien and unwelcome while everyone around me goes about their usual lives. The same questions cycle through my mind ad-nauseam: *Who can help me sell my house? Where will I go? What will I live on?* Overwhelmed, I don't know where to start.

"Don't make any major decisions for a year after a spouse has passed away" was the advice given to me when Lars died. *At least I can lay the groundwork for the upcoming necessary changes,* I reason. *And if worse comes to worst, I can join a circus or the gypsies. Or even find a nudist colony. Of course, I'm not sure my sons would approve.*

The home we lived in for twenty-five years was transformed from a typical boxy New England Colonial into a small-scale version of a South Carolinian low-country plantation. I dreamed about doing this for years. My house stands on a ridge overlooking two hundred and seventy acres of open space where Edward Steichen, a world-famous photographer, once lived and photographed the trees, stone walls, and creeks that I see every day on my long hikes. I always find peace and solace on the woodland trails that lead to Topstone Lake, where my sons spent their childhoods fishing, canoeing, collecting salamanders, and learning to swim.

Mark Twain was Redding's most famous inhabitant. In this beautiful town of about nine thousand people, miles and miles of footpaths meander alongside rivers, gurgling streams, and pine tree–covered hillsides. The whispering forests and the wetlands are carpeted with skunk cabbage, which, when brushed against, gives off a pungent odor. The thought of leaving it all stirs up an aching feeling that I can't shake. I know I will miss my solitary wanderings in nature and the frequent appearances on our property of white-tailed deer, pheasants, Canada geese, and male turkeys making weird noises, feathers all fanned out while strutting about in the midst of a clutch of admiring females.

That long year following Lars's death is filled with endless hurdles as one life shuts down and a strange, unwelcome, and unfamiliar life slowly comes into being. During that traumatic and devastating period of transition, I drift ghost-like through my house, crying and feeling abandoned, lonely, and hopeless. Teary-eyed, I think about how my sons lost their rock, their protector, their advisor. Lars, an empathetic father, always patiently listened to their dreams and hopes and shared his wise insights. I spend as much time as I can with them, but I can't replace him.

Every day presents a new, disorienting set of challenges, and I never know what to tackle first. The legal papers on the counter? The daily chores? *Everything* screams for my attention. Watching my life fall apart fast and furiously, I wonder if I will ever be able to trust anything in the future.

People are afraid to talk to me. What can they say? They have their lives. Their husbands. Their houses. Their security. Their normalcy. All of those things were wiped away from my life instantaneously, and I wasn't prepared. But how could I have been prepared? No one is. I, alone, have to figure out how to navigate my present hell.

So I go through all the motions while trying to look like I have it all together—though obviously I don't, to anyone looking closely enough. At the local grocery store, I hope no one will notice me. If I see a familiar face, I hide behind a magazine rack or a floor display. Or run to a different aisle. I can't handle their discomfort over not knowing what to say.

My mother-in-law, Maud, the daughter of a Swedish lumber baron, went through an entire fortune in her youth while cavorting in Madrid with jet-setters, Picasso, James Michener, bullfighters, and Spanish royalty. Now, after Lars's death, Maud calls me weekly for money. In a grandiose voice she says, "Dahlink, you must be *very* well off now! I'm sure Lasse left you a *lot* of money."

We always did our best to help her, but under the present circumstances, I can no longer afford to offer her the same financial support. Nevertheless, I continue to fetch her in New Hampshire for our bimonthly get-togethers in Connecticut. My right upper arm bruises from the way she clutches it when she wants to make a point. And the most sensitive place on my back yelps when she digs her finger into it.

But there is simply nothing to be done about it. The million-dollar life insurance coverage that Lars had claimed would keep me funded for the rest of my life is nonexistent. There are just enough funds left in Lars's retirement accounts to pay the monthly bills and the mortgage for one year, plus the hefty real estate tax in the early spring. Lars, like his mother, squandered away the money.

The endless rains that summer create a semitropical atmosphere in the basement. Mold is growing on the furniture and all the odds and ends that I store there. The mice have built a nest on the underside of Maud's Louis XIV chair, and the sterling silver is almost black. I don't care. I just want to get rid of everything.

———

It is time to move on and put the house on the market as soon as possible. Feeling overwhelmed, I don't know where to start, much less whom to turn to for advice or where to go after I sell my house.

I start by gathering together all the things I no longer need or want and put them aside for my upcoming tag sale. The evening before the sale, I hang my husband's collection of silk ties on a rack in the garage. Among them are his favorite pink tie with grey stripes and the green tie that he always wore at Christmas. Suddenly feeling weary, I ball up the rest and throw them across the room. *Why in the hell did I plan this tag sale?* I wonder as I gather Lars's leather belts and coil them on a shelf. The one he wore most often is the expensive brown leather one, which was buckled on the last hole. An admitted chow hound, Lars used to worry about his weight, which slowly crept up over the years. The daily assortment of fresh pastries offered in his company's break room was too tempting to ignore.

Each jacket that I hang on a clothes rack carries memories of international business dinners, live music venues, and evenings with friends. One still has the faint odor of cigar smoke. His red ski outfit brings back memories of our snowy vacations in the Northeast and Canada. I want to bury my face in the fabric and simply give up. *I'm so tired*, I think. *I just want to go to bed. But the tag sale is looming . . . I need to get this over with.* So I return to Lars's clothes entwined with memories. *I can't believe he's gone. He was here one minute. Then gone. Life is so scary.*

Audiophiles arrive at my tag sale eager to buy Lars's extensive collection of vinyl records and CDs. That same week, my neighbor's teenage son sells Lars's high-end stereo equipment for me on eBay while my sons and I divvy up what is left of Lars's massive CD collection.

I am filled with anxiety about this new, unfamiliar terrain. Everything in my life has changed. *How will I survive?* I wonder. *Where will I live? What do I do next? Will I be alone for the rest of my life?*

My two part-time jobs, one in floral design and the other in graphic art, will not give me the income I need to live in Fairfield County. The foundation beneath my feet no longer feels solid. All the knowns in my life that I take for granted have now dissolved into unknowns. A friend, gently patting me on the back, reminds me to focus on solutions not problems. I try but often fail.

It is heartbreaking that the house renovation I yearned for would not be mine to enjoy with my husband and my family.

I have no choice though. I simply cannot afford to live in my dream home. And even if I could afford it, the isolation of living in a small rural town would be a challenge for me as a single woman. Now in my fifties, would I become marginalized? Fall from grace? Never fall in love again?

Selling my house, on the other hand, would untether me from all the responsibilities that come with home ownership. I would *finally* have the opportunity to come into my own and create a brand new life. But what would that new life look like, and how would it be different than the old one? *Am I living the life that I really want to live?*

———

There are some bright spots amid everything going wrong. I continue working at hoity-toity Fisk & Company, an upscale Fairfield County flower shop frequented by rich women. Most important, my boss (the owner, Gregg) makes me laugh hysterically. Since I am suffering from brain overwhelm and consequently unable to make decisions, I even let him think for me. In short, his head becomes my head, which gives my brain a little respite.

One afternoon when I return home from work, Alex approaches me with a handful of telephone messages jotted down on small scraps of paper. Kim, the features editor at *O, The Oprah Magazine*, has been trying to reach me. When I *finally* get around to calling her, she comments, "You writers are all alike. You're impossible to reach!"

They want to publish my essay "A Budding Genius," which is about my landing a job at Fisk & Company. Totally inexperienced in the floral trade, I lied during my first and only interview about my previous floral design history, which was limited to designing wildflower arrangements for my mom when I was six years old.

"Have you designed flowers professionally?" Gregg asked.

"Yes, of course," I said in a slightly miffed voice.

"Can you do French provincial or the English country look?"

"Yes, of course," I said again while wondering how I'd pull it off.

Months later, feeling concerned about the upcoming Oprah article, I admit the truth to Gregg. What a relief it is when he lets out a loud guffaw.

Not long after, Oprah picks my essay to be included in her book *Live Your Best Life*. Her personal camera crew makes the trek to Redding from New York City to photograph me in front of Gregg's shop. It is a wonderful bright moment in the midst of everything. I am only sad that Lars—an author in his own right and the biggest supporter of my writing— did not live to see it.

2

Black Crows in Beaufort

In early June, almost a year after Lars's death, I awake with an intuitive sense that it is the perfect time to sell my house.

The day before, as I wandered down Main Street in nearby Georgetown, I noticed signs that said "Change is Good" on three different storefront windows. Maybe this is a go-ahead signal from the universe. So I put my house on the market that very day.

A few hours later, I receive an offer from the head of World Wrestling Entertainment. Oddly, it had been raining nonstop in Redding for weeks on end. But on this day, the sun comes out. It is one of those clear, dark-blue-sky days, and I begin to feel optimistic about my future.

Sorting out what to keep, what to give away, and what to sell is stressful. Friends often drop by the house to give me back rubs and words of encouragement. Six weeks later, a moving van hauls most of my belongings to a storage unit. The manager there helps me consolidate my furniture into a fifteen-foot by five-foot unit. He says, "I've never seen such nice things! No one here has the fine things you have."

Having noticed that the contents of twelve units there are about to be auctioned off, I say, "Whatever you do, don't auction off my things."

Following a friend's advice, I rent a small fifties-era cottage for one year in Milford, Connecticut. It's one block from a beach overlooking Long Island Sound in an old-fashioned, slightly worn-down Italian neighborhood where men in wife-beater shirts flex their muscles and occasionally drop half-smoked cigars on the sidewalks. The only sounds are the distant whir of cars on Usher Street, screen doors creaking, and the occasional startled yap from a dog.

A house down the street was once a flophouse. The local fish market, according to a neighbor, sells stolen lobsters. And Patrick next door calls his wife a witch behind her back. In spite of Milford's proximity to Long Island Sound, the air here brings back memories of when Lars and I lived in England, where we always had a layer of soot on our window ledges.

Why in the hell did I move to Milford? I ask myself almost daily. *Giving birth to a new life can be messy and uncomfortable.* It turns out suburban life isn't for me. I am used to a woodsy, private lifestyle. On the positive side, it is close to Hartford, where Alex will be entering his freshman year at Trinity College in the fall, so I will be able to watch his rowing events in New England. Conversely, it's an hour's drive on the backroads to my job at Fisk & Company.

On my days off I have time to catch up with myself, my

body, my brain, my empty refrigerator, my laundry, and the half-finished essay that I promised to write for the Milford newspaper.

On my very first day there, I receive a gruff call from the other next-door neighbor. "Your dog is making a lot of noise. *Do* something about it!"

That same morning, when I attempt to walk outdoors while holding a cup of coffee and Murphy on a leash, the creaky, hard-to-open screen door slams into me, causing the coffee to run down my arms and legs. Then, on my way back, the door slaps me so hard that I am propelled like a bullet into the house.

Every morning at sunrise, Murphy drags half-asleep me to the beach in the penetrating morning chill. Long Island Sound, sometimes as still as a lake, is usually hidden under a heavy grey mist in the early hours when the sky and the water blend together under the ashen fog. It is hard to decipher where the beach ends and the water begins. The seagulls standing watch on the dirty dark sand ignore us on these morning walks. Sometimes a neighborhood lady with sparse strawberry-blond hair, swollen eyelids, and possible short-term memory loss will try to pet Murphy, who spurns her attempts with a low growl.

That winter, it rains almost daily, and I start to feel as if I am in a *Blade Runner* movie. It is one grim, drab, depressingly lonely experience. When it becomes apparent that my attempts to befriend the neighbors are unsuccessful, I give up trying.

The owners of my rental, a cranky elderly couple, apparently believe they have rented me the Taj Mahal. Not *one* day passes without Shirley and Bob dropping in unexpectedly to inspect the house. *Do they think I am a kleptomaniac? That*

I will steal their tchotchkes? Sensing they are lonely, I join them occasionally for lunch at the local diner.

When spring *finally* arrives, Milford and I become friends. I love the sounds of the waves washing the shoreline, the hum of fishing boats, the loud squawks from the green parrots overhead, the coo of the mourning doves on the roof of the abandoned house nearby, and the lonely clang of fog horns in the far distance. The rosehip bushes out front are now sprouting new growth while a profusion of white and yellow daffodils bring color to the empty lot across the street. And the wonderful briny smell in the air brings back memories of my childhood visits with my parents to the Maine coastline.

By late spring, however, I am ready to exchange the long New England winters with a gentler Southern version. My friend Sharon suggests that Alex and I relocate to Beaufort, South Carolina, where she recently moved. Since I was a boarding student at Ashley Hall in Charleston during my teens, I was already familiar with the low country. I know that I will feel at home there, so I end my lease and pay for the remaining three months.

Shirley arrives on the morning of my scheduled departure to make sure I am actually leaving. "I thought you'd be out of here by four a.m.!" she says, her eyes narrowed and her face wrinkled up into a prune-like scowl. Suddenly the image of a shrunken head comes to mind—the one I'd seen as a ten-year-old when I visited the American Museum of Natural History in New York City with my grandparents.

"Well, things are a little out of control here," I tell her, trying not to snap. "In fact, I feel like I'm about to have a nervous breakdown." The tension in the air is onerous.

Furious, she parks her withered body and her balding,

red-dyed head in the small alcove by the front door so that I have to turn sideways to get out of the house. With Q-tips and dental floss falling out of my overstuffed purse, I head to the car as Shirley runs after me, yelling, "The phones aren't working! Call Bob!"

"Shirley, can't you see I've got my hands full?"

"Well, you'd better be out of here by two when the cleaning ladies come!"

She glares at me while I sit on my suitcase to latch it. By 2 p.m., when the Brazilian cleaning ladies arrive with buckets, mops, and Lysol spray, everything I own is sitting on the front lawn.

As I am trying to figure out how to pack my car, Bob shows up. It is obvious that Bob and Shirley are ticked off with each other when I overhear him say "Maybe you'd be better off without me!"

Alex and I drive in separate cars from Connecticut. His bright-blue secondhand Subaru is mud-splattered from a recent off-roading adventure with his buddies. Everything Alex owns is wedged into his car, and he can barely see out the windows. My car is also stuffed. Clothing, shoes, toiletries, food items, and basic necessities fill every crevice.

I wrap a seatbelt around my mother's antique Chinese lamp to keep it from falling onto the floor. I wanted to, but couldn't, ditch the family heirlooms. I wasn't able to pare down—perhaps because there were so many losses in my life. Murphy, looking perplexed, watches me from the pet carrier on the back seat.

We stop at Klara's Kitchen for "the best home-cooked Southern veggies in all of Dinwiddie County." On my way into the restaurant, I ask the heavy-set greeter at the entrance, "Are the vegetables fresh?"

Looking puzzled, he asks, "What do you mean by fresh?"

"Well, you know, grown in the soil then cut and sent to a grocery store."

"Ours are *really* fresh. Straight from a can!"

"But don't you have something *directly* from the ground? Like tomatoes or corn or even lettuce?" I ask hopefully.

"Yeah, the macaroni and cheese is fresh, and the salad is out of a bag. And it has strips of carrots in it."

Weary, my brain feeling bunged up, I give up and sit down.

———

I hope that Beaufort will offer me a gentler, more laid-back lifestyle than the Northeast. And I especially look forward to a more intimate connection with the sea.

After two full days of driving, Alex and I pull onto a crushed-oyster-shell driveway leading to an elegant, three-story low-country home with pale-blue siding and white shutters which we are going to lease for a year. On our arrival, a soft taupe-colored dove with iridescent pink and green coloration walks around us as we haul our belongings into the elevator in the garage. The elderly owners are currently at their chalet in France.

Once the cars are empty, the dove disappears from sight. *Was the bird a sign? A welcome to Beaufort from an angel?* I wonder happily. Birds have always appeared at important times in my life. They seem to portend change, and I pay attention to these heavenly messengers.

"We made it!" I exclaim as I give Alex a big hug. His bedroom is on the second floor, and mine, on the third floor, overlooks the wide brackish Beaufort River, which draws a profusion of sailboats and kayaks to it on the weekends.

We spend many late afternoons that summer sitting on my small wrought iron balcony, admiring the glorious view of Beaufort shimmering like a beacon in the distance. And when the sky turns a bright golden vermillion in the late afternoons, my room becomes saturated with the same ethereal light.

Art books line the low, dark wooden bookcases beneath the windows, and a well-used easel speckled with dried oil paint guards a corner. The husband of the couple, a former art director for a corporation, is an accomplished artist.

A small open kitchen has all the necessities, and I look forward to fixing simple meals for Alex and me. I didn't know it at the time, but this would be Alex's last summer living with me. He would be starting his second year of college in the fall, and life would take us both in very different and unexpected directions.

As I stand there looking around the large room, I think, *I'll be like the woman in a Matisse painting sitting on a wrought iron balcony. And I'll write in my journal while sipping Earl Grey tea in the misty low-country summer mornings as sailboats dart about below. My beautiful dreams will be wrapped in the finest silks with colors no one on Earth has seen before and ribbons of mist from the early morning sunrise.*

Murphy takes long afternoon naps on her red plaid cushion next to my bed while I go about my chores and journal writing at the desk. Eventually, Murphy becomes bored and moves over to sit at my feet while looking up at me with her sad droopy eyes. Feeling guilty, I say, "Okay! Do you want to go on a walk?" At that point, her tail goes into overdrive.

———

The summertime heat and humidity have yet to blanket the town. Beaufort is graced with ancient live oaks whose long elegant limbs and gnarled finger-like tips stretch low over the ground like ballet dancers doing a plié. In late spring, when the ocean winds pick up, the mossy branches of the oaks move up and down in the breezes as if invisible beings are swinging them back and forth.

I feel beautiful in my summer dresses, my bare legs lightly tanned. I am in a more relaxed state of being, which is something I yearned for after my recent full-throttle rollercoaster lifestyle in the Northeast. My new life is deliciously quiet, still, and profound on many levels, and I embrace it with all my soul.

During that hot and humid summer of 2004, my son and I spend many evenings on the dock below, where we stretch out on its weathered wooden boards looking for Orion, Leo, and Ursa Major. Our voiceless desires meld with the twinkling stars above and the clicking sounds of dolphins coming up for air. In the daytime, we explore Beaufort's barrier islands, driving past oak tree forests and meadows of cattails and low-land marshes where great blue herons stand on one leg. Our mainland explorations to Hilton Head Island, Savannah, and Charleston take us along estuaries that cut through fields of green spartina where hundreds of white egrets roost in the late afternoons. We swim in the surf at Hilton Head and St. Helena Island, slurp homemade ice cream at roadside stands, and eat the low country's famous Frogmore Stew and she-crab soup laced with sherry. We dig into fresh shrimp caught by St. Helena Island's shrimp boats and ride with a tour guide in an old-fashioned horse-drawn carriage down narrow streets where plantation homes hide behind walls of ancient oaks. As

Forrest Gump country slowly works its magic on us, I begin to feel relaxed—even happy—again.

That fall when Alex is back in college, I volunteer at the Beaufort Chamber of Commerce Visitor Center as an "Information Specialist." I greet glowing, proud parents who arrive from farms and small towns all over the Eastern Seaboard to see their sons and daughters graduate as Marines from Parris Island. One thing I never mention in my spiel to tourists is that it is still legal to beat your wife on the court-house steps on Sundays. Or that a Confederate flag flies over the state capitol.

After six weeks of mind-numbing boredom, I inform the marketing director that I want to leave. Within hours, she hires me to be her assistant. The two recent articles about Beaufort, "America's Happiest Seaside Town" (*Southern Living Magazine*, 2004) and "The Most Romantic Town on the East Coast" (*Life Magazine*, 2005), are empowering to me and give me the oomph I need to sell advertising space at the Chamber of Commerce to real estate companies. In my spare time, I moonlight as the American representative for an antique company out of Normandy, France—another job with a high learning curve. Everything is going well, and I am proving that I can support myself financially.

During the latter part of my sojourn in the lovely house overlooking the river, the cockroach population increases alarmingly. At first, it is just one here, one there, but soon it becomes a veritable cockroach army. They are *everywhere*. And the roach hotels aren't working.

"Don't you dare come near me!" I spew at them after writing this short poem:

They nibble on your ears
They nibble on your vitamins
And if they could, they'd nibble on your privates.
So it's time to leave.

———

Shortly after Alex returns to college that fall, I buy a white Greek Revival cottage that has a symmetric, temple-like appearance. The large front porch with four white columns overlooks a lagoon where egrets and grey herons wade in the shallows looking for small fish at sundown. Just a five-minute walk away is a community dock on an inlet where Murphy and I continue our evening star gazing and our one-sided conversations. Murphy, as always, is an excellent listener.

After so many years in rural Connecticut, where I could barely see my neighbors, I have to adjust to living in a neighborhood. The houses, many of which are owned by Navy pilots, are on tiny lots, and sometimes I feel as if I am living in a goldfish bowl. After sundown, Murphy and I enjoy strolling along the quiet, lamp-lit streets, and in the warm soft glow of the lights, I sneak curious glances into uncurtained windows.

The family next door befriends me when the dad, a pilot, goes to Iraq on an extended mission. I pay extra attention to his two young sons, who often drop by unexpectedly without telling their mother. Eventually, Vicky wanders over looking for them, her baby girl perched on her hip. When the neighborhood pilots leave for or return from long missions, large cloth banners at the three entrances to Battery Point say things like *Welcome Home Snoopy! Good Luck Tuna! We love you Squadron 15!*

Fighter planes roar almost constantly overhead, and then the sound abruptly disappears as they soar in eerie silence. Then, all of a sudden, the roar will resume, constantly reminding me of wars taking place in the world. Somewhere.

———

The following summer of 2005, Alex lands a job as a trainer at the YMCA where I exercise after work. A man I notice but ignore asks my son one evening, "Would you please introduce me to your mom?" Tom, short in stature, lean, with an athletic body and close-cropped grey-blond hair, hides his lively blue eyes behind a pair of glasses. His dark green backpack is tricked out with a carabiner holding keys, a small flashlight, and a Swiss Army knife. I am intrigued.

A divorced Navy dentist in charge of forty dentists at Parris Island, Tom is a beloved mentor to several young dental assistants who need a father figure. He steps into my life just as I am getting settled, just as my life is calming down. Refreshingly old-fashioned and polite, he quickly becomes my best friend and my lover. The chaos and trauma left over from my husband's death are soothed by Tom's steady, calm, grounded presence. His words, "Wendy, focus on one day at a time," become my mantra.

Lying next to him in his antique iron bed in the evenings, I curl up close to him, feeling loved and protected. Even now, years later, the high-pitched scream from a jet soaring overhead always brings back memories of Tom Hill. There we are, fixing dinner together in his pretty yellow house on a street overlooking Port Royal Sound. The naval airbase is just across the bay. On weekday evenings, the fighter planes race breathtakingly low over his neighborhood, and I love the sexy roar and vibration from their engines.

Tom's home holds special smells and energies that are comforting and pure like him. Knowing that we are meant for each other, we believe that our lives will always be inter-woven. It seems like yesterday. The details are so clear and vivid.

That fall, with Alex back in college, I concentrate on Tom. Between him and my job, I have little time to devote to build-ing friendships in Beaufort. I can't wait for the work day to end so I can be with this sweet, generous, kind man who has an angel in his eyes. Together we experience the fairytale side of this romantic Southern town as we stroll in the evenings, hand in hand, along the tree-lined narrow streets in the Historic District and past Federal, Neoclassical, and Greek Revival homes built in the 1700s. Their deep green lawns curve down to the water's edge where the marsh grass grows, and their gardens teem with magnolia trees, crepe myrtle, palmetto palms, and azaleas. The plantation owners sought respite here from their rice, cotton, and sugar cane planta-tions on Beaufort's numerous barrier islands in the pre–Civil War days. When General Sherman took over the town during the war, he and his officers resided in several of these elegant homes during his long march through the South. Perhaps this is what spared Beaufort.

In the evenings, we prepare gourmet meals together, then slow dance to '60s soul music in his candlelit living room. Before he buys "our" yellow house by the sea on St. Helena Island, Murphy and I stay with him in his bungalow on Parris Island, where I awake at 4 a.m. to the startling sound of male and female drill sergeants barking orders at Marines in the big grassy fields nearby. We buy food at the PX, party at the

Officer's Club, see movies at the Parris Island Cinema, and walk Max, Tom's golden retriever, down the streets of his neighborhood in the evenings after the heat of the day dissipates.

Tom is fastidious with his unblemished shiny black car, which he always parks at the furthest end of parking lots. I sigh sometimes over the ridiculously long distances we walk to shop for groceries, see a movie, or eat at a restaurant. An English antique collector, he surprises me one day with a beautiful mahogany sleigh bed for my master bedroom. During this early stage of our relationship, he teaches me navigation terms, which ignite a desire within me to sail the seas.

One night he proposes as we walk along the town pier where the salty marsh breezes tickle our faces. Without hesitation, I answer, "Yes, I'd love to be your wife." Things are moving quickly but naturally. We both feel we are destined for each other and decide to marry the following summer.

Tom wants to have a military wedding at Savannah's Air Force Museum, so it is settled that we will walk underneath the crossed swords of his fellow Navy officers, and Tom will wear his formal white uniform. We will grow old together in the pretty yellow house near the sea. We have so many wonderful plans.

Tom continues teaching me nautical terminology, and it is with him that my yearning for the sea takes an even greater hold through our imaginings of buying a small sailboat. We would take it out on the weekends and join all the boats darting to and fro across the bay. The sea comes alive even further through his stories of living on a carrier ship during the Gulf War. His house is decorated with nautical art, and he calls the bathroom the head, the kitchen the galley, and the bedroom the stateroom.

There's no better place for a budding romance than

Beaufort. No longer lost and lonely, I feel younger, beautiful, and relaxed with Tom by my side. On the weekends, we picnic at Hunting Island State Park, a forty-five-minute drive from town. We make out like teenagers and snuggle together on beach towels until the sun dips low on the horizon, painting the clouds with swirls of papaya, red, and violet. Then we race to the car laughing, hoping to make it out of the gate before it is locked for the night.

Twice a month, Tom sends bouquets of flowers with love notes to me at the Chamber of Commerce. Late one afternoon, as I am walking back to my car with a basket of gerbera daisies, purple iris, and fragrant white phlox, a yellow butterfly lands on an orange daisy and rides there until I open the car door.

Looking at me lovingly as I put on makeup one morning, Tom says, "Wendy, you're in a whole different league. I'm so moved that you're part of my life. I love your spontaneity, your warm smile, your way of looking directly into people's eyes. Most of the men here would be scared away by that, but at this point in my life, I can do nothing less."

Not long after that, my eighty-nine-year-old father becomes ill. Several times, Tom and I drive to Alabama to see my parents when he isn't on call. That October, Dad dies after a long struggle with pneumonia. Then two days before Christmas, my mother, age eighty-three, dies suddenly. Tom joins me for their funerals in Alabama and never leaves my side. He instinctively knows how to support me in all the ways I need.

The first week of January, Tom helps me pick out a diamond engagement ring. Placing it on my finger he says, "I will love you forever. I will love you for all eternity."

One week later, on my way home from Tom's on a cold January evening, a somber feeling sweeps over me when the street lights suddenly dim. A few days later, when I pull up to my house after work, three black crows are perched side by side on the large tree branch that stretches arm-like over my driveway. When I step out of my car, they rise upward into the wind in an ominous way. Something is amiss. I have this sense of impending doom.

A few days later, when Tom and I hold each other close, he says, "I'm afraid I'm going to lose you, darling. Not to someone else, though. I'm afraid something is going to happen." Of late, he seems half here and half somewhere else, as if he has one foot on earth and the other in heaven. Is it my imagination that I see an angel in his eyes?

We are both sensing the same thing. That night, we cling to each other, both of us crying as if we are saying goodbye forever. The next day, I slide a note into his wallet saying: *I am the fiancée of Tom Hill. If anything happens to him, please contact me.*

Not long afterward, Tom calls me midday. "You're going to be upset with me. I had chest pains and went to the naval hospital without letting you know. After the EKG and a few other tests, the cardiologist said the pains were caused by a spasm in the esophagus. They gave me painkillers, and I'm supposed to take it easy for a while. Don't worry, honey. I'm feeling much, much better. I'll spend the day resting then we can meet this evening. You can pamper me then."

Around 4 p.m., Tom calls again. "Darling, I just want you to know that this time with you has been the happiest time in my life since I was a little baby. I will love you forever. I will love you for eternity."

I've never heard anyone say these words before—or since. And I have never seen anyone glow from deep inside the way Tom glows at night when he sleeps next to me. I first noticed this other-worldly radiance in mid-December when he lit up the dark bedroom, and I wondered if a beam of moonlight had fallen on him. But the curtains were closed.

An ambulance rushes toward me in the evening dusk as I drive over the long two-lane drawbridge that connects the mainland to Lady's Island. Its siren breaks the stillness of the night, jarring my senses. Suddenly I feel a great heaviness pulling me downward. I keep repeating out loud, "Tom, please don't be in that ambulance, please don't be in that ambulance, please don't be in that ambulance."

As I careen over the small narrow wooden bridge leading to the tiny island where Tom lives, I try to soothe myself by picturing him fixing dinner under Max's watchful eyes. This island is one of dozens off of Lady's Island. I race past the large pond at the entrance that brims with water lilies, croaking frogs, and lush green mangroves where white egrets roost for the night; past the golf course where Tom and I intend to play golf one of these days; past a group of large silent oak trees dripping with Spanish moss; and onto Tom's street overlooking the Beaufort River.

When I open the front door, the window shades rattle softly as if they need to speak to me. The kitchen glows with flickering candles, and an open bottle of red wine stands on the counter. Quickly dropping the ingredients for chicken Marbella onto the counter, I walk from room to room searching for him, my shoes clicking loudly on the wood floors.

"Tom? Tom?" I ask the empty air. There is no answer except the echo of my own voice in that heavy nothingness.

My voice shaking, I say, "Tom, are you here? Where are you? Please don't be the person in the ambulance. Please be out walking Max. Please don't leave me. I love you so much. I can't bear to lose you."

On the kitchen counter, I see a note reminding Tom to call his sister in Texas. Oddly, Max isn't sprawled out in his usual place on the back porch. His food bowl and chew toy stare back at me like stone statues in that god-awful silence. Max's leash inside the cabinet is missing from the hook, and for a few seconds, I feel hope. Maybe that isn't Tom in the ambulance. Maybe he is still walking Max. As I head to my car, I imagine him walking toward me wearing his beige baseball cap and the green jacket from his stint as a Navy dentist on a carrier ship off Kuwait.

The entire neighborhood is as bleak as a morgue. The street, forking right and left, dissolves into the void like two black ribbons. I suddenly feel as if a huge granite wheel is rolling over me, flattening me under its massive weight.

I drive up and down the streets of his neighborhood, hoping to see him. Then, suspecting the worst, I call the naval hospital. The receptionist says, "No one named Tom Hill has been admitted this evening."

When I call the Beaufort Hospital, the phone is passed from one uncomfortable person to another uncomfortable person in the emergency room. Finally, a doctor comes on the line and asks if I am Wendy Fredell. Feeling fragile, my voice cracking, I ask, "How is Tom? Is he okay?"

"Please come to the hospital. I'll have someone waiting for you at the emergency room entrance. I would rather talk to you in person."

For weeks, I felt something coming. It had now arrived at my doorstep, uninvited and unwelcome—and familiar. Like a replay of past events with Lars. Suddenly, I feel like that terrified, abandoned four-year-old who keeps calling out, "Mommy, Mommy, where are you?" My mother was, at that moment, in the hospital fighting for her life, and no one explained to me what was going on. She pricked her finger on a thorn from a rose bush, and it became badly infected. The doctor had given her horse serum, which, it turned out, she was deathly allergic to.

A sense of utter aloneness sweeps through me again.

———

The nurse, avoiding eye contact, ushers me into a spartan room lined with grey lockers along two of its walls. She slips away before I can ask about Tom. Staring down at my folded hands, I sense that within minutes, I will hear something that will break my heart. Why hadn't I driven to Tom's in the afternoon? Maybe I knew intuitively that he needed to be alone. *Please don't leave me, please don't leave me.* The same four words run through my head on an endless loop.

How can one day be so magical, then the next so desolate and lonely that you wonder if you've stumbled into hell by accident?

The doctor, somber, sits facing me. He leans forward and takes my hands in his while looking into my eyes. Before he can speak, I blurt out, "Tom's dead, isn't he?" Tears spilling down my cheeks, I continue, "Can I see him?"

He leads me through the emergency room, past a group of office staff who try not to stare, to a nondescript back room where Tom lies dressed in his green naval jacket and the blue and beige plaid shirt his youngest daughter gave him for Christmas.

His shirt is ripped open, exposing his hairless chest. His blue eyes are staring into a space I can't visit. Unfurling his tightly closed fingers and gently closing his eyes, I tell him how much I appreciate the love he showered over me, and how much I enjoyed our nine months together.

How could I possibly live without this man who touched *everyone's* hearts? Who wanted to start a free dental clinic in Beaufort for people who couldn't afford dental care. Who was loved by all the people who worked with him at Parris Island, especially the young dental assistants who turned to him for advice and support.

Just as his words "One day at a time, Wendy" come to my rescue, the door opens. My friend Sharon tiptoes into the room, lifts me from the chair, and then gently leads me out the door with her arm draped over my shoulder. "I'm not letting you go home," she says softly. "You can stay with me as long as you want."

Holding Tom's picture in my hand and wearing his black diving watch on my left wrist and his Gulf War cap on my head, I slide between Sharon's pale blue sheets. I want to die. Holding up my left hand to look at the pretty diamond engagement ring he recently placed on my finger, I remember Tom's proposal. "Will you marry me, love of my life? I *finally* found you. I want us to spend the rest of our lives together."

As Tom's mystery fiancée, I feel like an intruder at his funeral. Linda, Tom's ex-wife, is shocked when she notices my ring. "Were you and Tom engaged? Did you have a wedding date set?" I realize he hadn't told her or their three daughters that we were planning to marry that summer.

We were never given the chance to explore Port Royal Sound in our own sailboat or grow old together in the yellow house by the sea. We were never given the opportunity to see each other's dark sides and walk through the truths of ourselves together.

After the funeral, Tom's best friend shares what he said the day we were introduced. "I met a beautiful woman at the gym today, and I'm going to marry her." His next-door neighbor mentions that Tom's dog stayed by his side until the ambulance arrived.

Replacing any sense of normalcy, a different life emerges with its raw, jagged edges. I feel numb, frozen in time, fossilized. People avoid me. Their expressions and their body language make me wonder if they just don't know what to say to this different version of me that is so colorless, joyless, and dispirited. I understand. What can they say?

———

Thomas and Susan invite me to visit them in a small suburb south of Boston. The day before my flight, I have a hairdresser cut my hair as short as a boy's—which may be an unconscious effort to heal myself, start anew, and create a brand new life.

Cynthia, my former college roommate and a deeply cherished friend, calls me daily. "You're being asked to rise to a higher level," she tells me. "You're entering a time of being in a cocoon, and you're going to emerge into a beautiful butterfly."

Our conversations help me reconnect with my inner strength and gather the courage to live. My grandchild Tori is a welcome and pleasant distraction as she toddles about, dragging Winnie-the-Pooh across the floor. Seeing that reminds me of Winnie's famous quote: "You're braver than you believe, stronger than you seem, and smarter than you think."

The healing process begins to germinate inside of me during the six weeks I am with my family. The marketing director of the Chamber of Commerce calls me frequently to see how I am doing. One day, as delicately as possible, she asks, "Wendy, when are you coming back to work?"

Back home in Beaufort, I try to avoid grief by staying busy and working overtime. I just exist, coasting through the days and nights. Everything reminds me of Tom—the streets where we used to walk holding hands, the small cafés we frequented on the weekends, the BayStreet Book Store where we browsed books by Maya Angelou, Nicholas Sparks, Pat Conroy, and other local writers. No longer a magical, happy place for me, Beaufort feels as if it is cloaked in sorrow.

Feeling very lonely without Tom, I focus on building friendships with the women at work. They try hard to support me, but they are clueless about how to communicate with someone in mourning. They go through all the polite moves, inviting me over for dinner and questioning me about the process I'm going through while not really wanting to know too much.

There are, luckily, some angels in town who appear just when I need them. A prominent businessman with an abrasive, abrupt manner does a double take when I burst into tears during my sales pitch. He removes a small honey-colored teddy bear with a silky blue ribbon necktie from his bookcase and places it in my hands. That man becomes my friend and my best customer. And the two little boys next door, with their own perfect sense of timing, always arrive on my doorstep just when I need a distraction from sad memories.

During lunch with Anne (my former landlady who has become a friend), she says, "You got to be with an angel for a while, didn't you? He just had a glow about him. When you were together, it was like there was a halo over the two of you."

Thankfully, Father Zanger enters my life. A converted Jew from New York City and a former chaplain on Navy ships, he is now an Episcopal priest in Charleston and a well-known grief counselor who periodically travels the country lecturing on death and grief issues. During our initial phone conversation, I know in my heart that he understands what I am going through. I drive an hour and a half every Tuesday to talk to him. This man reaches deep into my being, witnessing and validating the most wounded part of me. Those weekly visits are my lifeline to sanity.

To distract myself on weekends, I become a docent for a plantation tour where I end up representing the gun room with Jaquie, the eighty-two-year-old owner. We both come from the same world: upscale Connecticut, the world of "dahling," quail hunting, private country clubs, and not giving a hoot that the pale green shag carpet in the living room became outdated in the early 1970s.

In the late afternoons, I often drive to Hunting Island, where I wander its empty beaches. One day, I am feeling especially sad and lonely, and a motley group of seabirds keep pace with me as I walk barefoot along the water's edge. At that moment, it seems totally natural to have a flock of birds as walking companions.

When I turn to head back, they startle and fly away. Moments later, a park ranger in a green uniform races toward me on his sand scooter. "That's the most incredible thing I've ever seen! What just happened? Those birds were walking with you! Who are you? Are you an angel?"

Years ago, a woman from Atlanta who is known as the Angel Lady told me that I have seven angels around me all the time. I believe they sometimes visit me in bird form because I've had some very unusual experiences throughout my life involving birds, such as the bird that appeared on the bedroom windowsill every morning the week before Lars died. On one of my darkest days after his death, when I walked to Topstone Pond for comfort, I noticed three white swans in the middle of the pond. When I stopped to look at them, they lifted from the water and circled over me several times. And here are the birds again, walking alongside me at Hunting Island after Tom's death. I could go on and on about birds. They are my messengers. I love and appreciate their guidance and loving presence.

At the time, I don't realize their presence foreshadows something auspicious just around the corner. I feel the heaviness lift from my chest because I know at that moment that something I never imagined is waiting to manifest in my life.

3

My Crazy Dream

I grew up in Anniston, Alabama, as one of five kids. We were surrounded by loving grandparents, aunts, and uncles, plus four cousins on my dad's side and two on my mother's side. I had, however, a problematic relationship with my mother, which was somewhat alleviated by my close relationship with my dad.

An outlier from the very beginning of my life, I was *always* testing the limits. My kindergarten and first-grade teachers regularly put me in time-out, and I was even suspended from school for a day when I was in sixth grade. Miraculously, I came home with decent report cards. Finally, by seventh grade, I had settled into the school routine and was well-behaved.

After school, instead of watching TV, I climbed trees as high as I could go. Balancing myself on the widest, sturdiest branches, I belted out Henry Mancini's "Moon River" or pretended I was Mary Travers of the folk music group Peter, Paul, and Mary. Oddly enough, in my adult years, I became friends with Mary and helped her with gardening projects. We spent many magical hours together in her small turn-of-the-century kitchen in Redding, Connecticut, drinking jasmine tea and talking about our lives. If I'd been able to glimpse this future at age twelve or thirteen, I surely wouldn't have believed it.

When I wasn't risking my life climbing trees, I explored the acres and acres of forest around our house. And when I wasn't doing those things, I experimented with how long I could ride my bike down the steep hills without holding the handlebars.

My mother and I continued to have a testy relationship during my teens. Frustrated, she exclaimed one day, "You have a *thing* about me." Admittedly, I did—because I was afraid that she didn't really love me. When I was shipped off to boarding school at age fifteen, I surmised that Mom just wanted to get rid of me. After one year at Ashley Hall in Charleston, South Carolina, I managed to talk her into letting me return to Anniston for the remainder of high school while secretly hoping that we would have a closer, more loving relationship. I quickly realized that the magical connection I had dreamed of was *not* going to happen. It turned out she was pregnant with my sister Nancy, and I felt as if she had abandoned me.

Fortunately, I always had a very close relationship with my dad. During the summers, I worked at his office as a receptionist to help pay for the car repairs from my constant fender benders. Luckily, my parents never knew that the police frequently pulled me over for ignoring stop signs and driving too fast. But fortunately, they always gave me a break since my dad had delivered their children.

My desire to sail started early on when I was seven and

a group of college students (with my parents' permission) took me on a wild and wonderful sailboat ride off the coast of Alabama. I remember how alive and happy I felt with the wind whipping through my hair and the sun beaming down on my face. Perched on the side of the boat, I stretched my hand into the water and watched the sparkles from the sun dance across the waves. I felt so free and so happy in those moments, and I hoped that one day I would return to the sea.

When I was twelve, my dad, who also loved sailing, ordered a Chinese junk (a type of boat) from Hong Kong. I spent many weekends with him on a lake in the northeastern part of Alabama. Sailing is too strong a word for what we did. My siblings and I lounged on the fragrant, sun-baked teak deck, waiting for an occasional puff of wind. My handsome dad, with his Clark Gable smile, always wore his beige coolie hat and motored much more than he sailed. All I know is that when the wind showed up, I was enchanted by the sound of the boat moving through the water and the creaking of the deck.

Anniston is a very sophisticated small town. I was exposed to international travel at an early age because everyone with means traveled overseas. My grandparents sent me postcards from all over the world while my parents traveled to the Caribbean, Mexico, northern Europe, and the United Kingdom. One of my grandfather's best friends, John B. Lagarde, was a famous big game hunter in Africa. His other close friend was Thomas Kilby, a governor of Alabama.

The *Peter Pan* movie came out when I was five years old and had a huge impact on me. Wanting to be just like Wendy in the movie, I dreamt that Peter Pan would one day take me away on a wild sailing adventure.

Lusting after something more than just the yearly trips to

New York to stay with my grandparents, I filled my journals with pictures and postcards of faraway places. I imagined viewing Paris from the Eiffel Tower, seeing the changing of the guard at Buckingham Palace, and touring the ancient ruins of Pompeii. After my best friend Alice lived with a Swedish family for the summer, I decided it was my turn to see Europe. Against my parents' wishes, I applied to the University of Stockholm, and it wasn't until the acceptance letter arrived two months later that they finally gave in. It was there that I met my future husband, Lars.

My ongoing craving to be near the sea would eventually take me to Beaufort. It was as if the universe had this plan in mind for me all along. Beaufort felt right.

———

The vague image of a sailboat occupies my mind continuously. Where is this coming from? Something deep within must be reaching out to my conscious self to let me know that living on a boat will revitalize my spirit in unimaginable ways.

I want to be in charge, to be the creator of *my* world, to be powerful. I want to let go of the victim mentality instilled in me by past events. It is time to find myself.

I stop taking Murphy to the neighborhood dock where I once sprawled on my back looking up at the constellations while lazily tracing figure eights with my foot in the estuary's cool waters. Instead, every day after work, before sunset, I pick up my doggie pal, who waits anxiously for me with her stumpy tail wagging wildly when I walk through the door. Murphy loves these outings. I drive to the town pier, park the car under a large shady oak tree, and sit on a wooden swing under a canopy of sweet-smelling jasmine and trumpet vines. Sitting at my feet, Murphy looks up at everyone who wanders by.

Breathing in the fresh sea air as white pelicans soar low over the river, I gaze wistfully at the small and medium-sized sailboats bobbing about in the brackish water now tinged golden pink and soft purple by the setting sun. I wonder what it would be like to embrace that strange and mysterious life. Over and over, I repeat silently, "I want to be on a boat. I want to be on a boat." More than anything, I desperately want to escape Beaufort.

This whole habitual exercise begins three months after Tom's death. I long for the sea and it, in turn, calls to me ceaselessly in its mysterious and ancient salty voice. I want a new life offshore—one holding no sad stories or ghosts from the past. And I want an existence where my own needs are fulfilled, where I can actualize myself. During my marriage to Lars, I fell into the traditional role of wife and mother and consequently forgot my own desires and dreams. Once, when a therapist asked me, "What do you really need?" I was too separated from my own longings to answer his question.

Working with people involved in real estate and commercial properties, I go through all the motions mechanically. My body is there, but my heart has already merged with the sea, which ignites within me a sense of hope and endless possibilities. I sit on that wooden swing day after day, and soon, the melancholy that entwined itself around me starts to dissipate, and my current vision of the world, a place previously devoid of color, possibilities, and joy, starts to shift. I want to live again.

During one of these dream-filled afternoons, the wind (now dwindled to a light refreshing zephyr) brings back memories of the soft breezes that flowed through the hallways at

10th Street Elementary School in Alabama. Those magical, mystical currents of air carried promises of good things to come, of unimaginable, wonderful coincidences in the making. This one carries potential, hope, and faith that everything will unfold perfectly. It also carries the faint scents of newly baked garlic bread from the Italian restaurant nearby and the smell of lilacs from the bush next to us. It transports the laughter of young children, a baby's cry, and the barking of a dog. It touches the cheeks, arms, and lips of the people in its path and then touches me so that I become one with the breeze and the people. Suddenly, I have this inexplicable expectation of travels and adventures in exotic places.

I begin to wonder about the daytime routines on a boat. I watch a man working on his sailboat anchored nearby but can't visualize what it would be like to share his living space. In the past, sailing was a quick tack here and there or a simple sail down island and back. *What is it like to live permanently on a boat?* I wonder. *What is this crazy dream?* All I know is that I feel really good when I think about it. Somewhere deep inside, I know I am supposed to live on the sea. My dream is vague yet strong and heartfelt. It is abstract, simple, and delicious. No details are necessary in this amorphous daydreaming experience.

As if on cue, as if we are playing assigned parts on stage, Murphy and I continue to arrive at the pier just before dusk for our staring exercise. Days become weeks, and weeks become months. When people walk by, they smile at us as if they somehow know that a dream is being born. I am the sweet nymph calling the sea to notice me, to bring me a boat with a sailor to satisfy my dreams and my longings.

My desire to sail drives me to seek out sailors at the local YMCA. As I sweat on the treadmill or the elliptical, I ask the person next to me, "Do you have a boat? I'd like to learn to sail." A few offer to let me crew on their sailboats. At a silent auction, I buy a day's sailing lesson at the Beaufort Yacht Club. Each time I interrogate someone new, I gather more information about boating and, feeling more confident, start lining up future crew positions.

Beaufort begins to feel like a place of transition. How this new existence would materialize is a mystery, but I feel confident it will create itself without my help. I am the silent observer watching my life transform itself.

What I don't know is that my Peter is out there: a man who is obsessed with adventure sailing and who is dreaming of meeting a woman who will cruise the seas with him. While I am sitting on the dock dreaming, he is buying a yacht and steering a course toward me. We are on a collision course. He is heading to Beaufort to visit his cousin who lives on St. Helena Island, and admits to me later that it isn't his cousin but something more mysterious that lured him to Beaufort. Me: Wendy.

The universe is paying attention to my powerful thoughts and to me, a middle-aged woman dreaming big dreams. I know and feel that I am on the threshold of moving into a whole new place of wonderment, empowerment, and freedom of spirit.

4

Tai Chi with
Mud Crabs

"Mom, you're dying here in Beaufort," Alex announces dramatically on his arrival home from college that spring. "You've got to leave! If you stay, your life will be over."

He's got a point, I think.

My income is decent, Murphy is a great companion, and my home is lovely. But I am also stressed out with my day job plus my weekend job representing Les Antiquités de la Normandie. My journal collects dust on the bedside table and persistently reminds me to return to writing. Sadly, however, my most creative moment during the day is mixing interesting concoctions of coffee in the mornings. And the only thing that makes me feel happy is sitting on the dock, dreaming about being on a boat.

Languishing in Beaufort, I am going through my life on autopilot. My sense of humor shrivels up, and I am not exactly fun to be with. This is when Alex stages his intervention. "Your job is killing you!" he tells me. "Look at you. You're all strung out at the end of the day, and you're *always* mad at me."

He is right. I am in a big funk lately but have no earthly idea how to get out of it. Thanking him for being honest and brave enough to speak the truth, I draw him toward me into a big hug.

A coworker approaches me a few days later. "You're leaving, aren't you? Honestly, Wendy, you're too artistic and creative for Beaufort. I see you living on the West Coast. California, for instance. This is *not* the place for you."

California seems like too much of a stretch. I have a dozen valid reasons why I shouldn't leave Beaufort. *You're fifty-seven years old. For God's sake, settle down and be a normal grandmother*, I remind myself. *Why jeopardize a decent job?*

But not long afterward, a perceptive friend (possibly sensing something in the making) mentions, "The rules are different at our age. We have this big pond of our lives, but the bridge has narrowed. We have to constantly readjust our strategies and our thinking. And, most important, we need to be open to change. Even if it's scary."

All my fears and feelings of hopelessness come to an abrupt end the first week of June due to three men, three similar messages—and exactly three months after my boat fixation began.

Father Zanger remarks during our session in Charleston, "The darkest moments are always followed by the lightest moments. You're right on the brink of a huge change. It's just around the next corner. Six months from now, you're going to ask yourself, 'How did I get here?'" Goose bumps cover my entire body.

Two days later, my eyes land on the young minister perched on the bar stool next to me at a local coffee shop. His left arm is in a sling. Getting up my nerve, I ask, "What happened to your arm?"

"I was riding a surfboard with my son in Costa Rica and sprained my wrist."

I share with him the shortened version of my recent past. Before I can finish, he interrupts to say, "You're on the verge of a major life change. You can't see it now, but it's all being lined up for you. You have no idea what's ahead. Six months from now you will be in a different place, and you're going to be very happy. And you'll marvel over how wonderful your life has become!"

Three days later, I receive another message. Having decided to cut back on my hours at the Chamber of Commerce, I visit a local Indonesian antique shop to inquire about the owner's previous offer to manage his shop while he and his wife are on shopping jaunts to Bali. *Maybe this is a good way to slowly ease myself out of my present job*, I think.

Tim, who is sitting at a large hand-carved teak desk from Bali doing paperwork, looks up and smiles when I ask if his earlier proposition still holds. "Absolutely, I'll hire you," he says, "but six months from now, you'll be running away with a man."

The next morning, while frowning at my wrinkles and a growing number of irrepressible grey roots in the bathroom mirror, I sense that this major life change is going to occur on its own, regardless of what I do. It is all out of my control. Something magical is happening in the background, and I can feel it. While I shop for food, drive to work, or walk Murphy in the evenings, I keep wondering what miraculous event is in the making. For days, I ponder over it, enjoying the anticipation of a pleasant surprise waiting around the corner.

During a visit with my son Markus in Vermont, a massage therapist exclaims while working on a kink in my upper back, "You're right on the brink of a major transformation. There's an energy of metamorphosis all around you. It's very exciting!"

Three weeks later, while strolling along Bay Street, I stop to stare at a wild-eyed young woman in the large display window of an art gallery. Her long brown hair is a thick, matted mess, and her mango-colored T-shirt is stained with traces of food. When I edge closer to see what is in the bowl in the far corner, she presses her lips fish-like to the glass in front of my face.

"What's going on here?" I ask the owner while stretching my head inside the gallery.

"Oh, that's Carly," the woman answers matter of factly. "She's an artist. She's living in the window for a week." As if that is a normal occurrence. "This is day four. Come this weekend for a party celebrating her final day of living in the public eye."

I rarely go to art openings in Beaufort, but my curiosity takes over. Feeling shy, I dilly-dally and arrive at the art gallery downtown just before the party ends. Ava, a striking young architect from Toronto who is standing next to her boyfriend in the midst of the crowd that spilled out onto the sidewalk, smiles at me as I approach her.

Later on she admits, "When you were walking toward me at the party, I knew that something very special was happening. I thought, 'There she is! I've been expecting her. She's right on time!'"

That evening, we both jabber away as if we are old

friends. Oblivious to everything around us, neither of us notice that the big yellow double doors to the gallery are closed or that the interior lights are out. Or that Beaufort is shut down for the night except for the brightly lit low-country restaurant at the end of the block. All the snazzy, artsy people are long gone, along with Ava's boyfriend, who finally says, "I'm heading out now. See you tomorrow."

Before we part that evening, feeling safe in her presence, I blurt out, "Ava, I want to live on a boat. I don't know why. It just feels right."

Within days she introduces me to a woman named Sally who is visiting her cousin Fred on Lady's Island. During an impromptu dinner at Fred's house, I mention rather off-handedly my desire to live on a boat.

"*What* did you just say?" Sally asks, her eyes agog. "You want to live on a boat? How odd. My cousin Lee just bought a catamaran in West Palm Beach and he's heading this way in a few days. He's sailing alone and would *love* to have a first mate. I'm going to have to get you guys together."

Fred adds, "Just a forewarning, Wendy. I would be remiss not to tell you that Lee is very perfectionistic about his boat. He wants everything to be impeccable."

I think, *I'm sure I can handle that. I grew up with a perfectionist mother.*

When Lee arrives, Ava calls and repeats what he said to her previously. "I'm looking for a loving, sane partnership." She senses that there will be a huge spiritual connection between us and that we will be perfect for each other.

Our first date is at a small Italian restaurant off Bay Street lit by romantic candles. I spot Lee immediately. He sits at the bar, his back toward me. Maybe it is the light blue windbreaker that gives him away, or perhaps it is his untamed, unbridled energy. He seems out of place in the café—as if he belongs in the wild.

Lee must feel my presence because he turns toward me on my approach. His sandy blond hair, dappled with grey, is slicked back from his face, and his blue-grey eyes sparkle with light. Simultaneously I sense a slight hesitation—a contradictory, subdued energy, as if someone or something recently deflated him. We are both shy and self-conscious at first. During dinner, he admits that he is recovering from a disastrous relationship and has resigned himself to enduring a blind date with me. I must bring out his best qualities because he quickly turns into an exuberant, fascinating, charismatic man.

Heated up by our pheromones, we face each other in a booth, locking eyes intently as if we are both starved for love and affection. Lee is ruggedly handsome. I like his sculpted face, his big, toothy grin, and his muscular body. As a teenager, I had a massive crush on Robert Redford and here is his clone, smiling at me from across the table.

After Tom's death, I kept men at arm's length, afraid to get hurt yet longing to be touched. Halfway through dinner, Lee asks if he can sit beside me. I feel an electric current surge through my body as he slides his hand across my back. I am drunk from the intense chemistry I feel with him. *Oh no*, comes a voice from deep within. *I'm in trouble.* I am utterly dazzled yet simultaneously petrified by this man.

"You need to know my life experiences to truly understand me," Lee says as he launches into a description of when he and six friends borrowed his father's thirty-seven-foot sailboat following an icy snowstorm in New Jersey. After brushing off the frozen snow, they hauled the boat off the hard and dragged it to the shoreline, where they all jumped in. Everyone except Emily, who was eight months pregnant.

"I watched over her as if she was my little sister," Lee says. "I lifted Emily into the boat and made sure she had the most comfortable seat in the galley below. When she began to feel seasick, I gave her tiny sips of water and applied cold compresses to her forehead while her husband rubbed her back.

"That sail to St. Martin in the Caribbean was unusually rugged due to the winter sea conditions. My friends spent most of the time with their heads over the side of the boat. I was the exception. Luckily, I've never once had motion sickness."

"Lee, I hate to admit it, but I'd get seasick under those conditions." Just as I say this, the waitress, sighing heavily, starts turning chairs upside-down onto tables. My car is a block down the road, and Lee, in a moment of exuberance, picks me up. I laugh hysterically as he carries me to my car. I am mesmerized by him.

Lee is engaging, charismatic, and very articulate. He is truly one of the most interesting people I've ever met. From the way he talks about his experiences in life, it is apparent to me that he is a self-actualized person.

My shyness evaporates during those very first moments with Lee. Because of his genuine curiosity about my life, he has this way of making me feel smart and compelling. Unlike some people I recently met, he really listens to me.

I'm not sure where I want it all to go. After finally reaching the point where I am comfortable with being alone, I don't want to be too easy or too predictable. And I don't want to risk losing another man.

After that first date, Lee is somewhat muted when Ava questions him. "He looked like he had just been hit over the head," she says. "In a good way."

"The reason you're here," Ava tells him, "is to meet this woman. She's perfect for you. You're going to fall deeply in love, and you're going to be extremely happy. You and Wendy are meant for each other."

"Really?" he says enthusiastically, grabbing her hands.

Our second date is a 7 a.m. breakfast on his boat *Worldwide Traveler*, which is docked off his cousin Fred's large compound on Lady's Island. I mention to him when we talk that my calendar is fully booked for that week except for the early mornings. As I approach the elegant forty-seven-foot French Catana catamaran, the dock's wooden boards creak under my feet, and Lee bounds out into the cockpit to welcome me with a big smile and a hug.

In the spacious, light-filled salon, Lee serves me a breakfast of fresh strawberries and eggs béarnaise, which is followed by a golf cart tour of Fred's sizable property. "Would you like to see something *really* remarkable?" he asks while zooming across the deep green lawn toward the creek. As hundreds of mud crabs scurry across the sulfurous, froggy-smelling low tide flats, Lee does tai chi in their midst.

My curiosity is piqued. *This is a guy who notices things and appreciates nature. No wonder he has so many friends*, I tell myself. Most importantly, I feel relaxed and happy when we are together.

Later, as we tour the oak tree–shaded compound, Lee says, "I want to do charters with friends and sail the Caribbean, the Mediterranean, then the waters off of South and Central America. Eventually, I want to sail around the world."

Not only do I have great chemistry with this man, but we also share similar dreams. My childhood yearnings to travel are suddenly reactivated. And that is how I begin to visualize living on the boat with him.

On our second date, I feel a little miffed when Lee says, "I hope that beautiful women will charter my boat."

Deciding to ignore that red flag, I blurt out, "Lee, you're the type of man I've *always* wanted to be with."

"You'll meet someone like me, I'm sure."

"No, I want *you*, not someone else," I say in a needy, childlike voice, wondering why he pulls back suddenly.

I leave for work that day feeling uncertain, insecure, and crestfallen. Lee is putting out interested vibes, but what is this conflicting message? He seems as intrigued with me as I am with him. Wanting to protect myself, I decide to pull away from him before emotional involvement becomes a factor. When Lee calls the next day to invite me out, I say in a clipped voice, "No, I'm sorry. I can't. I'm booked up all week."

After a lot of prodding on his part, Lee convinces me to see him again. So I invite him over for dinner. There is this quality about this man that I've never seen before. A free spirit, he belongs in the wilderness where the wild creatures roam and the eagles soar. I am afraid to leave this restless untamed creature alone in my living room. It is like having a deer over for dinner.

After a few dates, Ava confides in me, "Lee is totally smitten. There aren't many women like you, Wendy. He's so lucky. I believe you're an incredibly special person."

The universe has, of course, stepped in. It was involved the whole time, setting up synchronistic events, one after another. Unconcerned that Lee is in Beaufort for only a few more days, I know that I am in the right place at the right moment, so it is pointless to worry.

Lee's original plan is to be in Beaufort for five days and then sail to New England. However, a series of boat system glitches force him to remain at Fred's for two more weeks, which gives us a chance to get to know each other better.

Meanwhile, everyone is encouraging him to hold on to me. Love is slowly developing as everything conspires to keep us together.

The one thing that worries me about Lee is his need to talk about his past girlfriends. Once, when he is mid-sentence in his rendition of his experiences with his ex-girlfriend Kathy, I interrupt him to say, "Hey, would you mind if we talk about something else?"

"But to really know me, you need to hear these stories."

"I'm not sure about that," I respond, nipping that in the bud—at least for the time being. "What about your childhood? What was your role in the family?" I figure that hearing about his parents and siblings will be easier.

"Okay, so here's the shortened version because I don't want to bore you," he says. "I was the oldest of three sons, and I had a *wonderful* relationship with my mother, who must have been one of the sweetest moms ever. She was always there for me and supported me in everything I did. When I was ten, she bought me a small sunfish sailboat and taught me how to sail. At first, it was just a little tack here and there until she eventually trusted me enough to let me sail solo along the New Jersey shoreline. It's because of her that I became an expert sailor.

"My dad, on the other hand, was very difficult to deal with. When he was angry with me, which was often, I'd go to my room, shut the door, and stay there for hours on end. My closed door was a normal sight, and my brothers thought as they walked past, '*Lee must have angered Dad again.*' Thank goodness I had the loving support of my mom, who helped cushion his hard edges."

It is amazing, really, how similar my experience with my own parents was. I was the troublemaker, the rule-breaker, and the nonconformist of the family, often sent to my room for mouthing off or disobeying. I spent a lot of time there reading *Wonder Woman* comic books, coloring, and writing sappy poetry. One day, feeling like I was treated unfairly, I took all my long-forgotten dolls, pulled down their underpants, and turned their butts so they'd be facing the door. Mom always came by to check on me after an hour, so I knew she'd get the drift.

Similar to Lee's mom in terms of being affectionate, my dad always softened the edges with his big warm hugs. He'd say, "You know how your mom is. Don't worry. She'll get over it."

———

With his departure date rapidly approaching, Lee invites me to join him, Sally, and her latest boyfriend, Bruce, on the passage to Rumson, New Jersey, where Lee grew up; then New York City; and then Stamford, Connecticut, where his brother, Nick, lived near an inlet with a boat dock. My first inclination is to say no. How can I leave my job on such short notice? For two weeks? What about Alex? And Murphy? Would it be irresponsible to sail to New England with a near stranger?

Feeling confident about Lee's sailing abilities, I recall Dad's words to me when I was a student in Sweden. While my mother napped one afternoon, Dad and I explored Stockholm together. Stopping to gaze at the sea from a footbridge, he turned to me. "Do you know what I admire the most about you?"

"What?" I asked, my eyes widening.

"Your courage."

After voicing my concerns to Alex about joining Lee on this potentially dangerous passage, he sees it as something much greater than just a sail. He exclaims, "If you don't join him on this trip up the East Coast, this chance may never come again. It'll change your life, Mom. You've gotta go! I'll take care of the house and Murphy."

How can I not go? Saying no will be telling the universe that I want to go down a safe and secure path instead of a more risky, mysterious one. My closest friend nicknamed me the "Yes Girl" because I am the one who jumps before thinking and flies by the seat of her pants. So I choose the route that makes no promise of a secure outcome—one that *could* make me look like a fool. Standing at a crossroads, I know in my soul that I can't grow if I stay in my comfort zone, so I say yes to Lee and let go of all my fears.

Are we actually Peter Pan and Wendy archetypes? I muse as I study my wardrobe for boat-worthy clothes. Oddly, in sixth grade, I played the part of Wendy in the play. Lee seems to be the kind of guy who embraces fun and adventure like Peter Pan.

"I'd love to go with you, Lee," I tell him on the phone as I glance over at my wise son, my sweet dog with the sad droopy eyes, and the stack of unfinished work projects nesting in the corner.

"I'm thrilled you can join me!" he says. "And I promise to do *everything* in my power to make this an experience of a lifetime for you. Let's be joyful together and touch as many lives as we can when we travel to different countries. The people we meet will color our lives in rich, beautiful shades."

Wow, I think. I am impressed by the way he expresses himself.

"Well, thank *you* for trusting me as your captain of the

seas," Lee goes on. "And just remember, Wendy, you are *perfect* as you are. Never change."

I can tell that he truly means it.

———

Only forty-eight hours before our departure, I begin to prepare for my first blue-water sail. In those two days, I miraculously make more sales than I made in the past several months. Customers I courted for weeks call out of the blue, requesting ad space at the Chamber of Commerce. Money flows toward me effortlessly.

I buy two pairs of quick-dry Columbia shorts, a windbreaker, and a pair of Topsiders at the local marine store and then anti-nausea medication and wristbands at the drug store. At work, I break the news of my upcoming adventure to my nine colleagues. Liz exclaims, "You're going to do *what*? I'm not sure if I heard right."

"It's true," I say.

Her response: "You must be crazy!"

As sweat runs down the insides of my arms, I decide at that very moment that I am willing to lose my job. "I'll return in two weeks," I promise Liz as she lifts her eyebrows skeptically.

As a contracted worker, I have the freedom to come and go if I keep my sales numbers up. What I don't point out to Liz that day is the irony that while I am marketing Beaufort as the most romantic town on the East Coast, I am actually becoming the most romantic woman on the East Coast.

Lee makes my skin tingle. When he touches my waist, electricity runs the length of my body. And when he hugs me,

I feel as if I was the only woman in the world. The thought of sailing with him is delicious, even if I know I will be taking a huge risk. From what Lee has told me, I know he is not only a very accomplished sailor but also someone I can trust implicitly.

Do I really want to make myself vulnerable, though, and allow Lee to witness all my weaknesses along with my strengths? I want so much to be loved by this man, yet the fear of rejection that plagued me from childhood still lingers.

It is impossible not to fall in love with a man who always wants to make everyone feel good. He can talk to *anyone*—whether it is another boat owner or one of the dock hands. He is genuinely interested in their stories. Everyone lights up when they see his big infectious smile.

Yes, I am love-struck, obsessed, and probably not thinking straight. But I don't care. Love is in the light, love is in the breeze, love is tapping me on the shoulder. I cannot stop its momentum, nor can I ignore the tiny voice inside that keeps saying, *He's a good man. He's the one!*

At this point, I am oblivious to the likelihood of challenging weather conditions and tumultuous seas. All I know is this: The universe has given me another chance at love, and I am ready for anything.

I also feel that I should take the leap because, oddly enough, this isn't the first time the universe put Lee in my path. I noticed him in 1970 while watching the movie about the Woodstock Rock Festival. As an international film student at the University of Stockholm, I was fascinated with American hippies. Of all the thousands of long-haired, bell-bottomed bohemians roaming about being captured for posterity in the grainy footage, Lee stood out. He was the handsome dude with wavy, shoulder-length dirty blond hair who was perched like Rodin's *The Thinker* on a large boulder in the middle of a lily-covered pond—nude.

Two men with a movie camera and a microphone approached him in a canoe. "Would you mind being interviewed?"

"Yeah, man. Cool."

"What do you think of swimming naked?"

"Man, it's the only way to swim."

Wow. He's sort of cute, I thought in a twenty-two-year-old way.

Midway through the movie, he appeared again in a scene where his head was cocked to one side with a pay phone cradled against his ear. He yelled over the din to his girlfriend Marsha at IBM, "The gates are down! It's a free concert! Come on!"

When I watched the film all those years ago, I had a premonition that one day I would meet this man. Those images of Lee remain in some distant, vague, long-forgotten file in my head until we watch the Woodstock movie together on his catamaran a few weeks after we meet.

Stopping the film in two strategic places, he says, "That's me."

"Oh my God!" I clap a hand to my mouth. "I remember you."

"That was one of the best experiences of my life," he says. "For me, it was a way to protest the Vietnam War through songs of peace and love. I consciously chose to put that message out into the universe through my personal choices and actions."

"I totally respect that," I tell Lee while trying to ignore my growing attraction to him. "I admire you for standing up for what you value in life."

How strange life is. This Woodstock man would turn out to be one of the greatest teachers of my life.

5

My First Blue-Water Sail

I drive slowly down Fred's long driveway, pull into an area that is designated for visitors, and then carry my duffle bag up the sloping wooden ramp to Lee's boat. Pulling off my shoes, I walk barefoot across the sparkling white fiberglass deck and step down into the cockpit where Lee, Sally, and Bruce are stuffing supplies into the hold. Fred, who has been watching all the activity from land, approaches the boat and yells, "Lee, let me know if you've forgotten anything!"

Lee's cousin Sally grew up as an only child in Baltimore with a widowed mother who was famous in the neighborhood for locking her daughter out of the house, forcing her to play outdoors even when she was being chased by bullies. As a result, she became fearless. Sharing the same family name, we were born one day apart in the same year. A dark-eyed brunette, Sally is long-legged and muscular with medium-length hair. She is a Rosie the Riveter who can repair almost anything mechanical—a very valuable asset on a boat.

A few years ago, Sally rescued Bruce from a life on the streets of San Francisco. Locating a renovated loft in an Edwardian-era brick building near the bay, she covered Bruce's monthly rent until he landed a job as a boat mechanic. A fit and attractive man with deep blue eyes, he hides his increasing baldness with a tropical bandana tied over his head like a pirate.

In the captain's cabin, I self-consciously stow my tightly rolled clothes into a ten-inch-wide cabinet along with my toiletries, a floppy beige hat with a wooden chin toggle, dark polarized sunglasses, and 50 SPF sunblock. Hoping to make a great impression, I packed sparingly.

Lee's original plan was to leave Lady's Island by 2 p.m., well before the tide begins to recede in this St. Helena Island inlet, leaving stinky, squeaky, popping mud in its wake.

Beaufort, one of the largest natural harbors on the East Coast, has tides that rise and fall six to eight feet every six hours. When 2 p.m. rolls around, however, Sally and Bruce are still swabbing down all the decks. Self-consciously, as if the boat itself is observing my every move, I stow two weeks' worth of provisions in the galley. I glance over at Lee, whose pockets bulge with odds and ends as he finishes last-minute chores, and I am reminded of my sons returning from exploring the woods with all sorts of odd objects sticking out of their pockets.

At 3:15 p.m., Fred releases us from the dock, and we wave goodbye as he fades into the background. The tall, bright-green spartina grass sways and rustles in the breeze as we make our way east. Seagulls, screeching loudly, soar high over the blue herons standing tall in the shallows where egrets perch and watch black cormorants disappear below the surface looking for fish. Lee and I, sitting shoulder to shoulder at the helm, gasp as the depth meter goes from twelve to five to four feet. Frowning, Sally and Bruce peer anxiously over the bow at the areas where mud has started to peek through. She yells, "It's looking pretty shallow here!" just as Lee shouts, "We're aground!"

The newly polished propellers dig deep into the sticky mud, and we come to an abrupt halt as clouds of brownish, brackish water swirl around the stern. Using the classic touch-and-go technique, Lee releases the keels from their muddy, slimy prison, and we continue on to the deeper waters of Port Royal Sound. To help me learn the basic rules of sailing, he explains that the red and green buoys are for direction and the red-and-white-striped clanging ones warn of shallow water.

While Bruce fills the two diesel tanks at Hilton Head Island, Lee and Sally study the local navigation charts spread across the salon table. Just as the sun is setting, we turn due east toward the Atlantic. Within a day or two, we will be in the Gulf Stream, which is seventy-five nautical miles east of the South Carolina coastline. We are all high on adrenaline, an interesting mixture of excitement and sheer terror, which actually feels good in a weird way.

There is a light chop on the sea. Feeling confident and marvelous, I move about nimbly, almost like a classical ballet dancer. *I am a born sailor*, I think. Lee and I chat happily as we prepare spaghetti and Greek salad for dinner while Sally and Bruce, at the helm, keep an eye out for lights from sailboats and ships. Under a sky brimming with stars rarely visible from land, we eat with hearty appetites in the candle-lit cockpit. After dinner, Lee takes out a legal pad and draws up the evening and the following day's watch system. Each person is assigned four hours on duty and then twelve hours off. I am assigned the first slot, which means I will get a good night's sleep that night. Lee and Sally are giving me a chance to acclimatize to life on a boat, and I appreciate their thoughtfulness. I realize this will be short-lived, though.

Exhausted after my first exciting day at sea, I walk down the four steps to the captain's cabin in the starboard stern. Lee, currently on watch, will join me later when Bruce takes over. Wishing I had a small ladder, I jump up onto the full-size mattress that rests on top of a large wooden bunk where boat paraphernalia is stored. Along the starboard side of the bunk is the outer wall and a large oval-shaped window with an incredible view of the sea. Along the right side of the berth is a wooden desk where books and personal things are placed. Above that is a small window that looks out into the cockpit. As I lie there reading my novel, it feels as if the boat is actually flying above the becalmed sea.

I awaken the next morning to something sinister. Feeling insecure about being a novice, I wonder how I will handle dire emergencies. Will I have the inner strength? I had read enough sailing books to know that challenges appear out of nowhere.

On entering the cockpit, it is apparent that the weather and the sea conditions have noticeably deteriorated. Lee, observing my worried expression, teases me. "Babe, you look like a deer caught in the headlights!"

As the sailing conditions continue to go downhill, Sally and Bruce, who are sitting side by side at the helm, appear calm and cheerful even when the winds howl like wolves and the seas lash their fury at us. Lee, the force that holds everything together on the boat, continues radiating self-confidence as he scans the raging seas. It is evident that he is doing what he loves and is brilliant at it. Every once in a while I glance over at Bruce and Sally to see if they still look calm.

The sailing conditions rapidly worsen, and I sleep fitfully that night to awaken early the next morning in a state of utter terror. I feel bad for Lee, who has only had a few hours of sleep. The captain of a boat, unfortunately, has to be on constant duty during challenging weather conditions. I hear Lee, Bruce, and Sally talking loudly in the cockpit. Sally and Bruce are both seasoned sailors from racing in regattas in the San Francisco Bay.

Bolting out of bed, already dressed after sleeping in my clothes, I put on my safari hat and my boat shoes then tenuously haul myself into the cockpit just as the boat lurches at the apex of a twenty-foot wave then free falls into the trough, causing sea water to crash over the bow, the canvas awning, the cockpit, and me. It feels like the boat is being drawn and quartered. Nothing in my entire life has prepared me for this storm-tossed rollercoaster ride on the sea.

The ferocious Gulf Stream and the inexorable forces of nature have taken over. Looking slightly dazed, we view daylight framed by shimmering, translucent, rainbow waterfalls as they cascade against the boat and shower it from end to end.

On duty and tethered to the boat, Lee sits at the helm, his eyes charged and hard as diamonds, seemingly unfazed by what is transpiring. I stagger and teeter about like a drunken sailor, crashing into things while grasping for something to hold on to. Every surface is slippery with salt, making it impossible to maintain a firm grip on *anything*. Deciding to leave the cockpit before an injury occurs, I topple down the slick steps to the salon and then slide open the glass door to the salon, where I should have stayed in the first place.

The salon is both a living room and a galley. A long curved light green couch sits under the large port windows, which overlook the foredeck. A round wooden table is anchored to the floor in front of the couch, and most meals are eaten there unless we decide to eat outdoors in the cockpit. To the right of the dining table is a small double sink and a stovetop. Against the rear wall is a marine refrigerator that opens from the top and has two large interior compartments. The compartment on the right is for beverages, and the one on the left is for fresh produce, meat, and fish.

The patch behind my ear, the blue sea band on my wrist, the lavender oil on my pulse points, and the ginger chews are not working. Feeling very nauseous, a small red plastic bucket is my constant companion. Every time Lee empties its contents into the sea, my fantasies about impressing him cascade into the water along with that. No longer caring about appearances, I sprawl on a cockpit cushion and take deep breaths of the fresh sea air while wondering when this ordeal will end. Sally covers me with a blanket and then gently places a pillow beneath my head. When she hands me a small plate of Saltines, the wily fingers of the wind toss all the crackers into the air. In the evening, as Lee sautés the mahi mahi he caught earlier, I disappear below to our cabin, hoping to avoid the fish odor. I toss and turn in bed while feeling sorry for Lee, who has to take over my night watch.

For two miserably grueling days, we lurch about in the Gulf Stream's swift northward current, twenty-foot waves, northern swells, and forty-five-knot southerly winds—a terrible combination. The sails rattle and shudder while the sea washes over the boat and us. In the dark of night, as we pitch about madly in the raging sea, I try not to worry. Suddenly I remember the promise I made to myself years ago:

> *Don't be afraid. Never be afraid. Walk into the fear.*
> *Draw on the strengths the past gave me.*
> *Step over the cliff.*
> *I will be caught in a beautiful safety net from heaven.*

On day four, Lee moves the boat out of the boisterous Gulf Stream. The bucking bronco motion tapers off into a gentle sway. My seasickness is gone, and my appetite returns. We glide through the motionless Sargasso Sea of the infamous Bermuda Triangle, also known as the Devil's Triangle. The subject of countless documentaries, it has been rumored to be the site of many mysterious disappearances of ships and planes.

On day five, we anchor for a quick overnight near a tiny fishing village on Chincoteague Island off the northern reach of Virginia, a place famous for its wild ponies.

Lee pulls up to a weathered grey wooden dock and throws the coiled-up line to a dock handler, who wraps it around a cleat. Since the dock is relatively low, we can just step off onto the pier.

What a wonderful feeling it is to be back on solid ground where everything is fixed in place and my legs have free range of motion. For the first few seconds, I have a vague sense of still being on something that is moving, but that dissapears quickly. It feels great to be here.

Sally and I have errands to run ashore, so we motor in the dinghy to the main town pier while Lee and Bruce wash down the salt-encrusted boat. When Sally inquires about transportation, a middle-aged couple who are walking along the inlet's grassy shore inform us that there are no taxis there, only wild ponies.

The husband, tall and burly, offers to ride in the dinghy with Sally and guide her to the grocery store situated near a pier while his flushed, heavyset wife takes me to a pharmacy on foot. "Where did you come from?" she asks. She is stunned to hear that I jumped onto a sailboat with people I just met. She is equally amazed that Sally went along in the dinghy with her husband, a complete stranger. "You're trusting souls. I would never do that! We could be axe murderers."

That night, as Lee holds me in his arms, he whispers in my ear, "I love you, Tiger Lily. You're part of my future." (Later, he tells me he'd nicknamed me this after rejecting Petunia and Daffodil—thankfully.)

Continuing on, Lee says, "You're brave to go on this journey with me. Just remember that when you do risky things, the outcome can be better than anything you could ever imagine."

"It's also brave of me to risk my heart on you," I answer.

"Wendy, I will always love you. I want you to soar! We will give each other inspiration, strength, and courage."

I can no longer ignore the synchronicity of our perfectly timed convergence. My life is now on an upward spiral, heading in a whole new direction—unexpected, yet at the same time, totally expected.

Day six. I graduate to the late-night and early-morning lookouts, depending on the schedule. I try not to worry about making dreadful mistakes, such as missing the lights of a barge or another sailboat that is on a collision course with us. Or failing to notice on the nav chart that we are heading straight for land. Lee has taught me how to recognize ships, sailboats, and fishing boats via their navigation lights. For instance, monohulls have a green light on the starboard bow and a red light on the port bow. On the masthead is a red light over a white light. In the aft is a white steaming light. A small powerboat will have the same lights, but the masthead will have a green light over a white light.

During our evening lookouts, we wear harnesses that connect to a line that circles the boat's length and breadth. Despite Lee's reminders about the importance of being secured while on duty at night, I notice that he often forgets to attach himself. When I signal to him to belt up while we do a maneuver after dark, I see a little flicker of irritation move across his face.

Day seven. Snapping my eyes open, I let out a loud snort when Lee rouses me from a deep sleep for my 3 a.m. duty. Once, during a flight from Stockholm to Atlanta when I was in my early twenties, a pilot walked back to me, tapped my shoulder, and then said, "I can hear you snoring all the way in the cockpit!" Maybe it is a blessing that Lee and I are on different sleep schedules.

The boat moves like a speeding bullet relentlessly ahead, ahead, ahead. I brace myself against the wall as I slip my legs into a pair of damp shorts, pull on my crumpled spaghetti-stained T-shirt, smooth down my wild curly hair, and zip up my windbreaker. I am groggy and odoriferous from days without a shower. With longing, I gaze back at my soft feather pillow, still warm from my body.

I watch the birth of dawn as the sky designs itself in shades of pink and lavender. The water has become an undulating rose-tinged purple mass, and I watch it mesmerized. As the boat glides through tranquil seas, I realize that I am in a state of constant meditation as I sit at the helm looking for boats and flotilla. It is just me, the sea, and the moment. I learn how to relax during my three-hour watches while trusting my instincts. It feels natural to be here, sitting at the helm—just me and the ocean. All the noise, all the commotion, all the insecurities of my former life disappear in one fluid, blissful moment.

This is how you slow life down to a simple state. This is how you drop life's distractions. For a long time now, I had wanted to live a less complex life but couldn't figure out how to do it. Now the answer is spread out before me, sparkling in the early morning light. As my morning duties draw to an end, an iridescent pink and purple veil lifts from the fuchsia sun and scatters itself into the clouds like dribbles of blueberries. I feel the sea speaking to me at a deep level.

Day eight. We anchor in a small cove near Cape May, the oldest seaside resort in the United States, which sits at the southern tip of the Cape May peninsula where the Delaware Bay joins the Atlantic Ocean. When we walk to the historic district for lunch, I sway as if I am still on a moving boat. It takes me several minutes to get my equilibrium back. I am told that the body eventually gets used to the transition from being on a moving boat to walking on solid land.

Feeling like we have entered a movie set, the four of us wander along the quiet, tree-lined streets past Victorian homes painted in bright colors; people working in their gardens; turn-of-the-century bed and breakfasts enclosed by rose-covered white picket fences; and cafés that smell of freshly baked bread, cookies, and vanilla-flavored coffee. Savoring the feel of solid ground, we wander around for hours, taking in the textures and colors of this lovely town.

The following day we drive a rental to Rumson, Lee's hometown. At a local bank, Lee flirts with his favorite banker,

Lubba, while I sit within earshot. I feel slightly jealous when I overhear, "Wow! You look gorgeous!"

Later, at an ice cream shop nearby, Lee invites me to choose a flavor for him, so I ask the server, "What's the weirdest flavor here?" I hand Lee a dill pickle–flavored ice cream cone while giving him a dirty look. If he understands why, he doesn't let on.

I stand at the bow wearing my aqua-colored bikini as we motor past Manhattan's East River then glide under its numerous suspension bridges filled with cars. It is so hard to take in the fact that I am actually standing here, half-naked, viewing one of my favorite cities off the port side. Glancing up at the stalled rush hour traffic on the Throggs Neck Bridge, I feel the intoxication of true freedom.

No longer motoring, the mainsail up and the jib unfurled, we sail into Long Island Sound to the coast of southern Connecticut, where we tie up to a pier where Lee's brother lives. When I am alone with Nick, he mentions that Lee would disappear into his room for days at a time when he was a teenager. The oldest of three boys, he came from a high-powered prominent Northeastern family and, unfortunately, was his dad's whipping boy. Consequently, he grew up with a need to show the world that he was okay and worthy of being accepted and loved. From the first day we met, I had sensed this vulnerability in Lee.

Like Lee, I was the scapegoat in my family. My mom and I were always locking horns. I believed, in a convoluted way, that misbehaving was the best way to get her attention and affection. I've concluded that Lee and I have a similar need to show the world that we're okay and worthy of being loved and accepted. *Maybe we have something to teach each other*, I think.

By the time our first journey together reaches its end, I don't want to leave this sweet man who has generously welcomed me into his life with open arms. But I have a one-way plane ticket to Beaufort, and he is to remain in the Northeast, where he can prepare the catamaran for blue-water sailing. As if coached by a romance writer, Lee takes me into his arms, leans me backwards, and plants a massively satisfying kiss on my lips in front of hundreds of people waiting in line at the airport. In that moment, it strikes me that Lee is a dream come true. Loving, attentive, and kind, he makes me feel like a real woman. His last words to me before we part are: "You're part of my future, Tiger Lily!"

6

Answering the Call

While sparks shoot back and forth through the ether, Lee says during one of our daily phone conversations, "I think about you all the time. It's making me crazy. Please hurry!"

I curb my enthusiasm a little so I won't come across as needy. In a calm, slightly sophisticated voice, I say, "I can't wait to see you too, Lee. I've missed you so much."

What attracts me to this man is his fun, childlike side, his curious and intellectual mind, his passion for travel, and, most importantly, his genuine love of people. It doesn't matter what background or income bracket a person comes from. A dock worker is treated the same as the owner of a multimillion-dollar yacht. Feeling safe in his presence, people let down their guard and open their hearts to him—including me.

That fall, we meet up several times in Hyannis Port, Massachusetts. Our first sail there is to the Woods Hole Oceanographic Institute, famous for its research on climate change. On following visits, we sail to Nantucket, Martha's

Vineyard, and Block Island. Thankfully, no one remembers Lee's infamous arrival at Martha's Vineyard when he was a young boater. On his approach to the Vineyard, he gunned the dinghy by accident and—much to the horror of onlookers—flew over the dinghies in the anchorage.

Just as we close in on the tiny harbor of Woods Hole, Lee disappears into the salon to work on projects. Sharp rocks line the narrow entrance to the anchorage, which is jam-packed with sailboats. Despite my attempts to steer the boat leftward to avoid the rocks, the steering system doesn't respond.

"Lee, the steering isn't working!" I scream. "We're heading straight for the rocks! Please help me!"

"Steer to the left! Steer to the left!" Lee shouts from below.

As we draw dangerously close to the boulders, he continues yelling commands from below. What am I doing wrong? I'm desperately trying to steer the boat away from the jagged headland, but nothing is happening. I shriek, "Lee, take the helm! Take the helm! The boat isn't responding!"

Like a jackrabbit, he sprints up the stairs, shoves me aside, and takes over the steerage. *Nothing* happens. We continue moving closer and closer to the rocks and the lighthouse as a fiasco of steering failure, current, tide, and strong wind converge. Out of desperation, Lee grabs the shifters to the port engine and thrusts the boat into reverse while simultaneously pushing the starboard shifter forward. Just in time, the boat swings to the left, narrowly missing the rocks.

Again, Lee leaves me alone at the helm—the *last* place I want to be. My heart throbbing, I try to guide us toward the marina, but I *still* can't control the steering as the boat recklessly careens toward a shiny navy blue mega yacht. Lee dashes to the bow and quickly hooks our line to a mooring ball. Under the glaring eyes of the yacht's captain, we pull right next to the yacht—so close that I can see my terrified self in its reflection.

Lee quickly changes into his mechanic's costume and repairs the starboard engine's steering mechanism. I'm impressed that he never complains about things going wrong. He tackles problems with great stoicism and never, *ever* kvetches about all the time he has to spend in the two hot engine rooms.

When things have calmed down, Lee high fives me. "You did a great job, sweetheart. You managed to remain calm during that whole ordeal and, partly thanks to you, we came out unscathed. This was your first initiation into the life of a sailor, and you passed the test! Bravo! I'm so proud of you."

I beam with pride, feeling that I'm on my way toward becoming a competent sailor.

Days later, we are safely tucked into a deserted cove near Edgartown, Martha's Vineyard. As we snuggle in bed one early morning, I notice shadows flickering about through the windows. Bird-like shadows. Light playing with dark in the air. Imagining I'll see only a few birds flittering about the cockpit, the view through the porthole is one of a thriving, chirpy hamlet of diminutive grey, white-breasted birds who have chosen our boat as their ritzy new home. They're on the stays, the safety lines, and the canvas awning. Neatly perched on these horizontal resting spots, the birds bask in the late summer sixty-eight-degree sunshine. It takes us hours to scrub away the mess they leave behind.

We remain for two more days in our secret romantic haven at the northeastern tip of the island. Ever since Lee tied the reflective tape to strategic areas, the birds haven't reappeared. Late one afternoon under a pink-tinged sky, I sit reading on the port steps in my black bikini while Lee putters about in the galley. *What's he up to?* I wonder as the balmy breeze grazes my skin.

Beaming, Lee appears with a platter of my favorite things: Ryvita crackers, black olives, roasted red peppers, marinated artichokes, sliced cucumber, mini tomatoes, and two types of hard cheese in wedges. In his other hand, he carries hummus and mustard.

I love you so much, I think, looking over at him adoringly. *I would be content living in a tent or a grass hut with you.*

As the sun dips below the horizon and the temperature falls, we pull on more clothing and move into the salon to watch *How to Lose a Man in Ten Days*. As I lean happily into Lee's shoulder, that unnerving title suddenly causes me to drop buttery popcorn down the front of my sweater. I have a sudden flashback to my innocent, twenty-year-old self, the young woman who never stopped believing in Disney magic, who sang "Moon River" as loud as she could when no one was in earshot, who thought that *anything* was possible. Then the older me who hung on stubbornly each time my life came undone. When I drove down the empty back roads of Connecticut and South Carolina and Vermont, crying elephant-sized tears.

Feeling frisky and playful after the movie, Lee chases me around the boat several times, then, finally catching me, throws us onto the trampoline on the bow, where we bounce and crash into each other like children. I'm laughing so hard that I need to cross my legs. I can't help but love this fun-loving part of Lee. I've never met a man before who is so in tune with his inner child. Or as romantic.

A boat's trampoline, incidentally, is made from a light-weight net that allows water to pass through the holes in the weave. Most important, it allows water to pass through the two hulls which helps prevent the catamaran from flipping over. On a long passage it's an awesome place for relaxation while the boat is traversing calm waters. The swishing sounds of the waves below are mesmerizing. It can also be an outlet for releasing pent-up energy because you can jump up and down on it. If the boat is going through rough waters, however, it's not the best place to be unless you don't mind getting soaked with salt water. But right now, with Lee, it's perfect.

Lying next to me in bed that night, Lee whispers in my ear, "We will love each other so much that everything else will be secondary. I want you to be part of everything. Let's sail to warmer climes and swim naked in the azure seas. My spirit is in love with your spirit, and even when we're apart, our spirits are making love in heaven."

There is no doubt in my mind: I want to spend the rest of my life with Lee. He has all the traits, all the qualities that I admire in a man—intellectual curiosity, level-headedness in dangerous situations, a charming romantic side, joyful child-like qualities, a sporty and rugged adventurous spirit, and a very alluring boyishness. And he is *the best* hugger! How could I say no to this man?

————————

During my third and last visit to Cape Cod, Lee, pulling me into an embrace, asks, "Can you stay with me? Can you sail the seven seas with me? I really want you to be part of this adventure of a lifetime. I've fallen deeply in love with you, Tiger Lily." Then moments later, "Oh, by the way, do you like to cook?"

"My dear Lee," I say, laughing. "I'm crazy about you, too. Yes! I would truly love to join you and share my life with you."

"But what about the cooking part?" he reminds me as he loosens his grip around my waist.

Deceitfully, I chirp, "Yes, of course. Cooking is my favorite pastime."

Ironically, I had recently admitted to myself that I was burned out with cooking from way too many years standing in front of a stove.

"Are you a good cook?"

"Yes!" I insist. Well, sort of. I used to be.

"We'll be doing charters with my friends, and you'll be cooking a *lot*."

Damn! What am I getting into? I can still get out of this, but I don't want to. I'll make it work. I'm in love, and there's no turning back.

Truthfully, I'm feeling a little edgy about impulsively running away to live on a boat with a man I just met. Plus, my sailing skills need work. And I'll be leaving behind my family. Something inside keeps nudging me on, so I repeat these words out loud: "Don't think, just go."

Adrenalized over the heady unfurling of my dream when I'm back home in Beaufort, I'm too preoccupied to eat. My blue jeans are beginning to slide down my hips. At night, I twist and turn in bed, left, right, left, wrapping myself up in the sheets like a mummy. I prop my head up on my feather pillow, flatten it out, turn on the bedside lamp, turn it off, get up, drink warm milk, wander around the house, look out my bedroom window at the moon-lit lagoon, then glance over at Murphy with jealousy over her ability to sleep soundly every single night without the assistance of chemicals. It's not fair.

The five-day sail from Newport, Rhode Island, to Bermuda, then five more days from there to St. Martin, is rather daunting. Winter brings with it the conclusion of hurricane season and mostly calmer seas, but I can't help but worry about what lies ahead. Will it be as rough as my first passage?

A major focus of mine, along with purchasing essentials, is to find some sexy tropical clothing. After work, I head to the only department store in Beaufort and scan endless racks of clothing. After loading my arms with options I head into a tiny changing room where, after observing my undressed body, I wonder, *will Lee still love me under florescent lights?* At Walmart I stock up on toiletries, knowing that my favorite brands will be overpriced or hard to find in the Caribbean.

Dee, a coworker at the Chamber of Commerce, approaches me during my last week of work there. "I just want to know if the rumors that are circulating about you are true."

"What rumors?"

"People are saying that you're running off with a man to live the rest of your life at sea."

I can't help the smile that stretches across my face. "Yes, I've met a man, and his name is Lee. And I plan to sail with him for an indefinite period of time."

"Well, when exactly are you coming back?"

"All I know is this: I'm going on a wonderful adventure, and I don't need to know the exact dimensions of it. Everything will unfold as it's supposed to. So, in answer to your question, I don't know."

Dee, eyebrows knitted together, stares at me as if I'm deranged, then shrugs her shoulders and walks back to her desk.

Only one person at the Chamber of Commerce wishes me well.

Liz hugs me. "I know you won't be coming back. I hope that you have the most wonderful life imaginable."

People in town grill me. Like a small, slippery goldfish, I manage to escape from Beaufort's strong, questioning tentacles. As a young child with a controlling mother, I became an expert at vagueness, a long-dormant skill that has unexpectedly reactivated itself.

"When are you returning to Beaufort?" everyone asks.

"I don't know," I tell them.

"Well, you have to come back. You have a house here."

"True."

"Where will you live?"

"On a catamaran."

"Does the captain of the boat have a house?"

"No."

There's silence for a moment or two. "What about your job?"

"I quit."

Tired of my abbreviated answers, most people give up and wish me safe travels.

When my two sisters call and ask penetrating questions about Lee, I'm ambiguous.

"I like him a lot," I say.

If I tell them too much, they'll question my sanity because here I am, impulsively jumping into a new relationship only eight months after Tom's death. Foolishly taking another chance on love.

I ask Mary, a waitress at a local coffee shop who was Murphy's dog sitter during my Cape Cod visits, if she can take Murphy for an indefinite period of time. Knowing what a kind and loving person she is, I'm confident that Murphy will be fine. After my last trip to New England, Murphy looked back and forth several times from me to Mary, unsure of who her mother was. My heart breaks over having to leave her, but it would be impossible to take her on the boat.

I call my family and friends in the Northeast and the South to say goodbye. Several people assume I'll be gone for years with little or no communication. I remind them that this isn't the 1600s, when people sailed away on ships perhaps never to be seen again. Nowadays, sailors have great communication tools. For instance, we have a Global Star phone system for emergency calls, and a single sideband radio through which email can be sent. Wireless connections are available in most countries.

The last item on my list is to buy an international cell phone in which I can insert SIM cards in every country we visit. This way, I'll have a local number and the ability to make extremely expensive calls to the US.

During my last visit with Father Zanger, he observes, "Wendy, you've come a long way, but you're still not there yet. There's always this struggle for self-confidence."

There's an awkward silence as I process this.

After discussing my traditional Southern upbringing, Father Zanger adds, "No matter how much I stick my knife in you, you still sound sweet . . . the Southern way."

As he says this, I realize that I've never figured out how to love myself and be authentic. Much less set boundaries with people.

"When there is self-love, everything falls into place, and the boundary setting and authenticity become part of the package," he continues. "Oh, by the way, how will you feel when a paying couple undresses, and Lee is staring at the woman? Looking is biology. Lee will look . . . just remember . . . but he chooses to be with you. He wants you, not

Barbie. If he's worth having, he'll be faithful. He has male hormones. He'll stare. Look but don't touch."

"That might be a problem for me," I reply.

Before I walk out of his office for the last time, he asks, "Is Lee worthy of you?"

After pausing for a moment, I say, "Yes, he is." *I think so.*

"Good. When you and Lee get married, I'd like to be the one to marry you. I'll come to where you are." Then, hugging me, he adds, "You're my friend. My good friend. I love you."

As I leave the church parking lot, I notice, for the first time, the signage over the door of the small floral shop across the street. It says TIGER LILY in big bold blue letters.

Leaving to sail with Lee feels right. And it feels good to give love another try. I'm eager to learn to sail, to be Lee's business partner, to step into the role of first mate—and most of all, I'm eager to explore new worlds with him.

Tom's words, "One day at a time, Wendy," keep coming back to me, so I make a conscious decision not to worry about the future. My desire is to be fully in the moment with Lee, regardless of the outcome, and to enjoy the journey of living and traveling on a boat.

October 15th. After only two and a half hours of sleep, I wake up and admire my lightly packed rucksack and carry-on duffle bag. I chose things with care, taking only essentials. The bills are paid, and Murphy adores her new mom, the waitress who has been taking care of her when I've been away. She was thrilled when I said a few days ago, "I'm leaving Beaufort permanently. Lee and I are planning to sail together for an indefinite period of time, so I need to find a permanent home for Murphy. Would you like to have her? I may be gone for years, so I'm going to have to let her go, unfortunately. I'm confident that you will take good care of her. "

She was thrilled. "Yes, yes! I'd love to have Murphy. Thank you so much!"

The grass will be cut each week, and my next-door neighbor will be keeping an eye on my home. Alex is back in Connecticut for his senior year in college. He's sad that he may not see me for months at a time, but he knows in his heart that this is a once-in-a-lifetime opportunity that could change the trajectory of my entire life.

I'm drunk with excitement. As if a memo was sent out to the neighborhood, people suddenly appear on my front doorstep to wish me well. I have a strange feeling that Beaufort will always remember me.

Here I am, just four months after I was given the three prophecies, heading for a brand-new life that's way, way beyond my wildest dreams, I think as I walk toward baggage claim in Providence. The air is charged with electricity as Lee and I, radiating joy, spot each other across the room. Our faces light up as if a switch is turned on. Everyone around us must be able to feel the energy of the molecules in the air that are now dancing with excitement.

Lee, looking handsome in his white T-shirt and light blue seersucker shorts, pulls me into his arms. We kiss each other deeply, then, giggling, slowly slide down the wall behind us to sit next to each other on the floor with our feet splayed out in front of us like happy children in a sand box. *The world is our playpen*, I think.

Now outside at a marina, I turn my face upward toward the warm fall sunshine as I wait for Lee to retrieve the dinghy from the jetty. Water slaps the sides of the boats along the docks while riggings clank noisily in the breeze at this low-key, bare-bones yacht club, where unfinished boat repair projects lay willy-nilly along the shoreline. In the distance, the low rumble of a weathered fishing trawler heading for the wharf fills the air as a young long-haired dock worker in navy blue overalls yells directions to the fishermen. As I inhale the pungent smells of salt and fish and seaweed, seagulls wheel overhead, screeching at each other.

Now on board *Worldwide Traveler*, Lee draws a large heart on the fogged-up sliding door to the cockpit. Inside the heart he puts our names and says, "When we go through the hard times, I want you to know that I love you. Remember that."

His boat is moored in Tiverton on the lower part of the River Exe, where the houses line up neatly along the river bank like pastel-colored boxes. Currently a dam is threatening to break upstream, and homeowners are evacuating.

During an exploration of my new home, I notice that the starboard forepeak is stuffed with toys: a yellow frisbee with colored lights, juggling batons, and windsurfing, kiteboarding, biking, and diving equipment. Definitely a bachelor boat. I've always liked men who are tuned in to their inner child. *It's all good! Men are just boys . . . always boys at heart!* I tell myself as I roll up my clothes tightly and squeeze them into one tiny cabinet, then place my journal, my favorite fine-point pen, and a book in a rectangular wicker basket on the cabin shelf next to my side of the bed.

Lee is exceptionally tidy except for a few blind spots. Mold has overtaken the cheese and hummus in the refrigerator.

"They're still okay," Lee says as he shovels questionable things into his mouth. "Help yourself! We Adamsons have cast-iron stomachs!"

Not me. Quietly, I dump rotten bananas, rock-hard

oranges, and other foods that have taken on unusual odoriferous properties into the trash as Lee completes boat projects.

Happy to be together, we enter our own private world
of complete silliness, laughing manically over the dumbest
things. Like children, we make silly faces, lick our plates after
meals until they sparkle, and then walk robotically around
the boat. I come close to peeing my pants a few times during
these moments.

Crinkly, curled-up brown leaves skip down the sidewalks of
Tiverton while we wait for November 30th, the official end
of hurricane season. Sally and Bruce will arrive the third week
in November to help us prepare for the passage to Bermuda.

While shivering in the cold mornings blanketed under
leaden clouds, I wonder if God has misplaced his color pal-
ette. Our bed is stacked with navy blue wool blankets and
an open, unzipped red plaid sleeping bag. After wearing the
same two pairs of long underwear and three pairs of grey
wool socks for two weeks now, I suspect the gamey smell is
coming from me.

Well, I think, *I smell pretty damn good for someone who
has only showered twice in the past week!* The boat's icy
water makes showering torturous. My hair's a mess, my nails
are dirty, and I feel ugly. I've started getting small, minor skin
infections that won't go away. Neosporin and Band-Aids are
now my constant companions. Even if I'm one stinky, smelly
woman, I know that summer is just around the corner, and
I'll be wearing bikinis in the warm Caribbean sunshine.

Hurricane Wilma is heading our way. By the time it reaches
Rhode Island, the winds will be between thirty-five and
forty-five knots. Under mushrooming evening thunderheads,
we secure the mainsail, double the lines to the mooring, stow

the covers to the winches, and put away all loose lines and anything that can blow away. As Lee prepares the boat, he periodically calls out my name as if he wants to make sure I'm not a figment of his imagination. When I answer in a soothing tone, "Are you okay?" he usually can't remember why he was calling out for me.

When the winds arrive, we are buffeted about like a plastic toy, joining in a wind-directed ballet with all the other boats moored in the river. Luckily, we're protected from the full brunt of the wind by the bank of houses, the hillside, and the woodland to the northeast.

It seems like yesterday that I stood at my kitchen window staring out at the neighborhood children playing, wondering if my life was all about solitude, wishing it was more about togetherness. Here I am now with the man I love, unable to imagine any other place I'd rather be. Our camaraderie and our desire to live each moment to the utmost fills me with happiness and contentment.

One week before we head to Bermuda, we pick up Sally and Bruce at the Providence airport. All four of us huddle in a warm group hug and then head to a large grocery store for last-minute shopping. Lee encourages us to pick out our favorite foods for the long passage ahead. On our return to the boat, Phil, a navigation technician, is meticulously installing *Worldwide Traveler*'s navigation system, while Lee kvetches over the price tag.

We have no weapons or guns on board. We hire a local woodcarver to chisel the bird of peace, a dove with an olive branch in its beak, into the wooden bollard on the bow of the boat. Most of the sailors we'll meet in the future will have weapons on their boats, but we decide to take our chances.

7

Riverton, Bermuda, St. Martin

The vast expanse of sea that stretches from Newport to Bermuda is famous for its terrifying storms. Some sailors have actually given up on the sailing life after they hobbled into a port in Bermuda with shredded sails, a broken mast, or both. Or even worse.

I'm having a nauseous relationship with a bucket on this grueling passage. The wind and the sea are lashing out at me from both sides, and I lay in the cockpit staring up at the bimini, wondering about my harebrained decision to take off on ocean voyages for an indeterminate period of time.

Lee, Sally, and Bruce, on the other hand, look rather blasé as the boat careens and pounds into the volatile seas. It's obvious that they've made peace with the capricious, dangerous nature of ocean crossings. As a newbie sailor, I'm finding the combination of gale-force winds and boisterous seas to be utterly terrifying.

Lee's primary concern is the navigation system, which sometimes performs only intermittently. When it's working properly, we can pilot the boat from inside the salon using autopilot, GPS, and radar without having to subject ourselves to unfavorable weather conditions. When the autopilot fails, the person on duty has to sit at the helm and steer under *all* circumstances—gale-force winds, cold pelting rain, and lightning.

On entering the salon to start my watch the third evening, I find Bruce, supposedly on duty, snoring away like a buzzsaw on the couch. I empathize with him because it's extremely challenging to stay awake and alert after midnight. Not wanting to wreck my sleep in a few hours, I stimulate myself with computer games instead of coffee. Every twenty minutes, I step into the cockpit, where I crane my neck in all directions, checking through the inky darkness for lights from distant ships or sailboats.

The crazy-making forward propulsion that we've experienced for five days *finally* ends. On November 21st, we join hundreds of boats from all over the world in a slow waltz in the peaceful U-shaped harbor of St. George's Town, the first permanent and continuously inhabited English town in Bermuda and the New World.

The early morning sun warms my face as I snuggle up to Lee as he sleeps. Outside our window is a dazzling view of transparent, shimmering, turquoise-blue water highlighted by the white roofs and pastel-colored bungalows of St. George's in the distance. In spite of all the drawbacks, I'm beginning to fall in love with the boating life. The fact that we made it here makes me feel good and even a little more confident as a newbie sailor.

Back on land, I feel as if I'm still swaying with the rhythm of the boat until my body returns to equilibrium hours later. St. George's is currently celebrating its founding, and the mayor flirts with me as I walk past. Removing his large faux gold mayor's necklace, he places it around my neck while Lee takes a photograph.

I'm baffled over having blurred vision in my right eye, which has now dilated into one large blackberry. *What the hell is this? It must be a brain tumor. Or maybe I'm losing my vision in that eye. Oh God, why now? Just as I'm starting this remarkable journey.*

Frowning, Lee says, "Honeybunch, we're going to the hospital!"

But first, we visit the local doctor, who looks confused and asks, "Are you on drugs?"

"No, I never use drugs," I answer in an uppity voice.

I've now morphed into my frightened little girl mode as Lee and I wait on a sidewalk bench for the next bus to the hospital. A man walking by reminds me to keep my sense of humor. While stretching his straw hat toward us, he asks, "Did you know it costs a dollar to sit here?"

Lee repeats his words out loud, and the man, grinning, replies, "You must be American! Americans *always* repeat what you say!"

We sit on uncomfortable, butt-numbing white plastic chairs while waiting to see a specialist. Lee rubs my back in a reassuring way, then pecks me on my cheek. "You're going to be okay, Tiger Lily. I'm sure of it!"

A physician stops by several times to let us know he's trying to get in touch with an ophthalmologist. Worried, he says, "I've never seen anyone before with one dilated eye." Then adds, "I think we should do some blood work. Then a CAT scan."

Seeing big dollar signs in my head, I reply, "Uh, no thanks. My insurance won't cover that."

The ophthalmologist, fresh from surgery, approaches us. "Have you come into contact with a chemical?"

"I've been wearing a Scopolamine patch for seasickness, and maybe I was a little lax about washing my hands after touching it."

"Aha! That's it! In twelve hours to two weeks, your eye will return to normal."

Suddenly reborn into a brand new, positive reality, I'm filled with exuberance and love for Lee who has remained by my side throughout the whole ordeal. Thankfully, our dream journey will continue to unfold.

Just as we're heading for the door, the first doctor stops by and quips, "So! You're not going to die after all!"

———

While admiring the aquamarine water in St. George's harbor, my thoughts are interrupted by the annoying sound of Sally and Bruce arguing in their cabin below. Like a grizzly older couple who've been together *way* too long, they bicker at each other as they board the dinghy for a daytime land excursion. Hours later, they're still arguing when they pull up to the boat.

I'm grateful that Lee and I don't bicker the way they do, although I can't help but notice that Lee has been somewhat distant lately. For the first time since we started sailing together, I've started worrying about our relationship. Deeply bonded with Sally, his only female cousin, his attention has been focused on her. She speaks his nautical language in a way that I can't, and, even worse, she can repair anything, even engines. Feeling invisible and out of my league with her around, I'm a little jealous.

Damn! I was hoping to forgo waiting on men at this stage of my life, I mutter under my breath as Sally fetches things for Lee. She reminds me of my Southern grandmother who declared at family dinners, "Save the biggest steaks for the men! Keep the largest slices of pie for our darlings!"

Sally, a feminist who devoured Gloria Steinem and Betty Friedan books in the late '60s and early '70s, has suddenly transmuted into June Cleaver. I'm tempted to slip into this mode myself since it seems to attract positive male attention. Maybe this kind of attention is better than no attention at all. I never offer Lee water. My God, I constantly forget to offer myself water.

Feeling needy and vulnerable, I scurry about in a flowered apron and fawn over both men while Sally is preoccupied with adjusting the jib. "Are you boys thirsty?" I ask timidly. "Can I fix you a snack?"

———

Commanders' Weather Service advises us to wait a few days before leaving for St. Martin. The current forecast is for thirty-five-knot winds with twelve-foot swells. Two sailboats recently arrived here with broken masts and booms and shredded sails. It's rumored that they didn't have the patience to wait for a good weather window, which is always a bad idea.

Their partnership no longer working, Sally and Bruce

decide it's best if he returns to San Francisco. Lee and I have been feeling very uneasy about their constant bickering. Sounds carry in a boat's small and contained space, so relationship problems between people are hard to ignore.

Pope, who is Sally's friend from childhood, will crew on this last leg of the journey to St. Martin. On his arrival, he immediately plasters zinc oxide all over his face, making him look like Ebenezer Scrooge. A prominent congressional lawyer, Pope is a slim, clean-cut, grey-haired man who has sailed his entire life. During his youth, while sailing nude off the coast of Virginia with his father, their sailboat capsized and sank. Swimming to shore, they endured the embarrassment of appearing naked on a crowded public beach.

While Lee studies the weather and the navigation charts, Sally, Pope, and I wash and polish the sides of the boat. We accomplish this by balancing like acrobats on top of the soft, bouncy inflated sides of the dinghy, almost falling into the water when it rocks back and forth uncontrollably from the wakes of passing boats. I've now morphed from a 1950s housewife in a flowered apron into a dashboard hula doll.

The afternoon before we leave for the next phase of our trip, we hear a knock on the side of the boat and are greeted by a boyishly handsome man and his pretty wife from Charleston, South Carolina, who have motored over in their dinghy.

"We've been admiring your boat. Would you mind letting us come aboard to see what it looks like inside? We've never been on a catamaran."

On board he introduces himself as Neal Petersen, from Cape Town, South Africa. He was the first man of Black African heritage to race single-handed around the world in a thirty-eight-foot sailboat that he designed and built himself. Neal currently travels the globe as a motivational speaker.

Over Lee's chicken curry dinner, Neal tells the story of his childhood. Born without a hip socket, he endured three surgeries and five months in a cast that stretched from his ankle to his chest when he was a youth. While he was immobilized in the hospital, people gave him sailing magazines to read, and he became intrigued with the idea of sailing around the world.

With the help and support of a wonderful mother who was a schoolteacher, he overcame his physical disabilities, his working-class circumstances, and the apartheid system of that time period that made it next to impossible for a Black man to get ahead. As a teenager, he managed to get a part-time job at a yacht club, and eventually, through sheer determination, he landed crewing jobs in spite of countless rejections.

After years of crewing in races, he shared his dream of sailing around the world solo with some high-powered businessmen in Cape Town. At the same time, Bill Pinkney, a sailor from Chicago who was on his way to becoming the first Black man to sail solo around the world, entered his life. During Bill's nine-month sailing odyssey, he stopped for a layover in Cape Town and rented a room at Neal's childhood home. Neal shared his dream with Bill, who promptly became the main financial supporter of his dream to design and build a boat. Not long afterward, several businessmen in Cape Town also joined in with financial support. And now, here we all were together.

———

Sally and I walk into town for one last provision run before our five-day passage to St. Martin. After she chooses the cheaper generic brands with weird names and odd ingredients, we fill her large, brightly-colored Mexican shopping bags with fresh beets, broccoli, cabbage, christophine, turnips, cassava, leeks, potatoes, and loquats, plus ingredients for fish chowder. Unlike me, she has *no* fear about figuring out how to prepare exotic vegetables, and I realize that I need to keep expanding my world.

Rounding St. George's jetty, the water shimmers pearly blue in the early morning light. Lee's big toothy grin welcomes me as I join him at the helm, and he pulls me closer. "I was hoping you'd join me, my sweet love. I can't thank you enough for joining me on this wonderful, crazy adventure."

Lately, he's been understandably distracted by the nitty-gritty preparations for our upcoming ocean passages. And somewhat aloof. I'm noticing that he completely focuses on one thing at a time and that I probably shouldn't take his aloofness personally. Thankfully, though, we'll soon have plenty of chances to be alone together. I look forward to having Lee *all* to myself.

———

Imagine traveling on a nonstop, around-the-world flight that is constantly hitting heavy turbulence that causes carry-ons to fall out of the overhead. During these alarming moments, you glance around to see if general hysteria is setting in. A long boat passage can be just like this. Except you're outdoors most of the time, breathing in fresh air. Not the recycled version.

Now that we've left the infamous Bermuda Triangle, I figure things will settle down. Sally, wanting to support me, suggested a few days before our departure, "Why don't you just fly to St. Martin? Why put up with the nausea?" But

I simply shook my head and explained that I was driven by my desire to experience the *complete* version of a sailing adventure. How can I call myself a true sailor if I'm only having the watered-down version? I'm okay with faking it while trying to appear like I know what I'm doing. Eventually, I'll be a pro.

The sun is warming my skin on this balmy, pleasant day. Persistent stiff winds propel us onward into large frothy rollers that explode like heavy logs against the boat's sides and underbelly. Slowly working my way to the galley to fix lunch, I trudge across the cockpit bow-legged with my feet planted firmly on the deck to counterbalance the boat's jerky, lurching movements.

Under conditions like this, it takes a lot of effort to do even the simplest things in the galley. Awkwardly, I press myself against the counter next to the stove to keep from falling while I warm up homemade split pea soup. Fortunately, pots and pans remain in place on the catamaran's stationary stove. The table, however, can't be set in the traditional way. To avoid having plates and flatware fling themselves across the room, I hand the soup bowls and spoons to everyone.

On this second day of our passage, I'm preoccupied with the boat's unsteady pitching and jolting movement. Lying in the cockpit with my head propped up on two pillows, I attempt to read while trying to ignore the fact that I feel dizzy every time the boat lurches upward violently. My book, as if it has a mind of its own, suddenly hurtles itself across the floor as seawater dribbles down my chin onto my T-shirt and my stash of Saltines fling themselves up into the air. Wishing I felt better, I peek into the galley window at Sally, who is never seasick. Lying on the salon couch, she is reading a yellowed, dog-eared paperback while Pope hunches over a crossword puzzle. Lee, on watch, hasn't experienced seasickness either. Not once.

When I head below, my body propels itself into walls and objects as I inch my way toward the head. To keep from being hurtled off the toilet, I grasp anything protruding, then nauseously bend over to pump the toilet ten times to force salt water into the bowl, then another ten times to release the water. During these extended flushing episodes, I think enviously about the famous female sailor who perfected the art of peeing off the stern in spite of her anatomical limitations.

Breathing in the salty air, feeling its wild embrace, I spend my woozy off-duty hours daydreaming and gazing at the ever-changing waves and the cloud formations racing across the sky. Often my thoughts return to my sons, and I wonder if they're missing me as much as I miss them.

By day four, we all need a shower and a change of clothing. Both men are bewhiskered. Pope has a porcupine hairdo and looks like a specter with his zinc oxide face and large beaky nose. Fortunately, my seasickness has vanished.

I don't even bother to respond to Lee's recent comment: "Wendy, you always look so frightened."

He's right. I am frightened, but I wish he'd stop pointing it out. What possessed me, anyway, to want to become a sailor? And live in a state of panic for long periods of time? I must be addicted to adrenaline. The *true* driving force behind my putting up with this, I realize, is my infatuation with Lee.

Night is upon us as we round the headland of St. Martin and move ghost-like toward the tranquility of Baie de Marigot, where the sea sparkles from the gold reflections from the shore lights. Alone at the port helm, I marvel over the tiny bioluminescent plankton that shine like stars from the water being stirred up by our slow movement. Maybe this is why I'm really here. To experience these everyday miracles of nature.

The island of St. Martin, which lies in the middle of the Lesser Antilles, is influenced by its strong ties to France and Holland. After the cruise ships have disgorged their passengers at Marigot, this little seaside town is transformed into a lively, vibrant place. Its fancy jewelry stores, designer clothing boutiques, and open-air markets suddenly come alive. West Indian and French eateries are thrown into overload and confusion as hundreds of people line up for local delicacies. Four hours later, the weary, well-fed tourists toddle back to buses blaring loud rock music.

We will visit the French-owned section on the island's north end and the Dutch-owned southern region many times during our year-long sailing journey throughout the Caribbean. The French end is called the French West Indies while the Dutch-owned area is named the Netherlands Antilles. The island's mountain slopes are covered with dry forests of cacti, spiny bushes, and low, compact trees. Running the length of the island are thirty-seven gorgeous white sandy beaches overlooking crystal-clear water. St. Martin's tropical, wet-dry climate supports agave plants, date and coconut palms, cacti, succulents, bougainvillea, and plum and fig trees. The becalmed Dutch-owned Simpson Bay is also populated by a pesky mosquito population, while the perennially windy French region has none.

Tourists relax at the numerous small cafés overlooking Marigot's pebbly beaches. Plates are heaped with locally caught fish fried to a deep golden brown in coconut oil, sweet-smelling saffron rice, shredded carrots, greens, orange mangoes, and bananas. Batiks, cottons, and silks in vivid tropical patterns are draped over tables in the outdoor markets, where long gauzy dresses sway in the breeze and brightly colored cotton sarongs spin on their hangers.

As I stand there admiring the colorful clothing, the shop-keepers suddenly throw wide plastic sheets over their wares as a short rain squall moves through. I lift my face toward the raindrops, letting the warm, gentle drizzle wash my face. Rain showers are part of the daily rhythm here during rainy season.

I've lost track of the days. Time doesn't matter. Our boat twirls around continuously in the constant December north-east trades. Last night, we were awakened by the rolling, toiling sea as it feverishly pushed us in all directions.

Lee continues to have problems with the navigation sys-tem. Thankfully, heaven intervenes. A sixty-foot luxury yacht anchors next to us with Lee's navigation technician from Newport on board.

Eyes squinted, brows deeply furrowed, Lee scowls as the technician clicks seemingly random buttons. Sally and I flee the boat and its nautical issues to enjoy a driving tour of the island's north end. She pulls over on a deserted hilly road bordered by dry forested slopes to study the map and locate the route to the seaside village of Grand Case, which is bor-dered by soft green rolling hills and tree-studded grasslands. While she stares at the map, a small spunky donkey with long black eyelashes sticks its big head and floppy ears through my window, planting its furry self onto my lap. Sally, a little annoyed, acts as if having a donkey poke its head through a car window is nothing out of the ordinary.

"How cute!" I shriek, giggling hysterically as its whis-kered wet snout tickles my legs. Regretfully, I gently push its head back out the window.

Sadly, Sally and Pope need to return to their busy lives.

We knew from the beginning that it was never their intention to live indefinitely on the boat with us. Sally has a lot of ongoing commitments in San Francisco, where she lives, and Pope has a law practice in Washington, DC. They don't want to leave, and Lee and I don't want them to either. We've been like a little family during their stay in St. Martin. Feelings of melancholia sweep over us for days on end after their departure. Now it's just us, reentering and redefining our roles and rhythm as a couple. How wonderful it feels though, to be the center of Lee's attention again. Without warning, however, as we're relaxing in the cockpit, he jerks me out of my reverie.

"Wendy, you're still an apprentice," he tells me. "We have a teacher-student relationship as well as lovers. We need to know the logistics of what we're doing." Then he adds, "We need to review the characters we want to portray when we have charters. How will we interact with our guests? How do we welcome them into our dance?"

He's right. This is certainly something I need to think about and put into practice when we have charters. I need to present myself as a professional when people come aboard.

What we need right now is a live-aboard mechanic who can fix the nagging problems with the generator, the water maker, and the two engines. As soon as something is repaired, another thing breaks. Wondering what will happen next creates a lot of tension on the boat. I often find myself wishing Bruce was here, even if he was messy. I'm learning that the cliché "Living on a boat is about doing repairs in beautiful and exotic places" is true. A boat is a floating Midas shop.

The previous owner of the boat, a man named Vlad, jerry-rigged an astounding number of systems on board as he was slipping into dementia. The yards and yards of wiring to the navigation system look like a Tanzanian snake pit, and there are a whopping number of white plastic pipes underneath the berths leading to nowhere. The transmuted generator is now called Frankenstein. After Lee debugs something mechanical, we both know but don't say that another repair nightmare will soon follow.

We take a break from boat issues to share a tiny shower at Shrimpie's Bar and Launderette in Simpson's Bay on the Dutch side. A boater friend recommended their free wireless service and delicious Dutch beer plus a shower. The space is also shared with spinning, swishing, slightly rusted washing machines and loud whirring dryers. A heavily bearded Englishman with boozy red, swollen eyes, wearing flowered bathing trunks and a white wife beater shirt, hovers just outside our thin see-through shower curtain, and I hastily cover myself. "When will the shower be available?" he asks the attendant gruffly.

Listen, bloke, I haven't had a shower in days, and I feel like an unmade bed. So go get a beer and chill out. I want to say this but don't as I luxuriate in the deliciously warm water flowing over my body.

In the corner of the laundromat near the shower is a rickety bamboo table upon which rests a motel-sized shampoo and soap and a clean mini brush that I run through my thick curly auburn hair, pressing hard until the bristles meet my scalp. Overhead is a dusty fan so enhanced with spider webs that it's almost unrecognizable. After this deliciously strange experience, I hand the attendant our damp bath towels and $2.50 for the take-as-long-as-you-like shower: a deal. In Bermuda, the showers at the marina were $2 a minute.

After that weird experience, we're ready to hightail it back to the boat, which is anchored out in the bay. After a quick lunch at a small café, we head back and relax in the salon with our books. Suddenly, Lee throws his book aside and races into the cockpit. He stomps across the deck so hard it's amazing the boat doesn't cave in. Grabbing my sarong and wrapping it around my naked body, I sprint toward Lee as if a motor is attached to my ass. A massive powerboat is drifting our way. While Lee attempts to wedge the dinghy between us, there is a loud grating noise as it cracks into our stern.

Propelled by a hearty dose of adrenaline and partially airborne, Lee leaps back onto our boat and turns on both engines while yelling, "Pull up the anchor! Fast! Run!"

I rush madly to the bow, where I start pulling it up while my left hand preoccupies itself with keeping the sarong on. In spite of that, one breast pops out.

The anchor's bridle is wrapped in a massive mound of mud and seagrass, so I try to remove a little before hauling in the anchor.

"What the hell are you doing up there?" Lee yells testily from the cockpit.

"I'm trying to get rid of the seagrass so it won't clog up everything," I say sheepishly as my sarong falls off, revealing my nude self to everyone at the posh Simpson Bay Marina.

The anchor is encased within a solid mound of mud and grass, so I dunk it numerous times while Lee motors to another location. Now I understand why this anchorage is almost empty. Most anchors, including ours, don't hold well in mud and grass. This will be confirmed over and over again in various anchorages throughout the Caribbean and the Mediterranean.

Now that we're alone and settled for a while in St. Martin, Lee turns his attention to me, the student. He loves teaching and is quite good at it. I keep procrastinating about learning to drive the dinghy since I have left- and right-hand coordination issues, which can be a liability on a boat. Admittedly my line and knot skills need help. Lee looked at me recently with an expression of wonder as he studied my knot-tying technique.

"Why can't you do the knots correctly? What's with the raccoon hand thing?"

Embarrassed and deflated by his heavy-handed approach, I am determined to show him that I can master the art of making knots. In secret, I practice this using a book I bought at the marina in Beaufort that is written by a woman who has included understandable illustrations, not the indecipherable hieroglyphic images I've seen in other books.

One day, I finally get it right—the king of sailing knots, the bowline. A fixed loop at the end of a line and easy to untie, the bowline has been around for centuries. It's the most important knot to master and has all sorts of uses. It sings in its elegant simplicity, and I realize I've created something beautiful.

8

Driving the Dinghy

From time to time, Lee asks me, "Why don't you drive the dinghy today?"

Whenever that question surfaces, there's always a valid reason why I can't, such as a sudden need to go to the head. But the truth is, after watching Lee struggle with starting the outboard motor, making sure the gas has been mixed with the right amount of oil, and that none of the lines are kinked, and after hearing words like clogged filter, carburetor, spark plugs, and coils, I don't want to have anything to do with the damn thing.

Yet the dinghy is my ticket to independence, so I need to learn how to drive it. Tomorrow. When Lee isn't present, I stare at it with intimidation as if it's my enemy. Realistically, if I can't operate the dinghy I won't be able to go places by myself whenever I choose. I like Lee's companionship, but there are times I'd like to be alone.

A dinghy is a small inflatable watercraft that allows sailors to get some space from each other. They may also visit land to buy food, supplies, boat parts, and, most important, an ice cream cone. Plus, there's always the lure of internet cafés where sailors can catch up on email, drink overpriced lattes, smile at people who sneer back, and make costly international phone calls. Lee's light grey dinghy is awesome because it has a hard bottom and room for eight adults who can perch comfortably on its inflated sides. Most dinghies are much smaller and have soft, trampoline-like bottoms that make boarding tricky.

I watch self-assured, debonair sailors racing over azure waters in their dinghies. I want to be like them. I want to learn how to increase the speed until the front of the dinghy rises high out of the water, and then, radiating confidence, decrease the speed only seconds before pulling alongside the dock, creating an impressive wake that rocks all the boats nearby. After that, I want to walk away for hours with total assurance and no scared-rabbit glances back at the dinghy to make sure it is still there.

Soon after our arrival in St. Martin, I tested my dinghy driving skills on Lee, Sally, and Pope. Instead of slowing down, I gunned it just four feet from the rear of the catamaran. It was one of those moments where things seem to move in slow motion and you're afraid to see the damage. Sally and Pope disembarked, heads still intact. Lee motored a short distance away from the boat, then, scooting over, asked me to take the helm. Knowing the psychology behind this, I took over and puttered around the anchorage until my confidence returned.

The next day, Lee encouraged me to take the dinghy out on my own.

"Tomorrow, I'll do it," I said, ignoring his crestfallen face.

We've been in St. Martin for over a month now, and it's

apparent that I've procrastinated long enough about learning to drive the dinghy. The day finally arrives when dinner is limited to Campbell's baked beans and Norwegian sardines in olive oil. Salty air creates hearty appetites, and we eat like lumberjacks. Food disappears quickly.

"Lee," I say, "we really need some food."

"So why don't you take the dinghy yourself and buy some food?"

"You want me to drive the dinghy?" I ask, horrified. "All alone? Without you?"

"Yes, *you*!"

"Sorry, I can't. I need more practice runs."

I visualize a spectacular crash landing at the Baie de Marigot pier in front of groups of startled tourists. I'd prefer a test run off a deserted island where wild goats are the only observers. *No, this is not happening today!* I tell myself.

Confident that Lee will surely back down and be my chauffeur, I slide on my backpack, put on my sunglasses and hat, and then wait patiently for him in the dinghy. Instead, Lee hands me the VHF and says, "Call me on channel twenty-two if you have any problems."

I'm stunned. What is he thinking? Then I realize that I have to get out of my own way. I have two choices: sit in the dinghy and go nowhere, or turn it on and head into town—alone. I look at our brand-new, black, 25-HP Yamaha motor. The green and red buttons stare at me as if daring me to do something.

"Now, which one is on and which one is off?" I stupidly ask the air.

Just as I'm heading away on my very first solo trip, Lee, grinning like a Cheshire cat, comes into the cockpit then leans over the lifeline and blows me a kiss.

As I'm heading to St. Martin's shoreline in the distance, I finally get the nerve to gun the throttle and bring the dinghy to a plane. Wow! This is so easy. And fun! I needed that little kick in the pants. Why did I wait so long to do this? As I near the small town of Marigot, I turn and look at the boat, which is now a speck in the distance among a throng of sailboats.

I wrap the painter around one of the numerous boat cleats along the shore. A dinghy painter is a lightweight polypropylene rope that's tied to the bow of the dinghy and secures the inflatable to a dock or a pier. I have a small padlock that I attach to the painter to prevent anyone from taking off with the dinghy. Lee and I only do this if we're in heavily populated areas.

I head over to a bustling outdoor café and order spicy Caribbean shrimp with rice then catch up on email with my family at the internet café next door. Alarmingly, an unusual plumbing situation causes dirty dishwater from the café to bubble up through the drain next to my feet.

Feeling very content after my delicious meal and the spontaneous acquisition of two lovely Caribbean sundresses, I realize that it might be wise to head back to the boat. Still feeling a little insecure about the dinghy, I reassure myself that the return trip will be just as flawless.

Just as the sun is setting, I encounter a problem while motoring through a canal. A heavy current pushes the dinghy onto a shallow ledge before I can lift the engine. The motor dies and I imagine the propeller looking pretzeled. A boy, watching me from the other side of the canal, hollers, "Do you need help?"

"Yeah, sure!"

He hops into the dinghy and removes the cover to the engine. "No problem here," he says after a quick inspection.

"I wonder why I can't start it up again . . . the propeller must have hit a rock . . . do you know of anyone who can tow me back to my boat?" I ask as I picture Lee's worried expression on my return.

After a quick investigation of the propeller with a flashlight, the boy says, "No problem there!"

"Well, what would keep the motor from turning on?" I ask him, looking bewildered. Then I glance down at the gear, which is in the forward position. Oh geez! Duh! In order to start the motor, the gear needs to be in neutral, of course.

As the motor roars on full throttle, I bring the dinghy to a plane, which means that it lifts up at a steep angle for a few moments and then rides flat over the water. It has to be going very fast for this to happen. Before it reaches a plane, passengers have to hold on to something to keep from falling backward. Once the dinghy is flat on the water, passengers no longer have to grip the side handles.

The dinghy purrs as I slow down the boat, creating a wave that rocks it gently back and forth. Lee, summoned from his book by the sound, appears in the cockpit. Leaning over the railing, he smiles. "How did your shopping adventure go?"

"Great! No problems! Easy peasy!" I say.

"Well done! High five!" he answers with gusto.

I did it! It may sound silly, but I'm really proud of myself for facing my fear of driving the dinghy. For months now, Lee has been trying to get me to go out on my own, but I stubbornly refused. The day finally came when I had to accept the challenge. I've noticed that when Lee pushes me beyond my comfort zone, and I persevere and succeed, my self-confidence soars.

That evening, I burrow close to Lee in bed while listening to him as he reads a book out loud to me. Leaning my head against his chest, I feel a primal vibration, and I realize that sometimes the small, seemingly insignificant things are what matter.

———

The red hibiscus Lee tucks behind my ear is really all I need for Christmas. While embracing me, he says, "Tiger Lily, I've searched for you my entire life. I am so lucky to have found you. Thank you, my love, for joining me on this adventure."

Overjoyed by his sweet words, I am, however, a little disappointed that he didn't buy me something small while we were shopping the day before in Gustavia, the capital of St. Barthélemy. A pair of dangly earrings or a locally made bracelet would have been perfect. On the other hand, what else could I possibly need when the whole world is sitting at my feet, waiting for me to explore it with the man I adore?

Located in the French West Indies in the northwestern part of the Caribbean, St. Bart's lies twenty-two miles from St. Martin's southern point. A volcanic island, St. Bart's is one mile wide and ten miles long and is encircled by shallow coral reefs. For almost a hundred years, it has been a colony of Sweden. In 1784, the French minister to Louis XVI ceded this island to the Swedes in exchange for trading privileges in the Swedish port of Gothenburg.

Marine plankton, known as dinoflagellates, sparkle and swirl in the dark emerald water like glowworms while millions of stars gild the clear night sky above Anse de Colombier, a tiny bay located in the far northwestern part of the island. We sit sandwiched together on the trampoline, our legs spread before us. As I relax into Lee's chest, I can just make out the faint hum of nearby voices flowing our way through light puffs of wind. As a low swell traverses the bay, we rock gently back and forth as if we're in a hammock.

Out of nowhere, fickle wind gusts turn our boat to the right, then to the left, then back again. Coming into view is a portly, bulbous-nosed man dressed as Santa entertaining young children in a cockpit. The background quickly shifts to a boat lit from end-to-end with multicolored Christmas lights and a young couple toasting each other on the bow.

Currently feeling enormously content, my earlier comical baptism into the life of being a sailor keeps replaying in my head. Every single sailor has at least one of these moments. Sally's happened when she crewed on a cross-Atlantic passage with six strangers. In charge of washing dishes one evening, she accidentally threw all of the flatware overboard with the dirty dishwater.

My own moment of initiation happened on our first Christmas Day together in 2006. Under a sky concealed with clouds that looked as if they had been smudged by an eraser, we motored toward a tiny arch-shaped beach sprinkled with sunbathing tourists. Lee yelled, "Jump out before we get too close! I don't want the dinghy to beach itself too fast."

Almost dislocating my hips, I jumped—fully dressed, with both my purse and my brand new camera slung over one shoulder—into crystalline water that appeared to be only two feet deep. The cold, salty sea rose over my shoulders and, hoping for a miracle, I tossed my wet camera to Lee.

Wanting to be a tough sailor instead of a wuss, I craned my head upward toward him while declaring enthusiastically, "We can still go on a hike! My shorts and T-shirt will eventually dry out as we walk."

"No, my dear, we need to head back to the boat so you can change."

Feeling befuddled and embarrassed, I hauled my ass back into the dinghy, and Lee motored back to the boat where I changed into dry clothing.

Now dressed in outfit number two, Lee and I motored to Gustavia, the capital of St. Barts, where we tied up to a pier.

I followed Lee along a hilly trail lined with low scrub, spiny cactus, outcroppings of dark basalt, green maidenhair ferns, and yellow daylilies. Orange butterflies flit around us in the flower-scented air as we peer cautiously at the azure sea far below and the rocky sides of the cliff, which form a backdrop to a long curvy beach pleated with volcanic stones.

We spend our last day at the Anse des Flamands beach, which is mostly crowded with young Americans. A gorgeous, bare-breasted young woman stands waist-deep in the water, stretching her arms overhead while a nubile girl with perfect buttocks saunters by, her tuchus jiggling seductively in her G-string bikini. Lee's eyes, now attached to springy coils, nearly pop out of his head and I feel a sharp twinge of jealousy. Sensing this, he looks over at me and laughs. "I'm with the most beautiful woman on this beach, Tiger Lily." Then he repeats his promise to me before we leave: "We'll love each other so much that everything else will be secondary."

Later, lying in bed next to Lee, who is slumbering, a sense of something mystical washes over me as a waft of air sweeps through the porthole and caresses my face. In the deep and abiding silence of the night, I can feel the soft shimmering of the Divine.

————

While traveling throughout the Caribbean, we listen to South Bound Herb's rather edgy and pontifical daily weather forecasting and routing service on the single sideband radio. Herb Hilgenberg, a Canadian who can be expressive and blunt in his choice of words, provides invaluable weather briefs to sailors crossing the Atlantic or cruising the Eastern Seaboard or the Caribbean. When he assures us that the swells—which are formed by windstorms hundreds of miles away—have dissipated, we take it as a go-ahead for our passage to Barbuda.

Leaving St. Bart's in the early morning, we sail past Saba, St. Kitts, and Nevis. Three miles off of Antigua's mountainous northern tip, we turn northwest toward Barbuda, Antigua's sister island. During my watch, I read a newly published book about the Leeward Islands, which states that we can only clear customs in Antigua. I rouse Lee from a deep sleep.

"Honey, I'm sorry to wake you up! There's just one little problem. Nothing major. The guidebook says we can't clear customs in Barbuda."

Disappointed, we change direction and head southward to Antigua and clear at English Harbor, where a customs official tells us this information is incorrect. The following day, I stand at the bow scanning for coral reefs while Lee negotiates his way through the shallow waters eight miles off Barbuda's flat western shore.

"Where's the island?" Lee wonders as he peers through his binoculars.

Three miles from shore, palm trees appear faintly. On our slow, careful approach, I'm almost blinded by the sun's reflection on the pale green water, which makes it difficult to spot the reefs. The foamy rollers help, however.

Slightly hard of hearing because of too many Jimmy Hendricks concerts, Lee continuously hollers back, "What did you say?" after I shout the directions.

So, with motorized legs, I sprint back and forth to Lee at the helm, giving him the latest updates.

"Make a forty-five-degree turn to the right."

Then minutes later, "Now go straight."

Then, "Make a sixty-degree turn to the left."

Safely past the reefs, our next challenge is anchoring in the untenable conditions.

"It's going to take me a while to master this second anchoring thing," I mutter wearily under my breath as I press my bony knees into the cold and unforgiving metal arm of the second anchor to keep it from slipping off the bow.

Sea birds soar over our boat, which is now snug and secure in the clear turquoise waters between Low Bay and Oyster Point. Anchored between several sailboats, we see a pristine white-sand coastline before us. I dive off the steps and almost collide with a four-foot-long barracuda with a massive overbite and a compulsive desire to follow me. Unable to shake the fish, I look into his cold, heartless eyes while pleading, "Please leave me alone!" Frustrated, I'm afraid to venture too far from the boat lest the barracuda decides I look delicious. In defeat, I swim back to the boat.

We reanchor the next day off Princess Diana Beach and the exclusive K Club Hotel, a remote paradise hideaway once favored by Princess Di, who frequented the resort with her children William and Harry.

From there, we zigzag anxiously through more reefs to the beautiful large and isolated Gravenor Bay on the island's most southern tip. A pod of dolphins jumps and swim between our pontoons as pelicans, seagulls, and ospreys soar overhead on wind currents.

There are two distinct faces to Barbuda. There's the wild and wooly windward side, which has numerous caves, cliffs, rocky overlooks, and crashing waves. And there's the leeward side, which has long, flat expanses of palm-treed deserted beaches interspersed with natural salt ponds. The island is twelve miles long and seven miles wide.

While we're here, I dream one night that I'm climbing a steep ladder to the entrance of a hospital, which is three stories up. A doctor in light blue scrubs follows close behind me, encouraging me and talking to me. My steps are labored and slow, so I start hauling myself up the ladder with my arms. Then suddenly, about halfway up, there's a change. I'm now floating up the ladder effortlessly, smoothly. Like a feather. Weightless. The doctor keeps pace with me. Suddenly we're both in a holding position at the top rung. Glancing down at the precipitous descent, I realize that I can't go back. There's no choice. I have to keep going. The entrance to the hospital is through a large open window over to the right, and as I stand there sizing up the situation, the doctor, smiling, turns his head toward me and says, "Don't worry! I'll help you get through that window."

Like a rock climber, I plant one foot onto a small ledge and attempt to haul myself upward. Unable to make it, I wait, knowing that when the time is right, I'll go through that window.

I believe this dream is about all the steps I've taken in my life to heal my spirit. It was hard, scary, and slow in the beginning. As I progressed, it became easier. The doctor represents the numerous helpers in my life who have supported me at every stage of my healing journey. Illumination awaits me through that window, and I'm almost there. I believe that once you've started the spiritual journey, you can't go back.

In the morning, Lee and I skin-dive off an exquisite reef decorated with an unusual mixture of yellow and orange coral, purple fans, and bright green seagrass that sway in the water currents. Nearby is a smaller reef shaped like a rectangular coffee table. Yellow-striped turquoise parrotfish, dark purple and yellow-tailed queen angelfish, and deep-blue tang move about inside the space as if they're in an aquarium.

We hike to the wild and isolated Spanish Point, home to the Sufferers, an extensive archaeological site where two-thousand-year-old Amerindian artifacts have been discovered. Happily disengaged from the world, we wander over to the windward side of the point where the cliffs meet the sea and the slate-colored surge crashes loudly against the limestone outcroppings.

Slipping on loose stones and searching for footholds, we work our way down the steep cliff to a small beach nestled between a cluster of large boulders. As the sun slips into the sea, our pockets bulging with multicolored sea glass and small pink shells, we inch our way back up the cliff face on hands and knees, grabbing onto shrubs and outcrops. Then, while ambling across a moonlit plateau covered with purple flowered vines and shrubs, we find a path that leads directly to our anchorage. Suddenly a loud snort startles us. Through the foliage, we see several wild donkeys eyeing us with curiosity. Lee, speaking in a soft voice, moves slowly toward them, but they skittishly back up into the underbrush. Horses and donkeys are owned by locals and are allowed to roam free in Barbuda with the deer, boar, feral cattle, sheep, and goats.

Lynton Thomas, a short, wiry, dark-skinned man in an orange Tommy Hilfiger shirt, picks us up the next morning in his four-wheel drive for an offroad tour of the island. I share our peanut butter and jelly rice cakes with him as we jounce along on hard-packed dirt through arid hills and valleys covered with scrub. He stops frequently to let goats and sheep traipse leisurely across our path.

At Codrington Lagoon on the northwest end of the island, we board a small red wooden boat for a visit to the Frigate Bird Sanctuary, home to over one hundred and seventy species of birds and five thousand frigate birds. It's the largest frigate bird colony in the world. George Jeffrey, a guide with Garden of Eden Tours, mentions that we just missed seeing Jimmy Buffett, who hired him for a bone fishing expedition the day before.

While edging closer and closer to the bird colony, the sky darkens with hundreds of large black female frigate birds making unearthly clicking sounds with their beaks while inspecting their potential mates twenty feet below. The males, which have eight-foot wing spans, perch in the mangrove bushes hoping to attract a female. Their red gular sacs are puffed out like balloons, and their beaks, long and curved into a spoon shape, beat on the rounded sacs. Black feathered heads, red spheres, and an occasional juvenile crowned in white down decorate the mangroves. Lee and I, utterly fascinated, try to absorb the sensory overload of birds flirting, courting, mating, clicking, darting, wheeling, and soaring only fifteen feet away.

As Lynton drives along a paved road flanking the ocean, I see a handsome, bare-chested, dark-skinned young male riding a racehorse bareback into the ocean.

"Wait! Stop! I need to take a picture!" I say.

Running to the pier, I watch a test of wills between the horse and the rider as he pulls the animal into a circular movement, taking them deeper and deeper into the ocean until only the horse's head is visible. As they resurface I take some of the best photographs of my life.

In Codrington's Madison Square, we creep past a tiny one-story white building that's a hive of activity and a handful of nondescript one- and two-story buildings. *Is this it?* I wonder. Hoping to refill our larder, which consists of peanut butter, rice cakes, and grape jelly, I cruise through the grocery store's five narrow aisles. Peering into a freezer full of hard-frozen unrecognizable meats and vegetables, I find a rock-hard chicken from the US. Lee finds freshly baked homemade bread pudding, which we share with Lynton as we drive toward the caves in the Two Foot Bay area in the island's northern region.

A magnificent deserted beach stands empty at the base of a cliff, where we rest for a few moments before ducking down into the cave. The tropicbird, a slender white creature that has an unusually long tail streamer, lives in the caves and cliffs in this area but never makes an appearance.

"I never take people in there!" Lynton protests as Lee and I veer off from the scheduled tour and crawl into the holes and crevices that branch out from the main cave, where ancient Indian drawings were found. Sighing loudly, Lynton gets down on all fours and reluctantly follows us as we tunnel like coal miners through rarely visited areas.

I feel like an adventurer in a Hollywood movie as I crawl through a narrow dark tunnel that's lit by only pinpricks of light from random small fissures above my head. Trying to fight off the mounting feelings of claustrophobia, I focus my mind on what might be ahead for me. Lee keeps mentioning Europe and South America, and I wonder how that will unfold. Reminding myself to live in the moment, I keep remembering Tom's words, "Live one day at a time."

But I can't stop the dreams that interrupt my thoughts.

9

Dominica's Mystical Fireflies

During the passage to Guadeloupe, we sail past the British island territory of Montserrat, which in 2006 is in the process of undergoing a minor volcanic eruption. Since heavy concentrations of gas bubbles in the waters off an active volcanic island can cause a drop in water density enough to make a yacht sink, we stay well outside of the exclusion zone. Streams of orange-red lava flow down the mountainsides of the Soufrière Hills Volcano, illuminating the night sky. In 1995 the volcano became active and by 1997 the capital city of Plymouth, the airport, and twenty other settlements were buried under forty feet of mud. The survivors of these traumatic disasters have suffered severe psychological distress and prolonged grief and melancholia. And, according to what I hear, this British island did not receive adequate help. I feel for these people.

Just before dark, we anchor off an industrial park in Pointe-à-Pitre, where rusting container ships and barges are moored. Our boat moves and sways as ferries speed to and fro from the Iles des Saintes. Our view continually shifts from the junky shoreline to the shabby, dilapidated monohulls surrounding us. Off our stern, a weather-beaten, compact aluminum boat covered with coiled-up lines and odds and ends retains only a small amount of its original sky-blue color. I see a lot of similar sailboats in the Caribbean, and I suspect that people live on these boats permanently because it's an affordable lifestyle.

A pre-Carnival party is heating up on the distant shore. Loud drums throb nonstop into the wee hours of the night. These primal sounds entwine themselves around me as I breathe in this highly charged, wildly vibrating air, then slowly slip into a drum-infused slumber.

The island's economy is on an unfortunate downturn from a lack of tourism. According to a French restauranteur here, the French turned their attention to Cuba and Santo Domingo and generally stopped visiting Guadeloupe in 2000. He added that St. Martin, Mustique, and St. Bart's were still thriving.

I make silly mistakes while trying to speak French. At a local grocery store, I exclaim to a perplexed check-out girl, "I love you!" when I mean to say, "I love this dessert!" Since my French is usually met with smiles, I keep trying. Once in a while, by mistake, eyebrows raise when I throw a few Swedish words into the mix.

On the first night of Carnival, we motor to the shoreline, where we watch hundreds of locals as they mill about, gyrating, singing, flirting, smiling, and laughing. Music with a loud tropical backbeat throbs in our ears as we warm ourselves at a small beach bonfire. Fireworks suddenly blaze overhead, illuminating the sky with streams of red, green, blue, gold, and purple, which trail across the sky like Mardi Gras necklaces and then shower down in long golden tendrils.

Never bothering to check into Guadeloupe, we dive illegally for two days in the Cousteau Reserve on the leeward side of the island. Jacques Cousteau claimed that this park is one of the best dive sites in the world. The colors in the reefs are exquisite. Fans, sponges, and brain coral are shades of mustard, violet, Chinese red, pale yellow, green, and creamy taupe. Reef sharks prowl while schools of needlefish, blue tang, groupers, juvenile damselfish, stoplight parrotfish, and triggerfish dart in and out of the reef's protrusions.

Days later, still anchored off Guadeloupe, I realize that this place has a few similarities to Coney Island—minus the hot dog stands and muscle men in wife beater T-shirts. The similarities include brownish sand, tacky souvenir shops, and oversized women of all ages wearing string bikinis. Dissimilarities, however, are the open ditches that transport fluorescent pink sewage. The smells from the effluent blend with the odors wafting into the air from mangos rotting on the ground and stale cigar smoke. And unlike Coney Island, random stacks of rubbish litter the surroundings where boney, starving, diseased dogs meander about looking for scraps. Lee and I, repulsed, head back to the boat. Time to leave.

The neighboring island of Marie-Galante brings us a brand new challenge—a boatload of unwelcome stowaways. Flying ants, better known as termites, cover the boat like a dark veil as we anchor off Folle Anse. Lee quickly puts screens on all the windows. Then he wonders aloud, "What does the water look like?"

Feeling grossed out, I ask, "What water?" as I look down at the hundreds of termites covering the cockpit. The sight of them makes me want to run and jump off the boat while yelling loudly. This is horrible!

As I steer the boat into the anchorage in nearby Dominica, I notice that Lee's hands are jammed into his pockets. "What's up?" I ask him. "You're looking a little uneasy."

Still feeling tainted by an unfortunate experience that happened over thirty years ago in Portsmouth, Dominica, Lee explains, "I was here with a group of friends, and we were swimming in a water hole deep in the rainforest. Suddenly, a huge dark-skinned man with crazed eyes came out of nowhere, brandishing a machete. Yelling wildly, he rushed at us. Miraculously we managed to calm him down, and he disappeared into the jungle. That experience has left me, unfortunately, with a bad taste for this island."

The smell of sewage assaults our senses as we pull the dinghy onto the beach and tie it to a palm tree. A few young boys sitting on the beach offer to watch the dinghy while we shop, but Lee rebuffs them quite rudely. As we're walking into town, an elderly man offers us yams from a tattered net bag perched on the end of a homemade surfboard. Lee replies curtly, "No!" Then, recognizing his cold-heartedness, he quickly rewords it. "No thanks, mon. Have a good day."

Unfortunately, his fear has infected me. In my current state of mind, everyone looks slightly unhinged—even the stooped-over elderly man with glassy eyes who shuffles past in a cloud of garlic and curry. And a forlorn rust-colored, flea-bitten dog that lounges on the sidewalk.

A barefooted Rasta wearing a tattered T-shirt comes toward us. His large deep-brown eyes peek out at us from a thick curtain of long black curly eyelashes. "Mon, I watch de dinghy for five dolla. Okay, mon?" Tired of saying no, we hire him.

The small, nondescript shops in Portsmouth have no signage except for a bakery and a bar blaring Rasta music into the street. Entering a murky, unmarked structure that appears to be a store, I quickly remove my sunglasses and try to make sense of a very odd assortment of random dusty objects that rest on half-empty shelves. Coco sticks and cinnamon bark sit next to four-dollar Chinese fly zappers and cans of corn with partially ripped-off labels.

I've often wondered if Caribbean governments purposely make it difficult for sailors to check in with their customs. We meander for over an hour along a curvy dirt road past abandoned rusty boats and a beached tanker that is currently being explored by five young boys. Feeling uncomfortable in the unrelenting heat and humidity, I try to ignore the dirt filling the spaces between my sandaled toes. Sweat trickling down my chest, I stop every now and then to yank up my baggy shorts which keep sliding down my hips.

Concealed behind a chain-link fence that supports a mountain of used tires and garbage, Dominica's customs check-in is a one-room concrete structure. Inside, a massive metal table reverberates while stacks of pink, yellow, and white stapled papers are stamped individually by a customs officer.

"Wow!" I blurt out. "This would be so much faster if you had a computer."

Lee gives me an irritated sidelong glance, silencing me.

The officer's dark wooden chair squeaks as he reaches for a rubber stamper that sits among a dizzying array of stampers—at least thirty. Peering over stacks and stacks and stacks of yellowing papers at least a foot high, he stamps our passports and then throws our papers across the room with disdain. "You're finished, mon."

In town, we eat lunch at the Iguana restaurant where, after rolling a forkful of food on my tongue and chewing it tentatively, I notice a weird gamey taste and quietly spit into my napkin.

On our walk back to the dinghy, we pass a little girl in a white dress that's covered with small hearts in pastel colors. Around her neck is a scallop-edged lace bib. She looks up and smiles shyly at me as I walk by.

———

The following day, we meet JC, a muscular, compact, exotically handsome Rastafarian who will be our Indian River tour guide. Before we climb into his canoe, Lee treats him to a peanut cream rum punch, which is the specialty of the house at the Bamboo Bar. After pointing out white crabs, doctor crabs, and mud crabs, JC shows us where *Pirates of the Caribbean: Dead Man's Chest* was filmed. The fictional islands of Pelegosto and Isla Cruces, with their lush mountainous jungles, are actually part of Dominica.

Lee and JC, now nude and tipsy, slide into a large, clear pool surrounded by flat boulders. Feeling prudish, I remain in my black bikini. JC drifts past me crocodile-like while touching my stomach with his hand. While Lee and I perform our customary baptismal dunking of our heads into the water three times, JC decides to do his own ceremony. With impressive speed, he shoves me against his erect penis, then forcefully dunks my head into the water three times as I splutter for air.

Next, after cracking open a coconut with a machete and then splitting the meaty sections into smaller bits with his teeth, he hands us tooth-marked wedges to gnaw on. For the grand finale, he masticates a piece of coconut, spits it into his hand, grabs me forcefully, and then quickly rubs the slimy mixture onto my chest and under my bikini top. Then, lightning fast, his hands slither down my body toward my crotch. Thrusting him away before he can continue any further exploration, I clamber out of the pond. What in the hell just happened? And why didn't Lee come to my aid? Truthfully, if Lee had noticed anything through the haze of pot and rum punch, it would have been a bloody miracle. Thankfully, I know how to fend for myself.

Back in town, I follow Lee's trust-fund swagger into a one-room car rental office, which is about the size of an American bathroom. Here, we rent a car for the duration of our stay in Dominica. On our way out the door, the salesman warns, "Be careful!"

Be careful about what? I wonder.

Lee's eyes are out on stems as we drive through the village. The women in Portsmouth dress very sexily, and I'm beginning to feel jealous as we pass women in clothes that are molded to their bodies.

On one drizzly day, while we're in the throes of cabin fever, a local recommends we visit Rita and Kirk, who live in the Layou River Gorge.

"They're American. And really nice! They'd love it if you dropped by."

During our search for their unmarked driveway on a curvy red clay road, we stop alongside five tired-looking men and women who are covered from head to toe in mud. A stooped grey-haired man in the group explains that they have been in the "wets," where they toil daily harvesting bananas and plantains with rusted machetes.

"You'll like them!" he adds while pointing to Rita and Kirk's driveway down the road.

We drive slowly past a tiny pale-blue cinderblock building with a sign that says "Massage Studio" and pull up alongside a bamboo hut that rests on a hillside covered with crocus, philodendron, and dieffenbachia. Rita and Kirk come out to say hello as if they've been expecting us. They are some of the most welcoming people I've ever met. Wearing a pink shirt tied over the waist of her beige slacks, Rita has wide blue eyes and dyed red hair that accentuates her freckled paleness. Kirk, lean like his wife, has short spiky grey hair, a sharp nose, and a pointy chin. One ear is pierced with a couple of earrings, and his left arm has several tats. Lee and I like them immediately. Radiating kindness, they welcome us into their home as if we're long-lost friends.

A rock painted with the words "Welcome to Zen" greets us as we enter their tiny living space of one bedroom, a kitchenette, and a minuscule pantry. The ceilings are high, and there's a space between the roof and the bamboo walls for hurricane protection. The window frames, glassless, have bamboo closures held open by thin ropes. A white mosquito net surrounds the jungle-print-covered bed, and Rita's half-finished acrylic painting of a young girl leans against the back wall.

The only place to have an in-depth conversation is in their bedroom, where we're offered a seat on a small wooden bench at the end of their bed. Fascinated with these charming people, we both start asking questions about how they ended up in the middle of a jungle and what keeps them here. They tell us, "We both felt unfulfilled with our corporate jobs in Miami, so we started checking out different Caribbean islands. Dominica has an infrastructure that isn't as well developed as the other Caribbean islands and the last three climate disasters wreaked havoc on the island. It's one of the poorest islands in the Caribbean, so we decided to focus on helping the small community where we live."

That evening, Rita offers us the two futons in her massage studio, where Lee and I are lulled to sleep by the gurgling sounds of a nearby stream. Early the next morning, after a light breakfast, the four of us slide down a steep slope while holding on to small trees and rocks, to a ledge over the river where we perch side by side on a boulder. Kirk and Rita describe their life's work in Dominica, which involves teaching young children, helping the people in their neighborhood, and supporting their community with their extensive knowledge of agriculture. Several families live on their land in bamboo cabins that they helped build. After meeting a few of the people in the neighborhood, it's very apparent that Kirk and Rita are loved and respected. They've created a self-sustaining enchanted oasis deep in the rainforest.

Their overall mission here is to educate the local people about agriculture and which crops do well in this specific environment and what natural remedies can be used to keep insects away. Their end goal is to help as many people as possible. The locals we meet love these amazing people. I'm so happy that we have a chance to spend a little time with them.

———

Two days later, we head to the village of Bense and Chauiere Pool in a rental car without seat belts. The two-lane curvy road to the island's northern tip has no guard rails and is edged by deep concrete drainage ditches on both sides. Meeting several cars head-on as we round serpentine curves,

Lee comes to a full, screeching stop as they obliviously race past. My job, while Lee zigzags to avoid potholes, is to look for road signs that don't exist while rolling about in the front seat like a marble.

The paved road we're on, unfortunately, turns into a secondary dirt road overwhelmed with water-filled potholes. Eventually, the middle of the road evolves into an impassable mound of red clay. Unable to continue and unsure of what to do next, we leave the car balanced precariously on a rocky ridge.

For two hours, the sun beats down on us as we tromp through shallow streams and fast-moving rivers where we jump from boulder to boulder. While sliding down an almost vertical incline to Chauiere Pool, we meet a minister midway down resting in the shade of a balsam tree after working on the steeps planting carrots and yams. Out of the heavy hard clay, he has carved out ledges along the hillside and planted vegetables "in neat rows like they do in the US," he tells us. Handing us a bag of grapefruit, he talks with pride about his thriving farm of citrus groves, avocados, nutmeg, bananas, mangos, coconut palms, pineapples, breadfruit, and papayas. Thankfully, he and his broad-shouldered son help us move the car off the mound.

The Rastafarians here are free-spirited, joyful, and totally in the moment. And, of course, super relaxed. Swept away by their charismatic personalities and getting used to their constant teasing, we laugh our way across the island with these delightful people.

Pancho, a charismatic and virile young man, enters our life at our next anchorage. Nicknamed "the Rasta Boat Man" by visiting sailors, he helps connect sailboats to the moorings in the rough waters off the town of Roseau on the island's southwest coast. He whips across the bay in his speedboat from morning to night, taking sailors to the town dock for shopping trips and tours. Soon after arriving at this new anchorage, Pancho takes us on a jeep tour to the Soufrière Sulphur Springs at the island's southern tip.

As we drive through the town of Roseau, Lee mentions to Pancho, "The Dominican women are some of the sexiest, prettiest women I've ever seen. Look at her in that sexy red top!" He points to a beautiful twenty-something woman walking across the road in front of us wearing a top that's more of a second skin and a super tight black skirt. "Wow! She's gorgeous."

Pancho glares at him. "Love the one you're with, mon!"

Finally, someone is calling Lee out on his behavior. I've wanted and needed support from someone. *Anyone!* I should have realized he was trouble. Truthfully, I knew what I was getting into after Lee exclaimed on our very first date, "I love women! I prefer them to men."

He had also admitted that he was a big flirt, a fact I chose to ignore at the time. When he had proclaimed that he was a five-year serial monogamist, I ignored that too. Most men tell you who they are in the very beginning, but I was sure that things would be different with me.

In the growing darkness, we arrive at the Soufrière, which is named after one of the island's volcanoes and is located near the Waitukubuli Hiking Trail. Flashlight in hand, Pancho leads us into the lush rainforest past a sulphur deposit area where the baking hot ground is scorched white. Sulphur fumes fill the air as we hike past bubbling mud to a large mist-covered, pale-green, geothermal pool in a clearing. With our heads resting on the soft moss-covered ground, we laze side by side in the shimmering hot water listening to the chirping of crickets and the hum of insects under a canopy of stars suspended overhead. As Lee removes his bathing trunks, Pancho mentions that it's frowned upon to be naked in public in Dominica.

A few days later, Lee and I drive to a national park surrounded by volcanic mountains to swim at Trafalgar Falls. On our way through the parking lot, a seven-foot-tall park ranger with long dreadlocks and coal-black skin approaches us to wish us a good hike to the falls. We smile as he presses his fist against our fists saying, "Soul Brother! Soul Sister!"

We hike along a dirt path for an hour or so, going deeper and deeper into the dense, musty rainforest teeming with bird sounds. It's a fairytale place, both luminous and dark, under a treed canopy. We continue until we reach the falls, where we swim in the cool, frothy water. Wearing a mask and goggles, Lee confirms that there's a white crab sitting directly under the waterfall. Just like every waterfall we've visited in Dominica.

On our way back to the parking lot, we stop at a mini waterfall. Sunset is approaching, so I suggest we stay only momentarily, but Lee loses all sense of time as he floats about on his back in the pond. As evening descends, I become anxious. Having forgotten our flashlights, we dress and feel around on the ground for odds and ends, then edge our way back to what we hope is a path as cricket chirping sounds break the jungle's silence. Since there is no full moon to light our way to the parking lot, we can't find the trail.

"Maybe we should spend the night here and wait until dawn to find our way back," I suggest, swallowing the urge to say *I told you so.*

Suddenly, an otherworldly ball of twinkling fireflies about four feet in diameter materializes in front of us, and we stare at it in wonder. One firefly approaches me, flying to my face and then down the front of my body. Another one checks out Lee. One very brave firefly passes between our legs while another lands on my arm and is joined by another. Then they circle back. To our astonishment, the whole group of fireflies splits into two and line the path to help us find our way out. They do this until we reach the parking lot, where they vanish as suddenly as they appeared. The park ranger meets us, saying, "Mon, I was afraid you were lost!"

When we mention our experience with the fireflies, he nods his head as if he's heard this story before. I know that we weren't alone that evening in the forest. We were in the company of angelic beings. Every time I think about this, my eyes tear up.

10

A Pod of Humpback Whales

It's an early spring day in the month of April, and we're still anchored off the island of Dominica. It's very easy to get a little complacent at anchorages. Lee suddenly puts his book down and turns toward me. "Hey, why don't we do an overnight to Martinique? You can provision at the grocery store on the bay while I look for boat parts."

Feeling complacent about leaving our cozy spot, I finally give in. We'll be giving up a private, peaceful anchorage in Portsmouth, Dominica, for a sixteen-hour sail to Grand Anse d'Arlet on Martinique's southern coast. Aware that it's important to arrive at this bustling bay during daylight hours, we time our departure for noon. Although it's not hurricane season, a period during which thousands of boats seek safe hurricane holes all over the Caribbean, this bay is always packed with sailboats, many of which lack evening anchor lights—we could run into them inadvertently in the dark.

Wearing quick-drying sailing shirts and shorts, nerdy black sunglasses that look like the kind you'd get after eye surgery, and big-brimmed safari hats with ties under the chin, we sit beside each other at the helm under an intense blue sky. Glancing over at me, Lee flashes his seductive boyish grin, which I'm starting to find truly annoying. That grin sets me up for all sorts of things.

Roughly five miles northwest of Dominica, I spot a heart-shaped whale blow in the distance off the port side. "Wow! Hey, Lee! Look over there. Are those whales?"

This deep basin area off Dominica's west coast is a well-known route for humpback whales heading north to New England for the summer months. During breeding season, they return to the Caribbean, where they remain from February to April.

"I think you're right," he says. "Let's head on over."

While he restarts the port engine and moves the boat off the wind, I pull down the main. While furling the jib, Lee asks playfully, eyes sparkling, "How would you like to swim with the whales?" As if this was a completely normal thing to ask.

"Excuse me, what did you just say?" I sputtered. "You want me to do *what*?"

I gaze solemnly at the whales breaching on the horizon. *That's insanity. Surely he can't be serious.* Once again, Alex's words, "this chance may never come again," start looping through my head, reminding me to step out of my fears and self-imposed limitations. Admittedly, the balmy weather and tranquil sea conditions are perfect for this once-in-a-lifetime experience.

The air is alive with presence as we inch our way closer to the whales. Their flukes swirl the water, while a blow from the largest whale shoots out countless gallons of water, which scatter like buckshot across the surface of the water.

Lee calls out, "Sweetheart, grab your swim things and be ready to jump into the water when we get there," as if I had said yes.

Nervously, I squeak, "What exactly do you mean? Get into the water with a bunch of whales? You must think I'm nuts."

Amused over my discomfort, Lee chortles, "You betcha, babe! You are a little nuts. You're the Yes Girl. You'll try just about anything. Now go get a line out of the hold in the cockpit and tie it to the end of the boat on the starboard side, then make a loop for your hands. When we reach the whales, be ready to jump in. You can hold on to the line while I navigate to bring you closer. I'd really love to do it myself, but it's better if I drive the boat."

I'm stunned. He actually wants me to swim with whales. After a brief moment of hesitation, I reply, "Okay, I'll do it. I would do almost anything for you but with one exception. Please *never* ever ask me to swim with sharks."

Lee, the magician, has once again cajoled me into risking my life. Now bikini-clad, I sit on the steps in the stern, holding my snorkel, mask, and fins while procrastinating over putting on my gear. Although the whales have temporarily disappeared from sight, fear washes over me as I realize that something utterly amazing is about to happen. If I decide to abort this venture, I may never forgive myself. So, to calm myself, I picture the boat towing me slowly past the whales swimming lazily about, seemingly oblivious to my presence. *Maybe this is actually doable*, I think.

Lee yells over the starboard engine's steady drone, "Man,

there are four of them. One is about fifty feet long. The others are about forty feet. They look like humpbacks."

As Lee hovers near them, I peer anxiously over the boat's starboard side to see four wild and splendid barnacle-encrusted creatures who are blissfully slapping the water with their massive flukes and giant scalloped-edged pectorals while rolling gracefully in the briny depths. Their dorsal fins, about a third of their entire body length, are long and black on the top surface and light underneath. Clearly visible are the blowholes on their heads. I learn later that the rounded, wart-like bumps that sit in front of the blowholes are unique to humpback whales and that they travel in groups of three to four during migration.

Lee, realizing that I'm stalling, says sharply over the loud din from the engine, "Hurry, Tiger Lily! Jump into the water before they take off! This may be the only chance you'll have in your entire life to swim with whales. Go! Do it now!!!"

This may be the only chance is my ignition switch, and Lee knows this. Trembling, I pull on my snorkel, mask, and fins in slow motion, then edge my way closer to an abyss alive with wild and ancient whale mystery.

With shaking hands, I climb down the submerged stainless steel steps then slip soundlessly into the chilly, dark blue depths while curling my fists tightly around the line. An insignificant speck, my body hovers over this deep underwater basin. As the boat inches forward, the salty ocean holds me in its grip as my body stretches out arrow-like across its surface. Baby waves slap the sides of the boat as fumes from the clattering diesel engines envelop me. I hold my breath until the gases dissipate into the air.

From this vantage point, I can't see the whales, so I assume they've moved on until I sense a powerful presence off to my right. The fifty-foot whale lines up alongside me, only four feet from my outstretched body. Gazing into its strange, large, unblinking eye, I realize that I'm being watched with consciousness and that we both share an interest in each other. Feeling more intensely alive than ever before and part of every living thing, I perceive love as it passes back and forth between me and this creature.

In wonder, I study its knob-covered head and its mug heavily encrusted with barnacles. Its long sturdy body glides past me in a slow, dreamlike way, and I can just make out the outline of its white belly through the water. Lee suddenly makes a quick turn to the left, and I slam helplessly into the whale's smooth, hard, slippery side. Fluttering my fins gently, I move myself away from the whale. As my body straightens out again, the tail passes within a few feet of me. Then, as quickly as it appeared, the whale abruptly vanishes into the silence.

Unexpectedly, I feel a deep sadness. Sighing, I think: *This ended way too quickly.* I wanted to revel in the whale's presence just a little longer.

Unable to see the rest of the whales who must have taken off, I peek under the boat. Amazingly, two whales are under each pontoon, and the third is directly under the boat's center. Almost as long as our boat and evenly spaced, they move forward in sync with us. Again, I feel the same sense of oneness and consciousness that I felt in the larger whale's presence. They remain there for a few minutes and then, with a perfect sense of choreography, accelerate swiftly as they move in unison off the port side. The obsidian sea encircles them as I mourn the closure of this supernatural experience.

I lift my head out of the water to see if the whales are nearby. Not seeing them, I submerge my head for one last check. *Oh my God!* The largest whale is heading straight for me. A surge of adrenaline rushes through me as I flap my arms wildly, attempting to swim away. At the last minute, the whale veers off to the right and disappears. *That was too close for comfort.* Lifting my head from the water, I remove the snorkel's mouthpiece to shout at Lee, who stands at the helm, his back to me.

"Lee! I'm ready to get out!"

After yelling again over the loud steady hum of the engine, Lee pushes the throttle into neutral. Treading water, I peel my stiff, raisin-like fingers from the line, finger by finger, then massage my chafed hands before swimming to the port stern. My heart still pounding, I toss my fins onto the deck and haul myself unsteadily up the steps. Lee chuckles at the sight of me as I emerge. My black bikini top is twisted into a narrow band under my arm pits, and my bottoms are plastered mid-thigh. My seaweed-like hair is clumped into a messy mound on the top of my head. I'm so moved and invigorated by this magical event that it doesn't even occur to me that I may look weird.

"So, what was it like to swim with four whales?"

My teeth chattering, I wrap a towel around myself.

"What was it like?" Lee repeats. Shifting my weight, I pull the towel even tighter around my body while I dribble water all over the deck. I search for words.

Centering myself, I answer, "That was the most moving experience I've *ever* had. Thank you for urging me to do that. I didn't think I had the courage, but *you* knew I did."

The decision I made that day to swim with the whales was actually a conscious decision to move to a higher level. The woman who emerged from the water was not the same woman who entered the water. Yet again, Lee had helped me let go of all my resistance, which then frees me to reach into the edge of myself to find the brave me. He knows that I have that within me, and he also understands that sometimes I need a little push. I love him for recognizing this.

———

Soon we will start our long passage across the Atlantic Ocean, and I'm not sure if I should view this upcoming experience with fear and dread or just plain excitement. There have been a number of movies made about hairy passages across the Atlantic. In particular, the ones about boats capsizing during terrible storms, sails being shredded to pieces in gale-force winds, boats being demolished by monster waves, and survivors holding on to a life raft in the middle of the ocean hoping the flare they shot into the sky will be noticed by a ship or a small boat. So I'm not sure what to expect.

Pushing my fears aside, Lee and I prepare the boat for all eventualities. And I adopt an attitude that I am going to do something exciting that few people will ever get to experience in their lifetime.

Our friend Pope is back! And the zinc oxide! Lugging an enormous dark green canvas backpack, he arrives from Washington, DC, in late May to join us in Le Marin, Martinique, as crew for the Atlantic passage. A complicated, unassembled storm drogue tumbles out of Pope's knapsack.

I feel a sudden sense of dread as I study the melange of small umbrellas attached to a heavy braided rope. I hope we will never need to use these in a terrible storm. Fortunately, we'll be crossing the Atlantic before hurricane season starts. Even so, this is a potentially dangerous voyage. It could be one terrifying, sleepless, Saltine cracker–full event for me.

Apprehensively, I watch Lee and Pope chat cheerfully as they assemble all the drogue parts in the cockpit. They are weirdly casual, like two chatty old ladies knitting baby blankets.

"A storm drogue," according to Wikipedia, "is a device external to a boat, attached to the stern and used to slow the boat down in a storm and keep the hull perpendicular to the waves. The drogue will prevent the boat from speeding excessively down the slope of a wave then crashing into the next one in a broach."

Broaching is when a monohull heels too far to one side. This happens when the bow of the yacht is not kept pointed into the waves in heavy seas and high winds. The waves will push the bow aside, turning the sailboat side-on to the breakers. Once this happens, the waves will roll the yacht side to side violently, causing severe discomfort to the crew, and may even cause the boat to capsize. Catamarans won't capsize in the classic "beam-wise" manner, but they may have a tendency to pitchpole instead. This happens when the downwind or leeward bow sinks into the water, causing the boat to nose-dive. In other words, catamarans don't sink; they turn upside-down.

Lee estimates the passage will take approximately three weeks, but we need to be prepared for twice that long. At a French supermarket, I bypass the bulky leafy vegetables to focus on long-lasting root vegetables and fruit that will stack neatly in the refrigerator. The red and green cabbage, the acorn and butternut squash, and the potatoes, onions, ginger, and garlic will be stowed in ventilated bins in the cockpit's hold. I'll hang the large bunch of lady finger bananas from a hook in the galley above the produce hammock, which will be stocked with apples, oranges, mangoes, and a pineapple. Canned goods, bread, pasta, legumes, rice, oatmeal, nuts, crackers, powdered milk, cereal, soup, condiments, tea, and coffee will stow under the salon seats.

When we get to Sint Maarten, in preparation for the possibility of seasickness, I wander alone down Philipsburg's main shopping street, where I buy Saltines, chicken bouillon, ginger ale, and candied ginger in a corner grocery store. Back on the boat, I fill my toiletry kit with baby wipes, which will be a replacement for the showers I won't be having, plus my toothbrush, a tube of sunblock, and a small hair brush. I store these, a pillow, and a blanket in the cockpit's hold in case I feel seasick and need to be outdoors where I can gaze at the horizon and breathe in the fresh air.

Before departing Sint Maarten, I contact my family and my friends. My best friend asks in her email, "Why do you stay on the boat? I would have left long ago if I was seasick!"

My response is, "Because I love Lee, and I enjoy our adventures together. I'm willing to put up with three-day nausea from time to time." *So bug off.*

Lee brings out the true adventurer in me. I was a daredevil as a child, but that went into hiding when I started having children. These long-dormant attributes are now being reactivated through Lee's confidence in me.

After the thrilling experience of swimming with the whales, I'm on an emotional high. No one has ever managed to push me beyond my comfort zone like Lee does. And each time it happens, I grow and evolve.

Beneath a vivid morning sky swirled with pink and purple clouds, we motor under the tall narrow drawbridge that connects Great Bay Salt Pond to Great Bay. Just as we depart Sint Maarten's waters, a long, intimidating ebony speed boat with four dark-skinned men dressed in black from head to toe pulls up alongside, causing our boat to rock violently back and forth. All three of us, now adrenalized by our justified fear of pirates, look wild-eyed. To our utter relief, they are waterfront police doing a routine check to make sure we're not hauling drugs, as the island has a reputation for such activities.

Five days later, we're already one-third of the way to the Azores. Lately, storm systems have been mild to nonexistent in the Atlantic, and the moderate trades out of the west have created near-perfect conditions. *Sailing at a reach is about as good as it gets*, I think as I gaze up at our wind-filled multicolored spinnaker.

No longer tethered to time, I love these moments of tranquility where it's just us, the sea, the sky, our stories, and the present moment. Strangely, the faint scent of roses and jasmine wafts mysteriously over me during my watch, and I wonder if my imagination is playing tricks on me. The Milky Way, Orion, and the Twins stare down benevolently as we journey through the profound silence. The only noise is that of waves splashing against the sides of the pontoons.

Pope entertains us with hilarious James Michener-esque tales of his solo wanderings across Europe and northern Africa during the late '60s with only a backpack. Lee regales us with his adventures while exploring the islands of the South Pacific in a sailboat he bought from the French singer Jacques Brel.

Unshowered and undeodorized, we are an aromatic blend of unwashed bodies and garlic odors from our meals. Both men, slightly disheveled, are sprouting beards. Not wanting to know what I look like, I avoid the bathroom mirror. My frizzy thatch of hair has taken on a life of its own, almost a free-standing entity. Just before we sailed away on this passage, a female sailor, frowning over my mop, mentioned that women should either have very long hair or very short hair, not in-between like mine.

Pope and I are moving about the galley laughing and joking while wondering what to eat for dinner, when Lee unexpectedly yells, "Come out! The dolphins are here!"

We sprint to the bow, where eleven dolphins are swimming upside-down between the pontoons, crisscrossing each other. Several of them move off to the port side and leap high into the air while twisting and turning. Laying on the trampoline with our heads extended over the front edge of the boat, we clap and cheer during their twenty-minute performance.

The air smells fresh and clean. Massive white puffy clouds chase each other across the sky on this gorgeous day. The boat swaying gently beneath me, I balance with my feet apart and pretend for a moment that I'm on a surfboard gliding across the silvery blue undulating sea in search of dolphins and mermaids. Shearwaters circle overhead as the setting sun paints the sky with purple and rose hues.

As we enter the Horse Latitudes, the winds have vanished. In this eerie stillness, the ocean has become a motionless, mirror-like reflection of the bright blue sky. A region of light precipitation situated between latitudes 30 and 35 degrees north and south, this area lies under a constant ridge of high pressure called the subtropical high. Well known for holding sailors hostage for weeks on end, its name derives from the era when Spain transported horses to their colonies in the West Indies and Americas. Lack of wind severely prolonged the length of their cross-Atlantic voyages and resulted in water shortages that made it impossible for the crew to keep the animals alive. Unfortunately there was no other choice than to throw the dying creatures overboard.

In this still, magical place in the very heart of the ocean, we take the sails down, and then jump into the water. Feeling refreshed and clean, we float carefree on our backs while the shearwaters, which have been following us for days on end, dart about overhead. Lee and Pope compete to see who can swim the fastest around the boat while I do water ballet, holding one leg straight up while fluttering my hands and then allowing myself to sink slowly and artfully into the sea.

We continue heading northeastward at a gentle pace for days. The air is cooling down in these higher latitudes, so I drag out my sweatshirt and long pants from beneath the bed. In the evenings, the only sounds, other than our voices, come from the steady rumble of the diesel engines and the hum of the autopilot. In the nothingness of these windless nights, our running lights bathe the surrounding sea with gold. As veils of phosphorescent light charge the water alongside us, I watch the clouds part for the moon as it slips effortlessly through this new open space, creating a silver path in front of us.

During these moments of solitude when I'm on watch while Lee and Pope sleep below, I feel more content than I have ever felt before, and I don't care how long it takes to reach our destination. In this quiet, magical expanse, I feel as if I've tapped into something much, much more powerful than what I can detect on the physical plane.

Soon, I smell land. The lightning in the distance briefly lights up the sky and reveals the mountains of Flores, the first island in the Azores. The whole landscape opens up on our approach and I take in the mountains and the water and the trees and the birds and the boats going by. Our tiny, boisterous anchorage is tightly packed with sailboats that lurch about dizzily in the grey choppy water now shrouded in darkness. Sailors, awakened by the clanking of our anchor chain, appear on their decks to watch as we claim our space. I reanchor a half dozen times in the muddy bottom until my rusty friend bonds with the earth. Encircling the area are tall black volcanic cliffs where hundreds of shearwaters roost at night and chat loudly in what sounds like Japanese. From my past experience in places similar to this, I know that sleep may be intermittent. The wind can change direction during the night and cause the boats to turn at the same time, increasing the chance of a collision.

It feels good to be on firm ground. I want to dig myself deep into the soil as if I'm a plant. My feet, accustomed to counterbalancing day and night, don't know how to function on stable ground. As I follow Lee and Pope up a steep dirt path to the top of the hill overlooking the small anchorage, I feel as if the ground is swaying beneath me.

We say goodbye to a transformed Pope. Now wildly bearded and dressed in crumpled cargo shorts and a stained T-shirt, he looks decidedly un-lawyer-like. He's enjoying his new swashbuckling image, and it wouldn't surprise me if he holds on to it for a while.

Lee and I explore Flores on foot, noticing its many similarities to Hawaii. The temperate climate here in the Azores encourages the lush green vegetation to grow amidst a profusion of wildflowers that grace every meadow, hillside, and roadside. Standing on a ledge overlooking a water-filled volcanic crater, we find it hard to take it all in.

Sally and her new boyfriend, Allen, join us on the island of Horta for the passage to Gibraltar. This is a major stop for yachts crossing the Atlantic. On the walls and walkways of the town pier, for good luck while underway, sailors leave paintings that include the names of their vessels, their crew members, and the date. During our two-week wait for a decent weather window, we befriend several boats in the anchorage. As we pull away from the pier to start our passage to the Mediterranean Sea, I watch as our hand-waving friends become small specs in the distance.

Six days later, on the eighteenth day of our transatlantic passage, we stop along the southern coast of Portugal for a quick layover with an old friend of Sally's. The next day, we cautiously approach the Straits of Gibraltar, where the Atlantic meets the Mediterranean Sea. The convergence of these two massive bodies of water creates two currents, one flowing eastward and the other flowing westward. I feel as if I'm in a washing machine that is gyrating nauseatingly and haphazardly from one rotation to another. This jarring movement makes it almost impossible to focus on the radar screen, which shows an overwhelming number of massive freighters, oil tankers, cruise ships, and container ships from all over the world as they pass through this ocean highway called The Straits.

As we head into the Mediterranean's most highly trafficked sea corridor, we are obligated to stay in the right shipping lane while simultaneously keeping track of every single ship's whereabouts and estimated speed—especially when we traverse both the inbound and outbound shipping lanes to reach the port of Gibraltar. This is by far the single most complex and nerve-racking maneuver we've ever undertaken.

Sally, Lee, and I, nerves on edge, are hunched over the computer keeping track of all the vessels while Allen keeps watch on deck. It feels like forever before we are safely tied up to a public dock in Gibraltar. We visit the Rock to see the famous tailless Barbary monkeys, which originally came from the Atlas Mountains and the Rif Mountains of Morocco. This is the only wild monkey population on the

European continent. There are currently over three hundred monkeys occupying the Upper Rock area of the Gibraltar Nature Reserve. Perching on the fences lining the pathway, they jump down onto the ground as people approach. Not wanting to be bitten or climbed on, I keep my distance as I watch several monkeys attempting to climb onto passersby like pet lap dogs.

Hugging the coastline on our departure from Gibraltar, we purposely avoid the bustling shipping lanes. During my watch, momentarily preoccupied while fixing sandwiches in the galley, I glance up to the horrifying sight of a freighter the size of a large building coursing forty feet in front of us—a preview of the epic sailing challenges ahead in the Mediterranean.

11

Just Me and Albania

Dreamlike, we skim effortlessly across the serene Adriatic Sea past pine-treed coastlines dotted with pastel-colored bungalows and tiny, mostly deserted islands with terraced slopes where wild goats pick their way across rocky ledges and scrublands. I am lost in this moment of traversing through water and air filled with the echos of a thousand voices from centuries past. In the distance, a fishing boat's engine interrupts the silence along with my imaginings of the Romans and the Greeks as they sailed from Venice or Athens to Dubrovnik or Trogir.

We anchor off an isle in the southernmost part of Croatia's archipelago, which encompasses more than a thousand islands. A modest hotel emblazoned with the words DISCO/FOOD in neon red glares at us from the shore, where pink and lavender bougainvillea decorate rows of clay-roofed homes.

On this bright cloudless day, craving relaxation and a break from being on duty, Lee, Sally, and I sit in the cockpit slowly eating salad with almonds and oranges. A furry gold and black bumblebee settles on an orange slice and then attaches itself to my wrist, its small wings whirling away, tickling my skin.

Our 1,124 nautical mile, 36-hour passage through the Mediterranean was grueling. It was by far the most exhausting passage the three of us have ever taken together. It made the passage across the Atlantic look like a picnic.

I'm feeling a slight let-down. This often occurs after the arrival at the long-anticipated destination. Everything in me has been building up for this moment, yet I have a *what's next?* feeling.

We enjoy a brief respite in Reggio Calabria. Situated in southern Italy on the slopes of the craggy Aspromonte mountain range, this city is located in the province of Calabria. In the fifth century BC it was a colony of Greece and was named Magna Graecia. It's now home to an infamous international crime syndicate called 'Ndrangheta, which has its roots in the mountains. Dating back to the nineteenth century, it's considered to be one of the most powerful organized crime groups in the world.

Unable to proceed any further without some sleep, I insist on having a rest stop before we continue. In my exhausted state, I trip over my own feet and narrowly miss falling into the fetid water when I climb ashore to tie us up at the commercial pier.

During the early morning hours, someone quietly boards our boat while we sleep below and leaves a mysterious brown paper bag just outside the sliding glass door to the cockpit. *What's this?* I wonder as I slide the door open to the intoxicating fragrance of newly baked pastries, which instantly disappear into our mouths. Attached is a note from a man named Giovanni, who promises to return with more surprises. At least, this is what I glean from his note in broken English.

Wearing a shiny pale-grey silk suit and a partially unbuttoned white shirt exposing a furry chest festooned with thick gold chains, Giovanni tours our messy boat. I rush ahead of him and throw yesterday's crotch-side up panties and stinky socks into a cabinet, then quickly straighten out the bed sheets. Standing back in admiration, I watch Giovanni's brows furrow as Lee, using overly expressive hand gestures, bastardizes French into his own unique version of Italian.

Giovanni's hairy, sausage fingers, bejeweled with two man-sized diamond rings, lift the trunk of his shiny black Mercedes to reveal wheels of pecorino and Parmigiano-Reggiano cheese, a sizable chunk of mozzarella, and medium-sized links of salami, prosciutto, and sopressata sausage. The scent of freshly baked bread fills the air, making my mouth water as Giovanni hands me an open-faced sandwich of Parmigiano-Reggiano and thinly sliced prosciutto.

After stuffing our purchases into the refrigerator, we join Giovanni for a driving tour of the city, which was totally reconstructed after the devastating earthquake of 1908. During our stroll along the palm-lined promenade overlooking the Sicilian city of Messina in the distance, Giovanni says excitedly, "Quaerere!" while pointing out a pod of dolphins diving and arching in the water.

Back on the boat, after many goodbye hugs to Giovanni, Lee and I marvel over how well we got along despite the language barrier, and how verbal communication isn't always necessary when you relate heart-to-heart with people.

The boat shudders, and the jib whistles in the twenty-knot winds during our sail to Korčula in the faint early morning light. The wind moderates to a gentle breeze as we near

Croatia's mainland. The sails now furled, we motor slowly past this medieval walled Dalmatian island renowned as the birthplace of Marco Polo and as a favored holiday retreat for Greeks over two thousand years ago. Korčula's round defensive towers and red-tiled rooftops recede into the distance as we follow a parade of sailboats moving toward a nearby anchorage.

At a popular restaurant in town, four gorgeous blond-haired Swedish women sit at a table across from us. While eavesdropping on their conversation, I look up to see a flirtation going on between Lee and the two women facing him. He seems to have forgotten who he's with. As we stand to leave, he encourages me to speak Swedish with them. I rationalize that his motives are innocent since he's seen me befriend and hug Swedes everywhere we go, so I introduce myself to them as Lee saunters past. Smiling and speaking in Swedish, I ask them what part of Sweden they come from. Snickering and acting rude, they treat me with disdain, and I back away in humiliation and embarrassment. I'm stunned. In all the years I lived in Stockholm and Gothenburg, I was never ever treated with such rudeness. In Swedish, I tell them they are thoughtless and mean before I turn and walk away while their laughs poison the air.

Hurt and angry, I tell Lee on the way back to the boat how he made me feel.

He has the decency to hang his head. "I've been an asshole, haven't I?"

Not answering, I think, *I love you, Lee. But I'm not sure if you really love me.*

Having no one to turn to and feeling unglued, I disappear tearfully into the safety of the port forward cabin and lock the door. I don't want to see Lee's miserable face. I'm tired of his annoying habit of staring openly at pretty women. Discreet looks I *can* handle. That's normal. During our past discussions about his undisguised wandering eye, he remarked that his past girlfriends actually put up with it. Not me.

The next day, yesterday's ghosts still bruise. Lee, having as much facial expression as Joe Friday from the 1950s *Dragnet* TV series, hides behind his dark sunglasses as he sits reading on the couch under the clicking, humming fan.

"I'm socially inept. You need to teach me how to have social graces," he says lamely. Lee's hands are folded in front of his chest as if he's trying to ward off something.

I realize now that any real discussion is impossible, and I admit to myself that he's really not as easygoing as he appears to be. I try to push the thoughts away, but they're impossible to ignore. *Maybe he doesn't even want me to be here*, I realize. For the first time, I feel so uncomfortable I can hardly stand it.

_____

The only official nude beach in the Pakleni Island group lies ahead. Cheap empty white plastic chairs line up three rows thick on a sliver of dark beige sand. From the distance, they look alarmingly like small gravestones. A man sells tickets for the day to throngs of tourists arriving in water taxis from the mainland. On our approach, Lee exclaims, "Let's leave! This place is too tacky."

Back on the boat, I peel off my bikini top and lay down on the trampoline. After noticing the outline of a man staring at me with binoculars from a nearby sailboat, I take a running, screaming leap into the water, followed by a furious swim around the boat. Bizarrely, while swimming, I have a sudden craving for fresh tomatoes and visualize them in my head. During my second lap around the boat I see what looks like small red balls bobbing about in the water. Oddly, the four red balls are Roma tomatoes.

I've been a little worried about the complexities of staying at a Mediterranean anchorage. It involves "Med mooring": backing up a sailboat into a small space that's packed with boats. Everyone moors stern-to, which means after you drop the anchor off the bow, you have to tie the two stern lines to something on the shore, such as a tree or a boulder. This is especially daunting because there are strong crosswinds here.

Just before nightfall Lee wedges the boat in a tight spot between two boats while the winds are trying to push us sideways.

"Would you please take the stern lines ashore either by dinghy or by swimming while I let down the anchor? All you have to do is wade through the water with the lines, then climb up the embankment. After that, you can tie them to a tree. I've seen other women doing this, and I think it would be a great thing for you to do," Lee says in his best marketing voice.

What? Are you nuts? Everyone will watch me make a fool out of myself.

However, it's not like I have a choice. Steeling myself, I slide carefully into the dinghy, which is jumping up and down wildly. "The motor won't start!" I yell.

"You have to pull the cord," Lee says, smirking.

Embarrassed, I motor the dinghy toward the small rocky island while watching the stern lines uncurl from the bottom of the dinghy and fall into the water along with the tail ends of the lines. Oops! I goofed. Returning to the boat, I scoop up the lines from the water, then motor to the shore, hoping Lee didn't notice.

My biggest worry is the jagged rock ledge that runs along the entire shoreline, which can puncture the dinghy. I slow down, turn off the motor, and then drift close enough to heave myself into the rocky shallow water while holding on to the dinghy painter and the two stern lines. Barefoot, wearing a fleece top and black yoga pants, my water-blurred glasses slip repeatedly off my face as I pull myself up onto a ledge. I step gingerly across dried weeds with sharp prickles, then climb up the steep, rocky hillside where I wrap the boat lines around a pine tree. Then, after wrapping the painter around my waist, I swim back to the boat, towing the dinghy behind me.

Lee yells, "Watch out for your glasses!" as I climb into the boat and sit for a moment on the steps, feeling good and strong and capable.

At 5 a.m., we awaken to our boat drifting in the dank greyness toward the British monohull next to us. As we continue wafting closer, heads pop out of a hatch to the intimidating sight of a huge catamaran bearing down. Lee turns on the engines to keep the boat steady as I pull in the main anchor then haul in the second one by hand until my strength leaves me and Lee has to take over.

After preparing the dinghy for another trip to shore, Lee unties the two stern lines and then drops them into the water. I start the dinghy's sputtering motor and head to shore for the reversal of what I did the day before. This time I'm feeling confident. I'm a fifty-eight-year-old Wonder Woman in a black bikini, and I hope everyone is watching.

Sailing the islands of Croatia is not for beginners. Intense winds and monsoon rains habitually come up in the late afternoons or evenings. In France, this strong cold north wind is called the Mistral. In the Adriatic Sea it's called the Bora and in Greece it's called the Maistros or Maistrali. The entire Mediterranean coast is heavily influenced by it.

You can go from gliding across golden-dappled seas with birds soaring overhead to Dante's Inferno within moments. During a brief sail from Brač Island to Trogir, we reef the main to the size of a handkerchief and then furl the jib as the apparent wind reaches forty knots while rain and lightning envelop us. After moving the cockpit cushions into the galley before they're blown overboard, we drape our sopping wet rain slickers and harnesses across them. We are now surrounded by a fog so impenetrably thick that it's hard to distinguish what's sea and what's air. Lee accidentally cut his finger earlier while trimming the sails and there is blood everywhere. Feeling chaotic, I don't know what to do with myself, so I just sit and stare at the radar and the grey shroud while letting my thoughts drift. Especially to Beaufort, which I realize was a place of great transition. I miss it in many ways but I don't think I could return.

Currently, I'm in the doghouse with my three sons, and I can't stop thinking about them. I miss them so much. A boat is its own country, and its leaders have a terrible time even knowing what day of the month it is or who's celebrating a birthday or an anniversary on the other side of the Atlantic. Thomas hasn't emailed me for weeks, and Markus is upset with me for sending him birthday congratulations on the wrong day. And Alex is mad at me for a host of other reasons.

I'm currently learning about who I am minus all the definitions: wife, mother, and grandmother. I always followed a role and was who everyone wanted me to be. It's a painful process, this pulling away. Will my sons forgive me and understand one day?

Storm clouds dash across the morning sky laced with pink tones. We're anchored in a bay called Uvala Statival off the island of Kornat. On its uninhabited southern coast, Lee drops me off onto a rickety wooden pier that looks like it might crumble under my weight. I trudge up a sharp pitch along a rock-strewn goat path bordered by thorny weeds. My T-shirt tied around my hat and my camera slung across my chest, I hike to the ruins of a sixth-century Byzantine Church on the crest of a hill overlooking the vast expanse of the Kornati Island chain. As Lee motors slowly back and forth, I photograph our boat far below and then create a small prayer rock monument at the top of the hill before wandering back down the steep path, stopping every now and then to pick purple wildflowers.

The following day, we sail northward toward Šibenik, Skradin, and the Krka Waterfalls. Our last stop in Croatia will be Plitvice Lakes National Park. Then we'll hitchhike to Zadar.

I will always remember Croatia as a place of nightmarish sailing and anchoring experiences—one after another. Winds and monsoon rains have an alarming habit of coming up in the late afternoons in the mostly exposed Croatian anchorages. The boat is now leaking in unexpected places and our anchor has developed a disturbing habit of dragging across anchorage bottoms at night while we sleep. It holds in sand but not grass and mud, which are common here.

This month-long voyage through the archipelago of Croatia offers me an opportunity for intense self-reflection. I'm learning to accept the fact that the traits I dislike in Lee— his stubbornness, his cockiness, his self-centeredness—are also in me. The parts of him I admire are his friendliness toward everyone he meets, his generosity of spirit, and his courageousness. I share these traits. We both love people. There's a saying that if you live on a boat for a year, you will become a better human being, and I believe this because there's nowhere to run from yourself. There are no hiding places on a boat, no car to take off in, no malls to escape to, and no TV to lose yourself in. My escapes from me are the occasional internet connection at a port, a swim in the sea, a good book, and watching a downloaded movie. Sooner or later, my dark side shows up.

In the beginning of our adventures, our personal disagreements sometimes led us to deep, soulful discussions about our respective childhoods. After these truth-telling sessions, we'd stand side by side at the stern for a sending-away ceremony of mental baggage, which we metaphorically tossed into the wake. Unfortunately, sometimes they've clawed themselves back onto the boat. Whenever this happens, I remind myself that I'm taking tiny steps in the right direction and that setbacks are normal. Lee still continues to push me to my edge. Sometimes I want to flee and pretend that there are no unhealed parts left.

Our first charter in the Mediterranean is coming up soon. Heading southeast toward Greece with Croatia on our left and the olive-treed Italian coast on our right, we pass the expansive finger of land that stretches along the coast of Croatia and then narrows to a slim band near Dubrovnik. Lee sleeps worry-free as I nervously sail past Albania's coastline. Okay, I'm a little scared, but I reassure myself that everything will work out. It's just me and Albania.

Repeatedly, I check the GPS and the chart to ensure that the boat isn't accidentally being pushed by an eastward-bound current into the no-entry zone that spans the entire length of the country. Our Mediterranean cruising guide warns sailors not to come too close to it because of numerous instances of boardings by Albanian pirates.

I feel growing relief as we enter the Strait of Otranto, which is more than two-thirds of the way down the Albanian coast. Lee anchors off the island of Corfu for a short break before we transit the Corinth Canal, which separates the mainland of Greece from the Peloponnese Peninsula.

My brother Taylor, his wife, Penny, my sister Joanne, and her husband, Tommy, are planning on joining us in Athens. Four hours before their arrival, we cast anchor off one of the two small islands of Poros, located in the Saronic Gulf off the eastern Peloponnesian coast. About thirty-one nautical miles from Athens, Poros, with its aromatic lemon groves and hillsides covered with olive trees, is a popular weekend destination for Athenians.

Weary after our overnight passage through the Corinth Canal, we ready the boat for my family, frantically polishing, cleaning, organizing, and making beds until just minutes before the Hellenic Seaways Flying Cat Ferry is scheduled to arrive. The ferry, actually a small water plane, looks like a strange red-and-white bug—not the typical Greek ferry I had pictured. Uncertain that they're actually on this ferry, I wave limply just to be safe while saving the big wave for the giant catamaran that's sure to show up at any moment.

Taylor and Penny are the first to appear, with bags almost as big as them. I don't remember his hair being so white. My younger sister, Joanne, and Tommy emerge with equally massive suitcases. With trepidation, they stumble awkwardly into the dinghy as it bounces about in the choppy waves. Joanne death-grips the dinghy handle as Lee planes the raft, bringing the bow high out of the water. I realize at that moment that I've become an old salt, because it all seems so normal to me now.

After stacking the salon table with all the boat supplies he requested, Lee takes everyone on a tour of the boat, pointing out their cabins, the teeny storage places for their clothes, and the accompanying heads.

"Pump the toilet twenty times before you flush," Lee advises.

This request is always met with disbelief and horror. I remind them that it's an excellent way to build up the biceps. They seem underwhelmed with our almost empty refrigerator, which will soon be filled with everyone's favorite Greek foods, including Penny's "I don't know what this is but let's try it!" mystery purchases.

Each couple is assigned to fix one meal a day. Taylor and Penny are in charge of breakfast, Joanne and Tommy have lunch duty, and Lee and I have dinner. This turns out to be a dismal failure. Lee seems to be more interested in cereal, cheese, and cold cuts, while Taylor's focus is on dinner. And I'm mainly obsessed with herding everyone about, not fixing food.

We consume our weight in baklava on our way from Poros Town—where we rented motorbikes and rode through the narrow cobbled streets where we could almost touch the stone-walled houses—to Hydra Town and its tiny harbor teeming with sailboats, crossed anchor lines, and red-faced, swearing sailors. Burros stand placidly next to their owners, who sip ouzo at the numerous waterfront cafés and bars packed with tourists who have perhaps lost track of their young children who can be found climbing on the ancient cannons that overlook the steep cobblestone hillside paths.

Intimidated by all the noise and activity in Hydra, we find a becalmed bay nearby that has only one small hotel, a taverna, and a large water trampoline in the distance. Early the next morning, Tommy knocks on our door. "Lee, the anchor must have dragged during the night." We look out a window to the sight of the trampoline now stationed beside us.

Bookending my siblings' trip is a major disturbance in Athens. Students are protesting to have their college tuition paid for by the Greek government, and there are protests and escalating violence. A group called Revolutionary Struggle fires bullets at the Ministry of Culture building, and students run wildly through the streets of Athens chanting and carrying banners.

My family spends their last day in Greece avoiding tear gas.

12

The Turkish Weather

The mountains, shrouded in clouds, stretch majestically into the ocean depths, and the ancient ruins crumble silently along the pine tree–covered rocky slopes. The Turkish coastline has the most magnificent and magical scenery I've seen in all of my travels. Remnants of ancient Lycian cities gaze down at the azure water that pushes itself into the braveness of it all. Turkey is a brave place. It borders Syria, Iraq, and Iran. On our way to a marina in Marmaris, we take a detour and head through a narrow channel flanked by bright green weed grass. Massive rock tombs, centuries-old sarcophagi on pedestals, and crumbling columns watch us from the steep rock-strewn hillsides as we follow the path of a small guide boat.

Now docked at the picturesque Marmaris Marina, Lee busies himself with repairing one of the engines. This huge marina, in the town of Marmaris, is jam-packed with luxury yachts and international sailboats. Within walking distance are restaurants, bars, and a mall.

The Turkish women I pass on my way to town are wearing long, bright skirts with blouses of contrasting colors and small gold earrings that dangle and capture the sunlight. And most of them wear burqas or headscarves. The men, dark-haired and intense, dress in jeans, shorts, and T-shirts.

During my daily walks there, I receive ego-boosting invitations to ride on the backs of scooters with rakish young Turks. Struggling with a very heavy grocery bag one afternoon, I finally break down and accept a ride to the marina with a young rug salesman with mischievous dark brown eyes. Ironically, we blithely cruise past Lee as he wanders down a sidewalk in search of boat parts, and I giggle over the fact that he doesn't even notice me.

When I mention to people that we're from the United States, people look confused. Their faces light up, however, in recognition of Obama's name. And when I ask the Kurds how they feel about the violence their brothers are committing in Turkey, they claim it's to get the government's attention because they're the underdogs here. Just weeks before our arrival, many foreigners were injured or killed in a bomb attack by the Kurds in Marmaris and Istanbul. But even filled with misgivings, we take a chance on Turkey.

At a small Kurdish lunch stand in Marmaris, the owner complains that the local government allows him only two small outdoor tables for customers while all the other cafés in the neighborhood sprawl out into the walking street. After learning that, I offer my outdoor table to a German family so that the owner will have more business and move indoors to sit on a stool at the counter. The owner, hugging me in gratitude, says, "If I wasn't married, I'd marry you!" Touched, I visit his stand many times while we're in Marmaris.

The Turks are some of the friendliest, most endearing

people I've met overall on my journey with Lee. And they're also very eager to talk about their country.

Turkish coffee, which is unfiltered and still contains fine coffee grounds, can taste a little bitter. The Turkish people add a little sugar to it and it's always served with some foam on top. As I sip my coffee in a small porcelain cup called a *kahve fincani* at a table in the bazaar, I'm entertained by the shopkeepers who are speaking loudly in rapid, choppy sentences.

Valerie, a young Oregonian medical student, and her friend Mahalia visit us for two weeks while we're in Marmaris. They join me on my daily excursions into the maze of bazaars in town. One afternoon, Valerie and I try on sexy belly dancing outfits and gyrate to Turkish music right in the middle of a shop. The owner flirtatiously asks me, "Where did you learn to belly dance?" Admittedly this is a ploy to encourage me to buy an overpriced outfit I will never use. Valerie and I giggle loudly as we jiggle our rear ends while tourists mill about ignoring us. Just as I'm trying not to wet my pants, Mahalia condescendingly asks, "*What* are you doing?"

Wandering through a public park the following day, I smile down at a family sitting on a picnic blanket and they invite me to join them. When I indicate with hand signals that I can't, the mother generously hands me tabbouleh wrapped in lettuce. I'm continually moved by the generosity I'm experiencing.

Kalkan. 3:30 a.m., October 10th. Our visitors from Oregon have left before thunderstorms and high winds become the norm. Awakened from a deep sleep by the sound of an anchor scraping over rocks, Lee chirps, "It's raining cats and doggies!" Bleary eyed, I look over at him and wonder how he has managed to keep his sense of humor.

The boat twirls around dizzily as massive amounts of water seep through cracks in the caulking in the salon, forming a stream down the starboard steps into our cabin.

The sight of Lee gathering together his foul weather gear always strikes terror in my heart. With great reluctance, I put mine on, then lumber upstairs to see what nightmare awaits. Rushing out into the cold angry wind, the torrential rain, and the lightning, Lee turns on the engines while I untie the line leading to shore, letting it drop into the turbulent sea while keeping it away from the props. Amazingly, one anchor is still holding as the other drags across the bottom. As we circle around under almost constant lightning flashes, the boat rolls madly from side to side in the big frothy waves. Staring at us, the rocky headland looms only forty feet away. Our survival plan is to share watches until dawn, when Lee can swim ashore to pick up the dropped line that's tied to a boulder.

4:30 a.m. A few stars appear overhead in the midst of the squall. Apprehensive, we wait it out, continually racing into the cockpit in between lightning flashes to check our position. The lights of the town in the distance beam at us alternately from bow to stern as the boat twirls in the wind. The dark silhouette of Kalkan's brooding mountains adds to the drama. Hair dripping wet, I sit on a towel in my no longer waterproof foul weather gear and stare blankly at a ginger cookie while Lee snoozes next to me on the sofa.

Later in the morning, the storm abates, and we are forced to reanchor off Kalkan's outer breakwater after giving up on finding shelter in its tiny harbor, already fully packed with large Turkish gullets, diving boats, fishing boats, and a handful of sailing boats. A Turkish gullet filled with middle-aged male tourists in high spirits anchors next to us. They congratulate Lee for having found a woman crazy enough to live on a boat with him.

"She's an amazing first mate," Lee says as he pulls me to his side. Momentarily famous, I bask in this brief glory.

Later in the day, while standing at the apex of the ancient city of Xanthos, Lee notices that the boat is turned sideways to the breakwater. Dark, forbidding clouds race like wild horses across the sky and the mountain ranges. The Turkish gullet parked next to us has vanished.

"This doesn't look good," Lee warns. Cold wind and sheets of rain pummel us as we run downhill to our waiting taxi.

"We need to return to the boat," Lee urges the taxi driver. "Now!"

"What? You no want to go on extra tour to third place? It only cost little more."

"No, we better return immediately. Weather no good for boat."

Rounding the jetty, the boat, now askew, swings around wildly in the twenty-knot winds and whitecaps. I quickly pull up the anchor as Lee motors westward under the grim clouds.

The coming front is announcing itself via an immense, angry, pulsating red blob on the radar. By nightfall, a terrifying green-tinted gloom surrounds us as the waves continuously break over the bow, washing the cockpit and us with cold salty water. In the midst of the bitterly cold swirling winds and all my fearful thoughts about outside forces and powers that I have no control over, I sense renewed strength and courage growing within me.

Early the next morning, under frigid temperatures, torrential rain, lightning, and high winds, we rock and roll our way to Kas, which is one of three stops on the way to Kemer and

Antalya. As we round a point on land, our destination marina emerges in the mist. What a relief to see masts bobbing up and down in the distance. Lee and I take deep breaths as we curve around the quay into calm water. I'm exhausted and tired of constantly being drenched. Will this rain ever end? God help us in these lightning storms. In a sleep-deprived, storm-induced daze, I navigate the boat too close to a buoy marking shallow water.

"What are you thinking?" Lee yells in an angry voice.

There's no room for a boat our size in this small U-shaped haven. Monohulls of all sizes are tied or anchored sideways four deep to a wooden dock. Told by sailors to back away, a sixty-foot naval training boat from Hafia fortuitously pulls out, leaving a space large enough for our wide catamaran. *Thank God.*

An English couple describes the craziness of the night before when charter boats, sailboats, and fishing boats slammed into each other during the storm. "People were screaming at each other in different languages. It was a Dante's Inferno! Lines were crossed, and chains overlapped each other. It was general chaos. You're lucky you weren't here."

Lee and I fall into bed, sleep six hours, wake up for dinner, and then fall asleep again. The boats are now tied five deep all along the dock. Within twenty-four hours, the purgatory scene we missed earlier recreates itself in an utterly terrifying way under menacing coal-black skies. The storm that ensues for the next twenty-four hours is like a giant boulder that crushes everyone in its path.

I watch people yell at each other frantically as their lines connecting to each other or the dock undo themselves in the strong winds. Boats are bouncing about like mad, out of control and headed for each other. A Swedish boat is almost skewered by the long, narrow prow of a gullet as it backs up to avoid plowing into another sailboat. The forty-knot winds suddenly grab the gullet and thrust it forward at high speed. Everything is happening so fast it's hard to take it all in. The winds, increasing and sounding like unleashed demons, shake masts and shriek through the stays.

Clattering lines whip about like Medusa's angry snakes. These conditions continue into the wee hours as sailors stretch four lines across the murky water at the marina's entrance to prevent boats from entering. A huge gullet charges toward the harbor's entrance while sailors yell, "Stop, stop, stop! No more room! Lines are blocking the entrance!"

Dozens of flashlights are now aimed at the lines, and the gullet halts just short of the first line, then backs up and leaves. More boats with panic-stricken sailors continually attempt to enter the marina during the night as rampages of angry words spill out like marbles, halting them. The sight of desperate, fearful people being turned away then having to head back into the dangerous seas is heart-rending.

It doesn't stop. A forty-knot wind gust rolls through the marina and pushes all the boats away from the pier. Sailors, yelling and screaming at each other, scramble about while rushing to reattach their lines to anything stable. I feel like I'm living in a Hieronymus Bosch painting.

Somehow, I eventually get some sleep, but then cold water dripping on my head jolts me out of it. Our blanket is saturated. The stove top in the galley is submerged under an inch of water, and the salon floor is covered with puddles. The boat next to us sways back and forth, making the fenders between us go *eek, urk, eek, urk, eek, urk.* Since Lee is still asleep, I throw on my raincoat and head out into the storm to add another fender, hoping to mitigate the annoying sound. I fall asleep again as the lightning flashes illuminate the boats across the way and the sailors in foul weather gear who are adjusting chains and lines.

At dawn, the sky clears. The winds are no longer howling down the steep slopes of the mountains like mad dogs. Newly born red waterfalls gush their way from the heights, turning the harbor water a scarlet color. Pieces of debris and water-soaked logs float by our boat, and the low clouds scattered overhead cast shadows over the muddy water. Exhausted, we stagger into the daylight and look around at our fellow sailors, who are also shell-shocked and discombobulated from last night's battles. Slowly, people begin to mill around tenuously, as if they don't trust the weather and expect the sky to explode again.

———

Kas is called the Adventure Place. Once in town, I find myself stupidly saying, "Yes, I'd love to go canyoneering!" to a salesperson at the Beaugonville Travel Agency. What was I thinking? I've just experienced several savage storms, and here I am, mindlessly agreeing to rappel down cliffs with Lee. For three days I pray it will rain the day we're scheduled to join the canyoneering expedition.

On the day of my potential demise, we arrive at the travel agency at 8:30 a.m. with backpacks stuffed with towels, hiking shoes, fleece pants, and sweaters. We're issued wetsuits that have holes, and I try not to imagine how the holes got there. On the drive up the mountain, we stop for a tea break at a café and sit under an arbor entwined with ripe red grapes. The air is clean and mountain cool. I remain silent while everyone chats. My thoughts are focused on what's ahead: going down cliffs with ropes into ice-cold water.

The people ahead of me disappear, one by one, over the edge of the seventy-meter cliff, and thankfully, I can't see what they're doing. Our two guides ask if I've done this before. Not satisfied with my evasive answers, they keep prodding me. The plump woman in front of me with curly blond hair and a snaggletooth smile freaks out three feet down and has to be lowered inch by inch, facing outward, down the front of the cliff. It's my turn, and instead of focusing on the scary depths below, I stare at the rock slabs before me and the deep blue sky above. I think of the cliff as bits and pieces instead of it's frightening entirety.

Like a mountain goat on speed, the guide, the last in line, comes down with a lit cigarette hanging out of his mouth and runs nimbly through the icy water to where we perch, bird-like, on logs around a fire, shivering madly. He throws a large black plastic bag filled with empty tuna cans, plastic bottles, and wrappers onto the flames. We all back away in horror, though none of us want to leave the warmth.

Exhausted, we return to the boat that evening. The next morning, tired and achy from the day before, we head back to the travel agency for an 8:30 a.m. bus trip to the villages of Ucagiz and Kaleköy for a kayaking expedition across the beautiful Kekova Roads Bay to the ancient sunken city of Simena. Lee and I share a double kayak, and he navigates across the choppy waters to a small bay where we explore sections of the city on a small peninsula. Brambles and twigs cut my legs and arms as we trek through thick scrub. Partially remaining rock walls rise above the dense vegetation, and we walk tight-rope style across the walled areas. Later, as we kayak over the sunken city, the tour guide, in unintelligible English, points out mosaics, harbor walls, and parts of buildings below us. In ancient times, Simena was a small fishing village, then it became an outpost for the Knights of Rhodes. I enjoy greatly all the adventures we're having in Turkey. This is going to be hard to top. And I feel proud of myself for facing my fears and pushing myself to do things that are risky. My self-esteem is at a whole new level.

———

By mid-November 2007, after visiting Tekirosa and Marmaris, we're ready to leave the boat for life on land for the winter season. Lee wants to introduce me to his friends in Oregon, Hawaii, and California. The boat will be left under the care of the eight-hundred-berth Yacht Marina, one of the largest marinas in Europe, where we'll be one of a thousand boats on the hard. We sign a contract for five months.

Before leaving Turkey, we have a chance to connect with many of the international women and men who live on their boats in the marina. For my own entertainment, I do a little survey and discover that the one thing most women in their fifties and sixties have in common is a keen desire to know their true purpose in life. The one thing most men of a similar age have in common is that they feel their lives ebbing away, and they want to live out their dreams before it's too late. What they all have in common is a need to know that their lives actually mean something.

———

At 5 a.m., the bathroom light burns out during my ice-cold shower in the head. This is followed by my tea bag ripping in two, the bursting of a bag of almonds that skitter across the galley floor, and the scuttling past of a giant cockroach. During most of this, Lee is discussing primates. Oh, how I love intellectuals. They're so much fun.

Our driver to the Istanbul airport is late. The uniformed man at the check-in counter informs me that our return reservations aren't "set" yet. *What exactly does that mean?* I wonder. My jeans rip apart in the seat area as I nervously squat to retrieve the return flight information from my carry-on.

While waiting patiently in the security line, I study a group of women who are dressed alike in long bell-shaped velvety black skirts and black blouses over which white satin scarves are draped. Their waists swivel like dashboard hula dolls as they pull out items from under their skirts like a magician pulling endless rabbits and scarves out of a hat.

Once the plane has leveled out at 35,000 feet, the American woman next to me introduces herself. While her long blond hair does its best to relieve itself from a bun, she explains that she lives on the Lycian coast in a small village with her Turkish husband and their young daughter and a handful of British, German, and Dutch expats.

"There are some strange implants in this village," she tells me. "Two hundred years ago, three men, each running from various places after murdering someone, settled in this village, and all the present inhabitants are descendants of them. The murderous inclinations have continued through today. Recently a local man shot his wife, although he really intended to kill his sister-in-law."

Looking at her quizzically while wishing she would just hush up, I pretend to fall asleep.

While winter drapes Turkey with snow and ice, Lee and

I are now landlubbers in Seattle. We're car drivers, movie-goers, cell phone users, and TV watchers. *Will I like this new land version of us?* I wonder. I'm sure that there will be a period of adjustment for us as a couple. We have lived together for eighteen months in a small space totally influenced by weather conditions and mostly devoid of mass media. The boat was a quiet, centered place where we felt proud of ourselves for just knowing which day of the week it was.

Like the characters in *Star Trek* with microphones embedded in their ears, people here appear to be tethered to their iPhones, which are really a modern-day umbilical cord. And unless a rare person prods us with questions about our boat adventures, we avoid the subject altogether, since no one is really interested in hearing our stories. What I can't help noticing is that children, adults, dogs, cats, squirrels, and even bugs seem stressed out. Does anyone nowadays ever glance up at cloud formations or birds soaring?

What I miss the most is the intense, authentic conversations that we have with our fellow sailors. A beginning and an end are automatically built into these relationships because of our gypsy lifestyle. We never know if we'll see someone again. Since *anything* can happen on the sea, we connect heart-to-heart immediately.

———

While wandering through downtown Seattle, I notice an object on the sidewalk. It's been stepped on countless times and is hidden under a thick layer of dust. What appears after I brush off the dirt is a beautiful necklace with an etched copper base on which a silver spiral rests. The words "Enjoy the

Journey" are engraved along the spiral, and they become a totem for my travels with Lee.

That evening, we sleep in a friend's basement on beds so low and small that I wonder if, like Alice in Wonderland, I have eaten an enlarging pill.

A few days later, we drive to Eugene, Oregon, to stay with Lee's longtime buddy Dave. His mountaintop home overlooks Willamette Valley, which is currently blotted out by a mist that covers everything like a sheet of cotton batting. During the evening, the fog lifts, and Eugene illuminates itself for me as I rest on a reclining chair in front of glowing embers from the outdoor fire pit.

The view brings back memories of growing up in the foothills of the Appalachians in northeastern Alabama. My childhood home perched at the apex of a hill overlooking two valleys, and I loved to wander across the yard, moving from one vantage point to another. At night, Anniston sparkled like a Christmas tree on the west side while the more subdued glimmer of Choccolocco Valley blinked faintly from the eastern flank. Part of the glow was probably from the PCBs that Monsanto thoughtlessly dumped into the valley's creeks and streams for years, but in my childish mind, that glow was something magical.

———

Our next destination—Portland, Oregon—overlooks the Willamette River, where in the early 1900s, many people lived on ramshackle houseboats. Wearing my faded jeans, an oversized sweatshirt, and worn-out tennis shoes, I feel very much at home in this city. Lending us their slightly beat-up dark purple van and fixing us delicious gourmet dinners,

Lee's friends Sue and Brad welcome us into their lives. While we're here, our plan is to reconnect with Lee's friends from his many years working for a technology company in Portland.

After cooking in a Lilliputian boat galley for months on end, I forget how magnificent the kitchens are in this country. Sinks are almost large enough for bathing a toddler, cabinet drawers glide in and out as if they're resting on air, and refrigerators are massive. Our marine refrigerator is a nondescript four-foot-high white box with two lids that open on the top. Inside are four plastic bins stacked two by two. One bin holds dairy, meat, fish, and chicken; one holds condiments; and the other two hold vegetables and drinks. Our well-meaning charter guests unintentionally reorganize the bins during their visits, which makes meal prep challenging for me.

"I'll travel around the world with you" flows from the radio as Lee turns on the van's ignition. "Love is on your side, filled with the knowing of beauty" plays as we head southward through Oregon's beautiful countryside toward San Francisco. The refrain repeats as we hurtle past evergreen-covered mountains and hills through the early morning haze. "Love, love, love is all around" fills the car as farms, tractors, and fields dotted with sheep, horses, and cows fold into each other in the rearview mirror. A bearded man in a puffy black vest holds up a lonely thumb as we fly past, hearing "Fill me up with love, love, love."

We spend Christmas Eve in Sally's light green 1950s-era cottage overlooking a very foggy San Francisco. Lee is working on his computer in the chilly attic-turned-bedroom, Sally is emailing friends in the dank basement, and I'm in the warm, cozy living room ensconced on an overstuffed antique armchair, chatting with my family back home.

Rather fetchingly dressed in Sally's bright-red foul weather gear with a navy blue knit cap perched rakishly on my head, I crew with Sally in an afternoon race in the Bay. Spending most of the day gliding through the unusually calm water under gentle December winds brings me a little relief from Lee and his strange and unusual unfriendliness that has unfurled since we've been on land. I'm puzzled by his attitude, and I wonder what I've done wrong. When he's worked on the website in the past, he never acted like this.

After a full day of museum exploration, including the de Young Museum in Golden Gate Park, Sally and I return to Lee, who is still toiling over our website. "Would you like some help with editing your website entries?" I ask hopefully. In the past, I've helped with the writing and the editing but this time, for some unknown reason, he refuses my offer.

Imperiously, he snaps, "I don't need your help!" Then, "You don't help me anyway!" It's odd how Lee can be so gregarious, kind, and open, and then the next moment be totally closed off.

Feeling hurt by his rude behavior, I turn away melodramatically and head outdoors. Walking briskly down Kansas Street's steep incline to a grocery store on 18th Street, I wander through the aisles like a ghost, wondering what the hell I'm doing here in San Francisco with Lee. Our website depicts us as a smiling, always happy couple—kissing, hugging, laughing—an illusion our charter guests bask in for their two-week visits to the boat.

On my return hours later, Lee is still hunched over the computer, his eyes squinted and rimmed in angry red. His forehead is scrunched up, and his eyebrows are knitted together as he toils away on the latest postcard he'll send out to potential charter customers. In his own world, he doesn't look up or speak to me. I'm flummoxed. What's going on with him? Have I done something wrong? I don't know how to relate to this different side of Lee. I hope this behavior is temporary.

Feeling dismayed and depressed, I decide to focus on doing things that make me happy—such as sailing in the Bay with Sally and exploring the city.

———

I'm relieved that Lee is finally finished with the website. Now back to his normal self, he suggests we take a break from San Francisco and fly to Maui for a vacation. After the conclusion of his South Pacific adventures with his girlfriend Kathy, they both settled there. Eventually, they split up, and Kathy remained in Hawaii while Lee headed back to the mainland.

Just a week ago, while we were relaxing on David's deck, Lee suddenly announced to my surprise, "Wendy, I want you to meet Kathy!" Unsure of why he thought this was a good idea, I decided to go along with it. Anyway, I've always wanted to visit Hawaii since I was a child gaping at photographs of my grandparents with orchid leis around their necks at the Maui airport.

Lee also wants me to meet Nancy, his spiritual guide. He has mentioned how much she helped him through some difficult times.

Soon after we arrive on Maui, I have an hour-long session with Nancy, who says, "Wendy, once you love yourself, you will draw many people to you. It's the key to your inner happiness and your inner peace. It's the lesson of your life. You need to know that you are lovable."

Nodding in agreement, I smile crookedly at her. On the

right side of my face, a slight tightening runs along my nose up to my eye. This is the part of me that holds back out of self-protection.

She continues, "The little girl in you is like an alley cat, looking around for scraps wherever she can find them. But wow! Does she ever have a personality!"

Then she turns to face Lee. "One partner is usually ahead of the other. It takes two years to get to know each other. Accept that you're the coach with Wendy. You're responsible for coaching her. You get to do it in emotions. Your protected heart is opening up and is committed to love. Wendy is the messy side of love, and there are places where you're the same. Enjoy swimming in the messiness. Watch out, though, for when you disappear. Her relationship issues will crop up."

During our dinner with Kathy in Lahaina, she stuns me by saying, "Lee, Wendy is the *first* decent girlfriend you've brought to my house. She's wonderful. I give you permission to marry her." Hiding my smile, I watch him squirm.

That evening at Kathy's house, we toss and turn in our sleeping bags, which rest on a cold concrete floor in an unfurnished room directly below her bedroom. A restless soul, she paces back and forth across the wood floor well into the wee hours. Drawers open and close. A chair slides noisily across the floor. My only choice is to accept what is. There will be no sleeping here in Kathy's house.

Her small, disorganized hillside home looks as if it's in the throes of a recent move, although she has been there for many years. Half-unpacked boxes line the walls, and dusty decorative items are clumped together as if they're waiting to be placed somewhere. Kathy's life seems to be on a permanent hold.

Back in the 1970s, Lee and Kathy sailed the South Pacific together in the *Askoy II*, a sixty-two-foot sailing yacht purchased for a song from an ailing friend. They were both twenty-five years old. I would guess that they were more innocent, perhaps more self-centered, and still not sure about what they wanted out of life. And at that age, a lot of women tend to be attracted to extroverted guys.

By the time I joined Lee, I had already experienced many of life's challenges. There's an old Swedish saying about having "skin on the nose," which means a person has experienced obstacles and setbacks in life. At this point in my life, I have a better understanding of myself and my potential. I'm more confident, fulfilled, and serene.

What are the similarities—or the differences—between us, I wonder?

During our visit, I watch Kathy and Lee as they navigate their way through the slippery, mossy memories of the past. Each painful memory is examined and then lovingly put aside. When it's my time to talk, I tell Lee about my desires and needs in our relationship. Then later, while the three of us are eating our take-out dinners, Kathy admits that she was never able to show her true feelings to him. As for me, I have this scary habit of walking out to the edge of a cliff with Lee, where I stand naked and poised with my toes dangling over the edge as I say things from the heart while risking utter rejection. Lee, thankfully, responds well to my courageous honesty.

———

Our lovely vacation in Hawaii now drawing to a close, I'm looking forward to being back on the boat with Lee.

However, I'll be leaving again in a few months. I'm anxious to see how Alex is doing in college, and I want to visit Markus in Vermont and Thomas and his family in Massachusetts.

Those three months back on the boat dissappear in a flash. I'm currently driving through Hartford's east end, where men in low-slung, baggy gangster pants sashay down the streets looking like they'd like to score a sale, shoot someone, or hold up a store. I'm more afraid here in Hartford than I ever was during brutal storms at sea.

I arrive unscathed at Alex's dorm in my sporty red rental rocket, fully loaded with roll-down windows and prehistoric door locks. After a two-second tour of Alex's dorm room, he quickly removes a poster that's taped to the wall. It shows a boat floating on a clear body of azure water in the South Pacific. This is instantly replaced with Edvard Munch's *The Scream*.

Later, I visit the dean of students to see if he can work directly with me if any issues crop up during Alex's senior year. Keeping his word, he remains in constant contact with me and becomes my son's biggest advocate at Trinity—and my friend.

Next, I set off to visit Markus, who, after floundering in a couple of dead-end jobs, seems to have found his true purpose in life. Inventive, resourceful, and creative as a child, he has created a lens that is breaking world records in optics for solar power. This lens allows scientists to observe the sun in ways never possible before. Markus was also involved in the lens design for the Moon Lander and the Martian Land Rover.

I spend my first twenty-four hours in Brattleboro languishing at a bleak motel furnished in a run-down 1960s style. The uppity beak-nosed owner from Pakistan has apparently recently been robbed by a man with a plastic butter knife.

Happily, Markus rescues me from this motel where mites reside on windowsills, chairs, ledges, tables, and beds.

Spookie, Markus's lovely sweet black cat, sleeps next to me and becomes my constant companion while Markus and his partner Star are at work. Star is deaf, and Markus, fluent in sign language, discovered that she's amazing at working with his lens and hired her along with a whole group of deaf people.

Back at Thomas's in Massachusetts, my two blond-haired granddaughters toddle, careen, and squeal with delight in the midst of loud dog barks and fresh coffee smells from the kitchen. Five-year-old Tori hums as her bare feet pitter-patter across the wood floor while Annika, two years younger, trundles after her. Two lively Jack Russell terriers almost knock her over as they stampede out the back door into the early morning fog. As the sun rises above the eastern side of the woods, the evergreens, gleaming like glow sticks, light up the rain-filled wetlands. It's nice to be here.

The girls will come to know me as their gypsy grandmother who comes for a visit once a year and tells fascinating stories about whales and fireflies. Periodically, Thomas will point to a map of the world and ask, "Where's Winnie?"

———

While sitting in an airport café with Thomas and his family, reminiscing over our relaxing week at their lakeside cottage in Maine, I'm bemused to hear my name called out over the loudspeaker. "Will Wendy Fredell please come to the gate? Flight 1824 is now boarding."

After hurried goodbyes, I sprint to the security check, where I'm annoyed to see a long line of people snaking around the corner. "How can I get through this quickly?" I ask an attendant.

"You'll have to ask each person in line for permission to pass them," he replies.

I look *every* single person in the eye as I ask this question. On some level this is actually fun in a slightly hysterical way. There are a few perturbed glares, but most people are intrigued by the novelty and excitement of the situation and cheerfully wave me past. While nervously trying to put on my sneakers, I hear my name called again, so I race barefoot to the gate, hair flying, eyes wide as saucers. The man I sit next to in the bulkhead chuckles. "You must be quite a character!"

———

Beaufort appears mostly unchanged. And I find, to my surprise, that my home has a buyer after only a month.

Lee, having returned to Turkey directly from Hawaii to fix some pressing boat issues, is arriving soon at the Savannah/ Hilton Head Airport. It's been a month since we've seen each other. Thankfully, he has agreed to help me pack up all my belongings, which movers will cram into a large storage unit. I'm now officially a gypsy, which feels good on one level and slightly daunting on another.

I've felt like a traveling salesman during our entire US visit after lugging my backpack from airplane to airplane and house to house on our tour of New England, the Pacific West Coast, and the Southeast. I'm patting myself on the back for doing such a good job of adapting to our hosts' personal idiosyncrasies. However, I have not done a good job of adapting to the land version of Lee. He's been a little cranky and difficult to live with while on land. I'm looking forward to being with the sailor version of Lee, who is expansive, fun, and happy. Whose company I enjoy so much.

The next day, he returns to Turkey alone while I drive to my family in Alabama in my grey Acura, which will be sold there. Following this trip, all my material ties to the US will be severed, and there will be no turning back.

Once again, I leave behind another empty house. And that's okay. I really prefer living on the sea with the sailor version of Lee. He seems so much happier when he's exploring the seas. I recall that when we first met and I fixed dinner for him, it was like having a wild deer in the house. That has not changed. Not one little bit. Honestly, I prefer the wild creature side of Lee.

13

Charter in Greece

I'm served an elaborate breakfast on the rooftop garden of Hotel Artefes in Istanbul's historic district. The dark blue ribbon of the Bosphorus Strait shimmers in the distance while I sip a delicious Turkish coffee and contemplate my next three days of sightseeing. Lee, alone in Marmaris and missing me terribly, calls. "I've been waiting for you all my life," he tells me. Overjoyed, I respond, "I'm so happy that I'll see you soon. It's been lonely without you, my love."

My hotel room is interesting. Three odd beds of different lengths and widths line up against the sage-colored wall as if they're waiting to be tested by the three bears. My shower door is a conduit for water, which spreads itself across the black-and-white tile floor. The tired furniture is a 1970s-style Jackson Heights pseudo-Mediterranean.

While I'm worried about being alone in a city of fifteen million people, the kind and helpful hotel staff reassure me that I'll be safe. Attempting to create a conversation with the driver they organized, I announce proudly while pointing toward the ships at anchor, "I live on a boat!"

Glancing at me in the rearview mirror, he responds, perturbed, "I no understand."

Gazing over at the ships scattered about the Bosphorus, I realize he might think I live on a container ship.

A tour guide recounts the history of this part of the world as we cruise up and down the coastline of the Bosphorus for the remainder of the afternoon. While visiting all the must-see things in Istanbul, the humidity in the Underground Byzantine Cisterns, a very complex and ancient system created to bring drinking water into Istanbul from Thrace, destroys my new camera.

Three days later, I'm sitting in the reception area of the hotel, waiting for my bill to be totaled by a man with shiny porcupine jet-black hair. He announces solemnly, "Ah, madam, you owe a *lot* of money for some phone calls."

"How much?" I ask, my voice cracking. He prints out a statement and circles, with a pronounced flourish, all the incoming phone calls from Lee. "You owe three hundred fifty lira extra."

Staring at him in disbelief, I answer, "What? That's more than the three nights here."

He lets it go, thankfully.

I feel like I'm a participant in the Talladega 500 as my surly taxi driver zooms to the airport. He ejects me at the domestic terminal amidst a throng of dark suits. Everyone knows where to go—except me. Confused, unable to find help, I wait in line feeling slightly uneasy about the two different sections of the airport until I realize my mistake. I need to be in the Dalaman terminal.

Twenty minutes before my plane's departure, I skillfully

and gently move a gold-toothed, scarfed young woman and her diminutive child to the side while I wield, with the help of my legs, two eighty-pound L.L.Bean rolling duffle bags and a forty-pound backpack, all of which are filled with boat parts, onto the conveyor belt.

"You're not on our passenger list," they tell me. "You were a no-show on April sixth. You don't have a ticket." There are two parallel universes at work here. I made the reservation in Universe #1. The reservation doesn't show up in Universe #2, which I am now residing in. I'm told that I won't be on the daily flight to Dalaman, which is the closest airport to the Marmaris Marina. Instead, I'll be riding on a bus to Antalya, a coastal city four and a half hours from Lee.

A supervisor directs flustered, crying me to the ticket sales counter, far, far away. Like an annoying grocery cart, my luggage carrier wants to veer to the left while I want to go straight. Trying to make myself feel better, I think, *Well, I've always wanted to go to Antalya.* Maybe I could spend the night and see some ruins. Then I visualize lugging my baggage to a hotel. No way—not happening.

At the Istanbul bus station, I'm pleased to see a Saudi family with even more luggage than me. They have a ginormous sack of grain, an overstuffed suitcase, and several extra-large Mexican plastic bags teeming with stuff. They are in the midst of repacking a suitcase right in front of the *only* ATM in the building. With magnanimity, they move their luggage aside for me.

The bus to Antalya is actually a land airplane. Two navy-blue-uniformed stewards continually offer us lemon water, Nescafé coffee, sodas, and Turkish newspapers. These two men give me more attention than I've ever received on an airplane. When we stop for lunch at a roadside café, I'm fearful the bus will leave without me since I don't understand the Turkish words for "the bus is boarding now." I perch close to our two bus drivers, a pilot and copilot, and watch them continuously out of the corner of my eye. Halfway through my meal of eggplant stew, they stand up to leave, and I quickly abandon my plate.

The two young women sitting in front of me aim their air conditioner vents toward my neck, shoulders, and arms. Politely, I ask them to redirect the air. Bewildered, they look at me blankly. With chattering teeth, I stand up and redirect their air vents while everyone watches. I am now the personification of the Ugly American.

We speed swiftly along roads that curl through snow-capped mountains and then straighten out as they traverse verdant, boulder-strewn valleys bordered by tall pines. Wizened men herd sheep and goats with their crooked sticks and the help of shepherd dogs, while the women, in long skirts with scarves wrapped around their heads, work the fields. We fly past green, yellow, blue, and red concrete houses with terracotta roofs. At a sharp turn, the bus driver swerves into the wrong lane, barely missing herders leading their flock down the middle of the highway.

In Fethiye, the bus pulls over. Unsure about what's going on, I stand at the rear breathing in diesel and cigarette fumes while paying rapt attention to the driver's every move. A tiny blue car hurtles past with two ladies, heads wrapped in scarves, and a toddler, mouth hidden behind a red pacifier, who is standing up and looking out the rear window.

During an extended stop near Antalya, I manage to communicate to the bus driver that I need to be dropped off as close to Marmaris as possible. Not long afterward, the bus driver stops and nonchalantly tosses my bags into a puddle of muddy water on the roadside, then speeds away, grazing my arm hairs. I am now on the outskirts of Gökova, an hour away from Marmaris. I burst into tears as I study the desolate road ahead. What do I do now? Feeling unsafe, I dismiss all thoughts of hitchhiking.

In my hopelessness and misery, I manage to pull myself together and focus logically on a solution. Ahead is a fork in the roadway. Looking at the position of the sun, I realize the route to the left is southbound, which means it's most likely the road to Marmaris. About one mile ahead is a one-story structure. *Maybe there's a pay phone there*, I think hopefully. My cell phone is low on battery and I'm unable to contact Lee.

Pulling one dirty, wet duffle bag at a time, I trudge southward while crying and feeling sorry for myself. I stumble into the graveled, pot-holed parking lot of a restaurant which, I discover, caters to bus loads of tourists.

After dragging each bag into the empty restaurant, I call Lee on the pay phone. His cell disconnects just as I tearfully describe my whereabouts. With resignation, I guzzle a large bottle of lukewarm Efes beer. Then another.

Hours later, Lee, driving a rental car, finds me. Sobbing, I fall into his welcoming arms. To my relief, he doesn't tease or prod me about my state. Instead, he knows just what to say to soothe me: "I've been thinking about you a lot while you were away. You have this *amazing* person inside, Tiger Lily. There's so much power and strength in your center. Do you realize that very few women would have the courage to take off on a wild adventure like you? All you have to do sometimes is stop, take a deep breath, and realize it's there. You can call on that inner spirit to help you when you face difficult situations, my dear."

And just like that, I forget about every unkind or dismissive thing Lee has ever said during one of his annoyed periods. I'm his again, 100 percent.

Every night, we eat dinner in the canteen with the marina workers. If we arrive late, the stew will be mostly broth with just a few vegetables bobbing about. The salad will be gone. But the rice and yogurt never run out. A friend, Dave, who often eats with us, regales us with funny stories. Last night he exclaimed, "My SIM card has gone tits up!"

———

Living on a boat is hard and strenuous, I think as I climb up the twelve-foot-long steel ladder to the boat after dinner. *Living in a boatyard is not glamorous*, I think in the wee small hours when I climb down it for a visit to the ladies' bathroom at the other end of the marina. The ladder rungs are slippery rounded rods a half-inch thick. One wrong move and you're plastered against a concrete slab. My legs are in terrific condition after going up and down the ladder count-less times during the day.

Toilets and sinks on a boat are nonfunctioning when a boat is on the hard. And there is no gentle rocking back and forth to lull you to sleep. I think about this as I polish the stainless in the cockpit.

The boat is shrouded in dust inside and out. The dishes on the drying rack are filmy with grit. The once-white floor of the captain's head is now brown. Not many women would put up with this. Perhaps totally desperate women would. Women missing limbs or hair or teeth. Maybe gypsies.

We'll get through this, I remind myself. So stop the inner kvetching! In spite of all the frustrations associated with liv-ing on the hard, we never complain out loud because we know it will soon be a distant memory, and we'll be back to doing our lovely dance together on the sea.

During the first segment of our stay at the marina, my observation is that the lives of the Turkish workers weigh heavily on their faces. Perhaps my own face projects the same thing. In order to survive this trial that has an ending, I need to change my thinking. So I turn my focus to enjoying the fact that I'm living in exotic Turkey. Wow! I'm so fortunate to be able to do everyday things in an interesting place like this. A simple walk to the bathroom across the lot is totally interesting. People are humming around like little worker bees, engaged in boat projects, tooling around on mopeds, and wearing interesting scarves on their heads. I'm so inspired by the head covers that I wrap a scarf around my own head.

————

After weeks and weeks on the hard, I have enough dirt under my nails to plant a tiny fairy garden. My legs, happily, are in great shape. The sailors who are living on the water look relaxed, maybe even a little smug. They've already experienced life on the hard and now they're enjoying, more than ever, life on the water. They dress well and swagger when they walk. I've given up on trying to look good. I'm now wiping my dirty hands on my shorts. We land-based sailors walk stooped over from bending over most of the time doing boat projects. The water-based people stop to chat with each other and invite each other over for happy hour. We rarely smile. Inviting anyone over is an impossibility. This is purgatory. I don't have the energy to walk up the hillside to see the ancient ruins or even observe the majestic mountains that dive straight down into the sea. On the bright side, as I walk stooped over, I notice little things such as the diminutive grey cat that lost its ear in a cat fight that took place during a forty-five-knot wind storm from Egypt. That cat, tough as nails, swaggers to the dock looking for food.

I start leaving the boat for outings to the Beldibi Market, often sitting at a small outdoor table at a café near the market where I write in my journal. One day, a waiter asks to borrow my pen. He turns it over, studies it, and then says, "I gave this *very* pen to an American woman fifteen years ago! You *finally* returned!" Oh, how I love these outrageously flirtatious Turkish men. That same day, I visit a flower shop to say hello to the owner, who always offers me tea. He's sweeping in front of the shop and is thrilled to see me. Seeing that I'm hot, he removes my sun hat and, taking a brochure from the desk, waves it at me. I feel like Cleopatra. He doesn't speak a word of English, and it doesn't matter. Before I leave, he brings out a toffee-colored cocker spaniel puppy and hands it to me. My eyes well up with tears. *How's Murphy doing in her new home in Beaufort?* I wonder. Not a day goes by that I don't miss her.

The man who's painting the bottom of our boat sees me at the bus stop, runs toward me, grabs my bags, pays the bus fare, and refuses to be paid back. The universe is affirming me in such a loving way. I decide to continue my outings every single day for my own sanity. I'm not sure if Lee would even appreciate my staying on the boat during the daytime because I would surely be in the way.

At the marina, I find a spot where I can be totally alone. There is a magical oasis on the other side of the rocky seawall. The salty wind is brisk here and the sun feels good on my face. This becomes my soul-soothing place.

On our last day in Marmaris, I'm happy to leave the

boatyard but sad to leave the Turkish people who've stolen my heart. I'm given the job of checking us out of Turkey while Lee refixes the rudder and replaces the undependable anchor. I walk through a large anti-American protest in front of a docked US Navy ship on the way to the Customs and Immigration Office. At customs, I sit next to a British couple who tell me a heart-wrenching story about the recent Fastnet Race off the southern coast of England. They owned a sailboat that survived the deadly storm because the crew stayed inside the boat, shut the doors, and lay down on the floor for the duration. The sailors on other boats who jumped onto life rafts died. "Even in a terrible storm, stay on the boat," the British couple tell me. "It's stronger than the dinghy or life raft."

———

Immersed in repair work on a wobbly rudder at the Marmaris Marina, we'll be at least two days late arriving in Naxos, Greece, to pick up our charter from Seattle. The Meltemi, the main weather influence in Greece and Turkey from mid-May to September, are strong and dry northerly winds caused by a high-pressure system that parks itself over Hungary and the Balkan Peninsula. These winds, strongest in the afternoon, come out of nowhere without warning, often causing dangerous and unpleasant sailing conditions.

An important rule in sailing is to wait until the weather conditions are decent. They don't have to be perfect. Against our better judgment, we set sail for Naxos and crash across the boisterous seas, which causes our plates and cups to clank musically in the galley cupboard. The starboard engine growls loudly as we bounce about in the sea. The winds are now forty-two knots on the leeward side of the island of Amorgos. In spite of reefing down the main and furling the jib to the size of a handkerchief, we're almost airborne. Speeding in the wind at a close haul at a forty-five-degree angle is actually quite thrilling. At one point, we reach a heady eighteen and a half knots of speed as we race past a second island, deserted except for a farm and a few goats.

Santorini is just as gorgeous as I had remembered from a previous trip. With our charter passengers Judith and Max on board, we pick up a mooring in the caldera below the town of Oia, which has spectacular sunsets. Walking up an endless series of switchbacks that curl along the steep volcanic mountainside, we stop midway in a shady spot to catch our breath. Thirty minutes later, sweating and panting, we reach the summit.

The town of Santorini is gorgeous, with its colorful stucco houses perched dangerously along the caldera's edge. Massive clusters of purple and pink bougainvillea drape themselves over the walls and arbors and door arches. The angles and curves of the buildings and the shadows they create look like sculptures against the background of the deep blue cloudless sky. Our drive across the island to see the lighthouse is terrifying. Tour buses fly down the middle of the narrow cross-island road where tourists, who are more interested in looking at the view than the road, lumber along its narrow shoulders.

When we stop at a gas station to put ten euros of gas into our tiny robin's-egg-blue car, a white dog walks across the parking lot to stand next to my door. The night before, a dog who had been wandering around the outdoor restaurant where we were having dinner came over to me and sat down on top of my feet. *He's so warm and cozy*, I thought. After the waiter nudged him away, the dog returned and lay down again on my feet. *What's happening here?* I wonder. Animals have been very attracted to me lately. Is the universe affirming, through them, that my desire to love myself is taking root? Something is germinating inside—I can feel it.

Santorini, arid, is 78 degrees in the shade yet still comfortable in the day's heat. The air, heavily scented with lavender, jasmine, and incense from the white-domed churches, is restorative. Grape vines cover large sections of this island, and the long arms of the volcano stretching into the sea are dotted with hot pink flowering shrubs. Lavender grows wild everywhere on this lush and rugged landscape. Stray dogs lounging here and there along the cobblestone streets and fieldstone sidewalks are just something to step over. No one minds. Shops, painted in beautiful shades of cantaloupe, sky blue, and mustard yellow with blue trim, have lovebirds in wicker cages at their entrances. Scarves of all colors, weights, and transparencies flutter like flags in the breezes that sweep through the narrow streets. I buy a cappuccino and a pastry in a shop with window displays of chocolate tortes and cream pastries decorated with lime-colored kiwi slices and deep red strawberries. As I stand poised at the apex of the steep path to our boat below, the sea shines bright turquoise blue close to the shoreline, then fuses into aqua leading to deep navy blue as the depth increases.

In Fira, Santorini's main village, white marble sculptures lure me into a shop where I buy a cotton purse swirled in orange, yellow, deep blue, and pink shades. Every structure, every potted plant, and every doorway is a work of art melded with the sky above, the cliffs, and the water below. As Lee, Judith, Max, and I wander through the village, we follow a set of white steps that curl along the mountainside to a restaurant perched over the cliff. Here the red geraniums pop against the white stucco of the building and the blue door and window frames. Am I in heaven?

I look like a true sailor in my worn-out beige shorts, a tired T-shirt, a camera slung over my shoulder, and a large-brimmed hat. The shopkeepers warm up to me quickly when I tell them that I sailed across the Atlantic and the Mediterranean. A shopkeeper, grinning, remarks, "You're famous!" as she shakes my hand.

Their charter now over, we take Max and Judith to the dock where they'll get the ferry back to Athens. Unexpectedly, at this very dock, we meet an unusual couple. They live in a castle in Scotland and Jules is a self-published author who *loves* the word "nanosecond," which features abundantly in his detective stories. We say no thank you to sundowners on their boat after Jules states, "Anyone who comes on board must take off all their clothes." We also rejected an invitation to visit their castle in Scotland, which has the same rule.

Now just wait a nanosecond, I think but don't say.

On our way toward Athens, we stop at Poros in the Saronic Gulf. This small town's narrow, twisting streets are clustered around a bay where grape vines, oleander, lantana, and lemon and orange trees thrive. We anchor for an overnight in a secluded aquamarine bay nearby.

Reflecting on the past two weeks that we spent in this wonderful country, I feel so lucky to be here with Lee on *Worldwide Traveler* at this precise moment in time. The anticipation that I had of good things to come while I was packing up my house in Beaufort has manifested into reality. Never in my wildest dreams, though, could I have imagined being in this Greek paradise.

14

The Italian
Coast Guard

The steady humming from the diesel engines almost lulls
me to sleep as I watch the early morning sun sweep
its golden glow across the Adriatic Sea. In the distance, a
cobbled-together Albanian fishing boat putters along the
desolate coastline of Albania.

Earlier, just before sunrise, I motored through the narrow channel between Corfu and Albania, which brought us
alarmingly close to a restricted zone famous for pirate activity. As forest fires glowed red all along the mountain ridges
of Albania and poisoned the air with black smoke, I wondered if a gateway to purgatory had opened up. Through
seemingly endless floating debris from the fires, I skippered
my way through this scary netherworld as Lee slept below.

Paul Theroux wrote in *Pillars of Hercules* that the
Albanians are "poor and downtrodden without soul." A

young shipping entrepreneur I met recently in Athens told me that illegal Albanian immigrants have brought crime and distrust to Greece. "They are brought up with no religion and would just as soon kill you as look at you," he said.

In the daylight, while angry flames devour the forests and add more smog to an environment already struggling with pollution, I can't stop thinking about global warming. Athens had the hottest day on record while we were there.

Two days later, now safely anchored, the early morning sunrise awakens us from a deep sleep. We are situated off the Croatian island of Lastova, where rocky fingers of land reach far out into the sea. A fishing boat, trailed by white-winged seagulls soaring and shrieking from above, leaves a wake that rocks us gently. A second one, white and blue in color, its bow weighed down with rusty crayfish cages, barrels toward a desolate island in the distance. At the bow stands a fisherman, his chest puffed out with his hands against his lower back like Napoleon. I'm thrilled to see birds again after the scarcity of wildlife in Greece and Turkey, and here the Adriatic actually smells like the sea.

In the afternoon, Lee and I scuba dive off Lastovo and gently cup in our hands a lovely, velvety, chocolate-brown nudibranch, a marine snail minus the shell. The Mediterranean's coral reefs, which were profuse millions of years ago, have mostly disappeared due to pivotal oceano-graphic and climatic shifts. It is, however, abundant with shipwrecks ornamented with purple sponges, feathery hydroids, algae, and some marine species that are found nowhere else in the world.

After relaxing off the island of Mljet for several days, we sail toward Trogir to pick up our charter guests. Under leaden clouds, a wild and wooly storm unexpectedly stampedes our way out of the west with twenty-knot winds gusting and screaming up to fifty knots. Nothing inside or outside the boat is securely fastened, so we scramble to batten down everything as loud clanging noises fill the air. Sidetracked by worries about whether port holes are closed, I dash down the starboard steps to do damage control. On my way below, I hear a gruff, "Tiger Lily, come here!"

"Be there in just a moment!" I call in response.

Then an angry, "Come here now!"

The mainsheets, flapping wildly, smack me hard in the face. When I attempt to grab a port line it rips across my arm, removing layers of skin. After wrapping and grinding the winches as quickly as possible, we pull down the rest of the main by hand as my blood pools on the deck. All hell is breaking loose. My arm is throbbing with pain. Three reefing lines to the mainsail whip around like angry snakes. We're both drenched and cold. My waterproof rain gear is soaked through, my glasses are fogged up, snot is dripping off the end of my nose, my arm is bleeding, and I feel like shit.

When I'm free to do a quick inspection of the windows below, I'm dismayed to find water gushing into the port fore cabin through the bottom section of a window with a faulty seal. Out of exasperation I throw towels onto the floor, leave the disaster area, then rest briefly in the cockpit while Lee, steering at the helm, is pelted in the face by lashing rain.

The weather conditions now calmer, we approach the island of Trogir, which perches like a sentinel under a star-filled sky. As we motor into the channel, the water forms into mounds behind the boat, and I feel my flagging confidence return. We've been here once before and I know exactly where to anchor.

A mountain of laundry and boat cleaning jobs now loom before the imminent arrival of Pope and his girlfriend, Amber, who have chartered for two weeks. We clean for hours until the boat is spotless.

Damn those Croatian bugs, I think ruefully while wishing they would make themselves scarce. Amber can't stand bugs—probably not even innocent little ladybugs and the tiny spiders that create lovely web art. During her last stay with us, one tiny mosquito bite on her left ankle produced an all-out emergency situation during an extensive bike ride through Mallorca. On our return to the boat, all screens had to go on the windows immediately before she went into insect sting anaphylaxis. At least, that was her story. That same evening, loud thwacking sounds wake me from a pleasant flying dream which includes soaring over Trogir like a bird. *Whack! Whack!* Beside me is a crazed man who is staring dementedly at the ceiling with a rolled-up magazine in his right hand. Hoping Lee would take the hint, I dramatically insert my earplugs and return to my flying dream.

Willowy and fragile-looking with pale, translucent skin, Amber has an oblong face and watery, slightly startled blue eyes. Her straight black hair is pulled primly into a long thin ponytail. She mentions she has the princess and the pea syndrome, by which she means that her super-sensitive skin bruises easily and she has a low pain threshold. Just before their arrival in Croatia, Pope emails to say, "Amber is now allergic to dirt and air!"

I'm having my own issues. My new reading glasses sailed off the boat in a gust of wind, the lens of my prescription sunglasses popped out and joined the reading glasses, and my third and last pair of glasses are missing a screw. The arm is now duck-taped to the frame, and I look like a nerd. Is the universe trying to tell me something? Perhaps I need to see my life more clearly.

As the master and commander, Lee's role is that of the perfect charter captain who reigns over a sparkling clean, flawless boat. Distorting reality through his charming personality, he puts a spell on charter guests who buy into the illusion and have no idea that the engines are malfunctioning or that the water maker doesn't work or that we're about to run out of fresh food, fuel, or toilet paper. Or that his partner, unable to portray the perfect first mate, is currently confronting her shadow sides and has no idea what to fix for breakfast, lunch, or dinner.

Happily, though, I feel something stirring and growing inside. I have a new confidence about myself and my abilities. Because of this, I'm moving more and more into a teaching mode with charter guests, showing them how to do things correctly and standing back to admire their progress. As I've started to let them manage the boat and take over my responsibilities, I revel in seeing them excel as sailors. Even Amber likes this new approach because it helps her turn her focus to learning how to sail instead of worrying about environmental perils. It's gratifying for all of us to see Amber excel in seamanship. In fact, I have to pry her fingers away from the wheel so I can do my watch.

We're closing in on the dreaded Strait of Messina, which lies between the eastern tip of Sicily and the western tip of southern Italy. This narrow strait is well known for its strong tidal currents and natural whirlpools. In Greek mythology, Odysseus managed to avoid the two monsters Scylla and Charybdis as he traversed these narrow waters.

After all the build-up in the pilot guide about the straits

being a shipping hazard, I'm expecting mayhem, such as fierce and agitated waters that nearly overpower the boat. The guide is very specific about choosing the transit time carefully to avoid passaging during strong ocean currents, which can make navigation difficult. It also advises sailors to steer clear of charted whirlpool areas. The two main currents here alternate every six hours, which means one moves north to south while the other moves south to north. Then they switch.

This time, however, there are no jagged rocks, no fierce waves, no helpless swirling around a whirlpool, no sea horrors to cart us away, and no close brush with death. Our trip through the narrow, funnel-shaped channel is one of the most ordinary, tranquil passages Lee and I have encountered so far.

Luckily, Pope and Amber are now leaving for the States after having been totally ignorant of the port engine's steady death march during our explorations of the Amalfi Coast. We were the flawless hosts. Nothing amiss. At every port we visited, Lee, looking very professional, maybe even a little cocky, sidled our yacht up to docks while I, a bikini babe with cellulite thighs from eating too much fried chicken and lemon ice box pies during childhood, sucked in my stomach and tossed impeccably coiled lines to deck hands.

Why, I wonder though, does everything always have to look perfect?

———

With remarkable timing, the port engine sputters out shortly after Amber and Pope's departure. To avoid crashing helplessly into the breakwater looming nearby, Lee slams into a fuel dock under an impassive moon shrouded by menacing black clouds. A force seven storm is about to rip over the Amalfi Coast with thunder, strong wind gusts, and pelting rain, so we cleat all twelve lines to the dock instead of the usual four or five.

The thirty-eight-knot wind whistles *wooooo* all night through the dozens of masts and halyards in the adjacent marina, creating an otherworldly harmonic chiming melody. I almost expect to see spirits hovering about. If the winds continue tomorrow, it will be almost impossible to leave the dock with only one engine functioning. Technicians at the last harbor said the port engine needed to be lifted out of the boat to be properly fixed. At the time, Lee decided to wing it until our arrival in Malta, where people speak English.

In the high winds and waves and strong ocean currents it feels as if the boat is being pulled apart. I keep expecting to hear a loud bang followed by a violent release from the dock and an unstoppable fast drift into the twenty sailboats and motorboats tied stern-to at the neighboring pier. "Aren't we having fun!" Lee says in his best party voice as we lie next to each other in bed, afraid to fall asleep.

Bleary-eyed after a restless night on the port side guest cabin where we had hoped to escape the *yeehah, yeehah, grunch, grunch* sounds of our white starboard fenders grinding against a row of dirty red plastic-covered tires lining the dock, we stagger into the cockpit where we quickly check the lines then head into the galley for our first cup of coffee.

My feet propped up, I relax into a cushion while sensuously sipping my delicious coffee as if I'm at a resort. I'm embracing the denial that we are illegally moored at a fuel dock. I'm ready to chill here for a few days, maybe even longer. Alfonso, a dock hand, breaks my trance unfortunately by yelling from the pier, "You've got to leave! Now! Harbormaster's orders!"

"What? Oh no! Holy crap!" I shout.

Turning toward the salon, where Lee is absorbed in a book, I pass on the bad news.

"Alfonso says the harbormaster wants us to leave *now*."

"Motore discontinue!" I relay to a grim-faced Alfonso in pidgin Italian, hoping to gain a little sympathy and a few more hours here.

The wind has now switched from southwest to north, which is more favorable for departing the dock. However, after the last line is cast and we've motored away with our only working engine, the wind suddenly shifts and pushes us helplessly toward a nearby concrete breakwater.

I radio for help. The Coast Guard arrives within minutes and hovers nearby, waiting to tow us to the safety of the commercial dock in the distance.

"Get a line ready to throw to them!" Lee shouts from the helm.

What? When? How? runs through my head. Never having been in an emergency situation quite like this, my hands shake as I tie a line to the bollard, pull it through the second anchor roller, then brace my body to toss it across the swirling water. Lee yells, "Undo the line! Catch the line from the Coast Guard instead!"

As the breakwater draws dangerously close, a heavy line hurls toward me but is whipped away by the wind. The fifth throw reaches me, and I tie it to the bollard and haul it through the pulley. The slack instantly disappears as we're jerked forward.

Lee yells, "Get the anchor ready in case the line breaks. It doesn't look like it'll hold up!"

"Oh shit!" I yell, thoroughly fed up with the whole damn thing.

We usually make a glamorous entrance when we arrive at foreign ports. On our approach to the filthy industrial port in Salerno, Lee stands at the helm looking like a movie star captaining over the most perfect, unflawed yacht. Traumatized and disheveled after our near collision with the jetty and the frenzied rope-catching scenario, I try to collect my wits as I stand at the bow with a coiled line in my shaky fist.

The Coast Guard pulls alongside a massive cruise ship pier where two dock hands grab our lines, drag us in, and tie us up to gigantic ship cleats. While dust from the yard whips into my eyes, ears, and mouth, I hand over fifty euro for an alleged dockage fee and then accept a free ride to the grocery store in nearby Salerno.

Our new neighbors, ships as gigantic as buildings, blot out the sky. Insignificant in comparison, we've just entered the world of ocean liners, cargo ships, tankers, huge cranes, burly dock workers, and oily grime.

In the shadowy, narrow alleyways in town, the men from Africa glide past me, ghostlike, wearing brightly colored tribal robes or cheap, shiny suits. Their dark eyes, secretive and haunted, size up the pedestrians, hoping to sell them Chinese knock-offs. The sounds of people walking along the cobblestone streets and the church bells fill the air with mystery as I wander past empty park benches that hold untold stories. A gypsy woman with long black hair, high cheekbones, and a prominent nose squats on the sidewalk, a young child by her side. She glances up at me with her sorrowful kohl-lined eyes. Designer-clothed people glare down at her as they wander past. A group of grey-haired, ruddy-complexioned Italian men crowd behind two men playing cards at a table while young girls sashay by in skin-tight jeans with sparkly back pockets and snug T-shirts boasting slogans in Italian. A small golden-haired boy, holding his dad's hand, wearing baggy shorts that skim his teeny feet, toddles clumsily toward me. I wonder how I appear to them, the archetypal sailor in my Tevas, multipocketed cargo shorts, and a pale blue Asa Wright Nature Centre T-shirt. I can feel them watching me, just as I am watching them.

————

A soft melancholia wraps its arms around me as we weave our way through the towering ships entering and leaving Salerno's harbor. Never expecting to fall in love with this city or its people, I've discovered that Salerno found its way into my heart once I explored it beneath the surface.

There is the old lady dressed in black with gnarled arthritic fingers who always slips an extra handful of asparagus and haricot verts into my shopping tote. She is proud of the superior quality of her green grapes and her homemade mozzarella, which she packs neatly into small, sealed bags. Then there is the young, brown-eyed woman in my favorite corner café who speaks fluent English and makes me feel welcome. And the man who always appears when I need help—but expects nothing in return.

Salerno's old town speaks to me with its cobbled streets and its colorfully dressed singing bards. The sounds of classical music floats on air currents from a dozen violinists playing in front of a cathedral from Byzantine times.

As Lee motors past the breakwater into the glimmering moonlit sea, I watch with sadness as the city lights fade away.

During the night watch on this initial leg of our Malta

passage, I spot a container ship with red and green lights approximately six miles away. We're on a direct collision course. The average speed of these ships is twenty-one to twenty-five knots, so it will need plenty of time to adjust its bearing to avoid a head-on. Knowing that small sailboats don't always appear on radar, I hail the ship's captain on the VHS. No response. Not wanting to wake Lee, I shine a high-powered flashlight onto the mainsail to make sure we're seen. Not long after, the massive ship sweeps past our port side and rocks us violently back and forth with its large bow wave, which washes over me as I stand at the helm. Sighing with relief, I celebrate our survival with a handful of the best green grapes in Salerno.

The following day, off the island of Stromboli, Lee shuts down the engines and we drift about all afternoon in silence. This volcanic island is located in the Tyrrhenian Sea off the north coast of Sicily and has one of the three active volcanos in Italy. Nicknamed the "Lighthouse of the Mediterranean," this volcano constantly has minor eruptions.

Anchored, the boat barely moves in the calm cobalt-blue water framed by black sandy beaches. After snorkeling past the lava rocks far below where the sea urchins nestle, we swim over to the warm, ticklish thermal springs. Every once in a while, we bob up and down like a cork when a puff of wind from the volcano, two miles away, is expelled. We can almost taste the acrid sulfur fumes.

Later, while writing in my journal at the bow, I hear muffled rumbles coming from the island almost every five minutes. A large plume of dark brown smoke curls upward into the sky from the volcano's caldera. Handing me a glass of pineapple juice through the galley window, Lee says, "There isn't much time left for you to write. It's almost sunset."

Standing together at the bow, we watch a catamaran a quarter-mile away drift close to the shore where grey smoke rises from a river of lava rushing seaward from the volcano's base. As darkness envelops us, we have also drifted closer to shore. Sitting side by side at the helm, we are mesmerized by the orange and red lava shooting up into the sky, creating ribbons of fire that flow down the steep slopes along with pumice stones which sound like millions of marbles rolling down a large glass cylinder. I can hear them landing in the sparkling water all around us.

It's fascinating to be near something so magnificent, so otherworldly, so powerful. Our boat bobs in the blackness of the sea as the wind whispers into our ears and we sit for hours not saying a word. Suddenly, we both awaken from our volcanic dream and Lee turns on the engines, the navigation lights, the radar, and the navigation chart, and we head under the moonless sky to our next destination: the Messina Straits and the eastward passage between Sicily and the boot of Italy, then Malta.

From childhood on, I've looked on the outside for happiness. Someone or something would kindle the fire of happiness inside of me. The fix was always short-term, however.

Mary, a mindfulness-based cognitive therapist, joins us for a ten-day charter. Everything about her is round and soft and gentle. Her slopping shoulders melt into a cushiony chest, her back curves into a generous waist, and her light brown wavy hair frames her pillowy cheeks and sympathetic hazel eyes.

During our first joint counseling session with Mary, she turns to me and says, "When you fall in love with yourself, you'll be happy, and everyone will want to be with you. Then you will fall in love with the entire world."

Haven't I already fallen in love with myself? I exercise and eat healthy. In general, I take good care of myself. Perhaps truly loving myself is understanding that this perfect being inside of me doesn't need to be fixed. Since looking on the outside for fulfillment is always fleeting, the only place to go is within. Maybe this is what my journey with Lee is really about.

Unfortunately, right after Mary's departure in Malta, Lee criticizes me in a heavy-handed way. My attempt to rinse away his words in the salty sea fails. Since there are no chocolate chip cookies or ice cream on board to lift my spirits, I head below to sit cross-legged on my bed and say Stuart Smalley's affirmations. "I'm good enough, gosh darn it!" I realize that my sense of humor is my saving grace.

15

The Wild Water Woman

Off the coast of Spain in the Balearic Islands, seventy-eight-knot winds terrorize Mallorca during my shopping expedition in an enormous, eerily quiet underground grocery store. On my reemergence from the depths, people are milling about, looking dazed. At the marina, Lee meets my taxi. "The dock has folded up like an accordion!" he says, shaking his head. "This is unbelievable. I've never seen anything like it. We can only reach the boat with the dinghy."

Amazingly, our dinghy is still attached to the dock and is the only one left intact. There's some minor cosmetic damage to the bow of the boat but nothing that will delay our departure. The rest of the boats, having escaped their tethers, are heavily damaged.

As the sun dips low under a brilliant, orangey-red horizon, Pelle and his forty-year-old daughter Marie arrive from

Sweden to help crew on the journey to the Canary Islands. There we will join cruisers from all over the world for the Atlantic Rally for Cruisers. The rally, known as the ARC, is the largest and most celebrated trans-ocean annual event in the world.

After unloading their luggage, Lee invites Marie to join him on an errand to buy gas for the dinghy. Pelle and I are given the glamorous job of lubricating the closures on all windows. Marie is wearing tight, low-slung jeans that expose her muscled midriff, and as she prepares to board the dinghy, my gaze turns to Lee, who is placing both hands on her bare waist to assist her. I feel a big wave of jealousy and wonder how I'm going to survive Marie's presence.

The following day, Pelle—thin and long-limbed with pointy, arched shoulders capped in fuzzy white hair—sunbathes on the trampoline with one long arm stretched above his head. Marie, brown as a berry and clad only in a bikini bottom that allows her youthful buttocks to peek out in an eye-catching way, sprawls next to him.

Marie decides she'll join Lee during his 11 p.m. watch. Knowing this, I thrash about restlessly in bed. Peering through the small porthole to the cockpit, all I can see is a pair of calloused, dry heels in bad need of exfoliation. Why can't I just relax? Marie will be gone eventually, and I'll have Lee all to myself.

On the fourth day, Lee snoozes below while Pelle settles into a comfy spot in the cockpit and immediately dozes off. Marie, bare-breasted, sunbathes on the foredeck. As we plunge through the navy blue Atlantic waters off Morocco's coast I'm listening to a Turkish belly dancing CD while writing. The sails are perfectly trimmed. We are right on course. Everything is perfect except the jealousy churning in me.

That night in my dream, I break up with Lee. And for the first time, I can see how tiny he is. Only two feet tall. With blinders on, I haven't been able to see the truth. Everyone else has. Giving away my power, I've made him bigger and more powerful than he really is. This dream is a big turning point for me.

On November 6th, we arrive in Las Palmas de Gran Canaria. Pelle and Marie have thankfully returned to their homes and their spouses in Sweden. Lee comes and goes like a will-o'-the-wisp. After all this time, he remains a mystery to me. Out of the blue, he's suddenly brushing his teeth, washing his face, and getting ready to leave the boat. Before he heads out, with no intention of saying goodbye, I ask uncertainly, "Are you angry with me?"

There is still this dichotomy within me. Even though I've come to the realization that I'm giving my power away to Lee, I live in my heart. That's never going to change. Since I was a child, the grownups in my life recognized this and said, "What a beautiful trait to have!"

Owning this, I treat this fragile part of me with love and patience.

"No, I'm just focused on projects," he says over his shoulder as he jumps onto the pier.

While I'm crying in the shower at the marina, the hot water quits abruptly after only sixty seconds then turns into ice-cold water. Maybe the universe is trying to get my attention. Yesterday, I had a full five minutes of warmth. On my return, I find Lee lying on his side at the bow, caulking cracks on damaged areas. He acts as if everything is normal. But nothing is normal to me.

"Why did you leave in a huff without speaking to me?" I demand.

Shrugging, he answers, "I need to focus. I don't want to get caught up in conversation with you." Noticing my crestfallen face he adds, "Go into town. Walk around. Take pictures. Take the day off. You don't need to go shopping. We have enough food."

As I walk past a long row of international sailboats, I glance back to see Lee having an animated conversation with a young sailor who just arrived.

Wandering slowly through the old section of Las Palmas, I stop for lunch at a quirky vegetarian restaurant called Hippodrome, where a collection of troll dolls overwhelms my vision. They are *everywhere*. Even in the bathroom, where they grace the top of the toilet tank, the window sill, and the sink counter. In Scandinavia, they're used to remind people to laugh, and according to legend, luck follows when you laugh.

The night before, I had a dream about a man who stayed afloat in the dark choppy sea by holding on to a wooden board. A wide-eyed, visibly anxious young boy, his son, kept disappearing beneath the ocean's surface. The father was apparently oblivious to his plight. In the next dream, I was at a seaside park. I saw an enormous python that was inside a large container with holes in the sides. As I walked across the top of the crate, I wondered if the snake inside could feel my body warmth through the hard plastic.

I think about the parallel between these two dreams and my actual life. Perhaps these dreams signify that my unconscious mind is begging Lee to pay attention to how he makes me feel when he says insensitive things to me.

The air is humming with energy as the festivities for the ARC gear up on our thirteenth day here. Soon after their arrival, sailors queue up outside the main office to register for the upcoming crossing, purchase ARC T-shirts, and receive the program of activities. Locals and sailors stroll the docks, watching crew members check boat systems, inspect sails, and change engine filters. Our mainsail is looking pretty worn at this point, but we'll wait until we're in Martinique, where Lee knows a well-known sailmaker.

In twelve days, more than twenty cruiser yachts will head across the sea for Rodney Bay in St. Lucia, in the Caribbean, which is 2,700 nautical miles away. Lee estimates the passage will take three weeks with the assistance of the eastward trades. The fastest passage on record for this event is eight days, and the longest is thirty-one days.

I drink a strong Cuba Libre at the Vela Luka happy hour, which will surely wreck my sleep. I watch Lee and our new friend Steve, whose sailboat is docked close by, as they attempt to fix our moody water maker—at midnight. Apparently, they're also jazzed up.

In between daily happy hours, costume parties, and courses on provisioning for long passages, boat safety measures, and man overboard procedures, I clean the bilge and the large storage cavities under the queen beds in the stern and the twins in the forward port cabin.

To clean the bilge, I lie on my stomach and lean head-first into the three-foot-deep, stinking, oily cavity with my legs splayed out. As I'm wondering why Lee insists I do these seemingly unnecessary cleaning jobs, he emerges from the engine room with black engine grease smeared across his sweaty face and hands.

Young internationals, pretty girls with a certain toughness and handsome boys with long curly sun-bleached hair, knock on the side of the boat periodically to see if we need crew.

Today we're taking a break from boat chores. I do yoga, meditate, and journal while Lee sleeps below. The boat bobs side to side, and the newly washed laundry behind me lifts itself into the soft breeze as I watch men work on their brightly colored racing boats, each of which represents a province in the Canaries. Their wives, meanwhile, prepare food for their weekly Sunday feast at the Vela Latina pier. Plates and cutlery clank while an aroma of newly baked bread permeates the air around the Norwegian boat off our bow. Palm leaves overhead clatter in a quick gust of wind as a young sailor speeds past on his stainless steel fold-up bike while talking into his VHF. Following him is a young girl whose feet slap loudly against the concrete as she runs past. Sailors from the Japanese vessel off our stern talk quietly in their cockpit while the Venezuelans across the pier unload large boxes of provisions.

In the evening, I wear a multicolored silk Caribbean dress to a party at the yacht club and feel beautiful and don't need anyone to tell me so. I can feel something shifting in my psyche as if a little seed is slowly germinating within. During my last visit to the East Coast of the US, a massage therapist remarked, "There's a lot going on in your solar plexus. You're at the brink of a huge transformation. Something really wonderful is happening to you."

Lee and I join a bus tour of Vega de San Mateo, a town in the mountainous part of Gran Canaria. In the bus, out of the bus. Herded here, herded there. Lee's having another aloof day, and truthfully, I'm getting tired of his moodiness. My solitary explorations of Las Palmas have brought me much more joy than any explorations with Lee. For instance, I constantly giggle to myself over my bumbling attempts to check out the city. Unable to decipher hand gestures from the locals, I nod yes while saying in a very charming voice, "Si señor, si!" as I wander off in the wrong direction.

Buses can be challenging. Asking for directions in English ends up involving the help of *every* single passenger on the bus. *All* I wanted yesterday was to find Tom Miller Street, which is one of the best shopping streets here. How difficult could that be? During a long-winded, energetic group discussion in Spanish, I glanced out the window to see the sign for that very street. I jumped off in front of a Swedish pastry shop run by a young Scandinavian woman who seemed confused over my elation at seeing her.

We've bonded with our hilarious boat neighbors, Carlos and Sebastian. Carlos, an Olympic diver from Venezuela, is quite charming, and Sebastian, attractive in a rounded way, is a producer for the Hispanic MTV out of Miami. In the galley of their large catamaran, a massive gnawed-at pig leg nestles in a wooden holder. The hoof daintily points outward like a ballet dancer. Carlos explains that this specially cured pork comes from the best place in Spain and keeps well at room temperature, which makes it perfect for long passages. He adds, "It's like prosciutto."

Lee responds, "We should get one. I just saw a store that has them hanging out front."

We wouldn't have room for something so massive. Our galley is half the size of theirs. I'd go for a much smaller version, but I'm not sure if that's possible.

A week before race day, we are given an ARC login address, which is unique for our boat, and instructions on how to email position reports every day at 12:00 Greenwich Mean Time. All of our interactions will be through the single sideband radio. Daily at 11:00 Coordinated Universal Time (UTC), we'll be emailed weather forecasts, and on Mondays, we'll be contacted on the VHF by the net controller. It's mandatory that we keep a log of the hours we motor each day.

We've been designated position 200 out of a group of 223 sailboats, so we'll be among the last to leave the breakwater.

The committee boat will be positioned at the start line. At 12:10 p.m., we'll hear a warning signal on the VHF from a warship. From 12:10 on, we'll have to keep the VHF clear. At 12:50, the countdown will start. At 12:55, there'll be a short signal followed by a long signal at 13:00. On our approach to the finish line at St. Lucia's Pigeon Island, we'll be instructed to call channel 18 on the VHF at five nautical miles, and then two miles.

The weather looks decent for the next few days. The trades are fifteen to twenty knots on the lee of the island. Since there is less rain activity south of the Canaries, we will initially head in that direction.

Our two crew members are Lee's friend Teresa from Portland and Sebastian, a former Navy captain from Sweden. As we prepare for their imminent arrival, I fret, "Are we going to be ready in time?"

"Not to worry," Lee answers brightly. "We'll put Teresa and Sebastian to work."

The list of to-dos is long. As project #1 is checked off, project #2 is added. Food supplies are my chief concern. Yet anyone who sees us at the prepassage festivities would guess that we're pretty much set. We look that laid-back.

Race management is currently performing rigorous safety and equipment inspections on all boats. We will not be able to join the ARC unless we pass inspection.

I take a bus to a huge grocery and department store complex, which is the recommended place to shop. This time, I have a tool chest of information that I've garnered from the ARC's provisioning course, and I feel totally confident about this excursion.

After a confusing trip on an up escalator instead of the down escalator and some interesting wrong turns, I find the grocery store's entrance. Four aisles later, my brain is fried from attempting to read labels in multiple languages. My cart isn't heaped as high as the other ARC people, and I soothe myself by remembering that this is just a test run.

A camaraderie has blossomed among the international sailors. We recognize each other immediately. I don't know if it's our clothing, the VHFs attached to our back pockets, or our weathered faces, but we are truly kindred spirits.

Too busy talking to other sailors, I focus only on bread— twelve loaves of it. I choose slightly undercooked ciabatta bread sealed in clear plastic packaging that just needs ten minutes or so in an oven.

On my next shopping attempt, I bump into my two young Swedish friends at the check-out and feel slightly agitated after seeing their three shopping carts overflowing with food. My cart is half-empty.

On my third venture to the grocery store, my confidence returns. I'm now helping other sailors. I leave my cart to take an American woman to the flour section, where I help her figure out which flour is self-rising. Then I lead someone else to the dairy section. I'm having so much fun helping people that I forget to shop.

The following day, I get sidetracked by the lure of an underwear shop where I try on twenty bras, of which I pick out four to buy. Then I head into the bowels of the grocery store for another half-hearted attempt at provisioning. I'm distracted, however, by a café and head there for a latte. I run into Paul, our English friend whose boat is moored next to ours, and pick his brain for the inside scoop on what was discussed during the skipper's briefing.

My daily four-hour attempts to shop are spent mainly socializing with sailors. Unconsciously, I'm avoiding the checkout, which is complicated and time-consuming. An interpreter has to arrange to have chicken, fish, meat, and other items vacuum-packed, deep-frozen, and delivered to the marina. Worried about our temperamental freezer, I am hesitant to buy anything that needs to be stored in it. And people have mentioned that their deep-frozen items arrived partially thawed.

Sebastian's luggage is lost somewhere between Stockholm and Barcelona. "A toothbrush is all I need," he says brightly. The next morning, Teresa and Sebastian help Lee with boat projects while I return to the grocery store again. I'm now feeling *totally* at home there. Even the locals are asking me for help.

During my last shopping trip, my young Swedish buddies approach me with an interesting proposition. "Would you mind being interviewed for a documentary about live-aboard sailors?" they ask. The whole country is keeping track of their whereabouts, and there's a lot of buzz about this documentary they're filming for Swedish television. After a two-hour interview, I buy six pounds each of frozen chicken and hamburger meat and arrange to have them delivered to our boat.

On my return, Lee, Sebastian, Teresa, and I wander the long wooden docks watching frenzied sailors completing their final, frantic preparations. As we walk along, I wonder if we're really ready. Have I covered everything that could possibly go wrong? No matter how well we prepare, there's always something lacking.

———

On November 25th, in a rush of true adrenaline, we untie from the dock and motor toward the starting line. It's a heady sight to see 234 sailboats gathered together in one area. Our position is toward the back, so we bounce about in the choppy waves as we wait for a warship's countdown on VHF channel 77. At 13:00, a protracted signal goes off as we hover in position as the boats in front take off. These starting boats jockey frenetically to be first, and at times barely miss running into each other. Our sails filled with wind, we head southward to avoid the western squalls.

December 2nd, day nine. Our fresh food is either going into our tummies or into fish tummies. All the vacuum-packed, flash-frozen food is now thawed after the freezer shuddered and death-rattled itself to a grand halt during the night.

Teresa and I sauté all the defrosted chicken, then make Northern Italian Bolognese sauce with the ground beef. I toss the moldy carrots and the sprouting onions overboard. Yesterday, after we caught our first fish (a mahi mahi), Sebastian said, "Less fish is wasted if you cook it Swedish style." So I marinated it overnight, and today I'm cooking it whole.

We bump about as the waves repeatedly smack the bottom of the boat as if saying, "Naughty child!" Every day brings different cloud formations and different waves in an ever-changing landscape. Today, an early morning rain shower has rinsed away the red Saharan dirt from the cockpit and the bow, leaving the boat sparkling white. While the sun peaks out from the heavy cloud cover, a gorgeous vivid rainbow with a large deep purple band appears as the mainsail and the jib, now filled with wind, push us relentlessly forward.

Our brightly colored spinnaker blew out in the wee hours

of the morning while Lee was on watch. The winds, unexpectedly increasing from seventeen knots to thirty-two knots, caused the sail to split down each side resulting in the midsection falling into the water between the pontoons.

Lee wakes us. "I have some bad news. The spinnaker blew out, and it's trailing behind the boat. I need your help pulling it in."

It's always a bad idea to leave a spinnaker out overnight, but against our better judgment and perhaps feeling lazy, we decided at our late afternoon crew meeting that we'd risk it. In the cloudless, calm early evening, we comfort ourselves that we've made the right decision. But things change very fast when you're in the middle of the ocean—especially at night.

December 3rd, day ten. Report from the ARC net control tells us that boat 181 is unable to charge its primary batteries, boat 242 has a broken main, boat 179 has broken battens and cans on the main, boats 24 and 40 have broken booms, and boat 35 has issues with water leaking through the keel bolts and the crew is currently pumping out the bilge. Their engine is no longer working, and they've been diverted to Cape Verde. There are also still a number of yachts in the Canaries that are unable to join the ARC due to ongoing boat issues.

Water is leaking into our aft port cabin. After a process of elimination, it turns out to be a faulty seal around the windows. In the port hallway, water is leaking under the berth, and we can't figure out where it's coming from. The set of batteries under the salon seats aren't recharging, so we recharge them by turning on the engines. Our fuel is now half gone.

December 9th, day fifteen. Foul weather gear moves ghostlike on the laundry line in the captain's head. Wet towels lie in a clump on the floor. A mountain of wet sheets and mattress covers sit in the corner of our cabin.

Today we are moving through a seemingly endless cloud front all day and into the evening. On the radar, this weather shows up as a red-dominated grain. The sky is pitch-black when I start my 6 a.m. watch UTC time. It's actually 3 a.m., but I lie to myself by saying, *It's sort of 6 a.m., and I'm not even tired.* I brew an Earl Grey tea while eyeing the radar monitor instead of stepping out into the downpour. Glancing over at the sliding door that opens to the cockpit, I notice what looks like a mini bathtub filled with three feet of water in the enclosed bottom step area. The water slaps against the glass door while I stand pondering over how to handle the situation. At some point, the sliding door needs to be opened, but if I open it now, water will flood the salon.

Holding a bucket against the bottom of the door, I inch the door open. After it fills, I slam the door shut and then fill six more containers. Clear, pristine water! Deciding not to unplug the drain, I contemplate having a bath. Instead, I wash my hair in a bucket of water and give myself a sponge bath.

Three hours later, I've filled twenty containers total. The rain has now tapered off to a soft drizzle. Teresa staggers up the steps for her watch and is greeted by Wild Water Woman. Wearing a black bikini, my wet hair is seaweed messy. My eyes resemble enlarged flying fish eyes. I must have gone a little crazy in those moments of eager water harvesting.

December 10th, day sixteen. The boat resembles a gypsy camp. When we sailed out of Vela Latina over two weeks ago, we were the proper yacht. Everything was neatly tucked away, the boat was spotless, and we all looked impressive in our foul weather gear as we waved, full of pride, to hundreds of people lining the pier on our way out to sea.

Now everyone is dirty and has worn the same clothes over and over again. In the evenings, I change into a tropical cotton sundress. The other night, my dress suddenly flipped up like Marilyn Monroe's during a squall and an emergency sail change.

December 11th, day seventeen. "We have a sailboat behind us!" Teresa yells. This is the first boat we've seen the entire passage. The VHF crackles with the news that a number of boats have been dismasted. Sadly, a sailor on one boat who was recently knocked unconscious by the boom has died.

A request goes out from the ARC headquarters to us: We are told to immediately change course and head to a sinking boat. Another boat, however, beats us to the location, and we're notified by ARC to return to course.

December 12th, day eighteen. We arrive at Rodney Bay in St. Lucia. We spend the next two days catching up on laundry and self-care as our crew members prepare to leave. I've enjoyed both of them, but I'm ready to enjoy my solitude. Unfortunately, after they depart, Lee angers me by saying, "We need to discuss what you *didn't* do right."

Damnit, I thought. *I did a great job! I knocked myself out to make our passage a pleasant one.*

The ARC behind us, we leave Rodney Bay at 7:30 p.m. and begin our slow approach to beautiful Vieux Fort at 1:30 in the morning. The seas along St. Lucia's leeward side have become boisterous as we close in on this well-known mecca for windsurfing. Careening nauseatingly to the right and the left, then up and down, the boat makes strange growling noises as if it is dissatisfied with the choppy seas continually washing over us.

We're five nautical miles off brightly lit St. Lucia. As we motor past the mountain ranges, the island's lights disappear and reappear as each large mountainous shape recedes silently into the distance. I remain in the cockpit the whole time, deep-breathing salty air, looking ahead while trying to cope with a bout of nausea.

Around midday, we dinghy over to a boat from Finland to recover the kiteboard that Lee loaned Janne when we were docked in Rodney Bay. I only saw Janne in passing, but Lee connected with him at some of the social events before the ARC send-off. I become fascinated with Janne, who has an odd way of speaking without moving his lips. His boat mates, all Finns who are shy about speaking English, look relieved when I speak Swedish, their second language.

I'm *thrilled* to be far from the madding crowd at Rodney Bay—especially from the two women in the monohull next to us who cleaned their boat in décolletage sundresses. One, whose dress barely covered her tuchus, continually fought a losing battle with her naughty breasts, which refused to be confined. Her friend's thoroughly unleashed ones swayed back and forth rather hypnotically. I was extremely happy to escape all that massive, jiggling buxomness and the obvious wanderings of Lee's eyes.

———

Christmas is coming soon, and I'm missing my family. They feel so far away. Every day I wonder how Alex is doing. During our charters and passages, I'm usually too preoccupied to miss them, but now that things are calmed down, I can't ignore the sadness inside of me. And I wish I had a female buddy to confide in. I always enjoy the companionship of the women who join us on charters, but they eventually leave and return to their own lives.

I park the dinghy at a fishing dock in Vieux Fort among gobs of floating trash. A NO ANIMALS sign is ignored by a group of small muscular short-haired dogs with question-mark tails. They sashay about as if they own the place. As I approach the town, a wild-eyed, stick-thin woman in a pea-green house dress stares at me as if she needs to ask me something. A couple wanders by. She's wearing an animal skin ensemble, and his outfit looks like something dug out of a garbage can. They chuckle and sway, their large flat bare feet moving in time to iPod music. I leave the sidewalk for a moment to let a middle-aged woman wearing an inside-out top stagger by me. It all feels a little dangerous, like I've stepped into a world with its own rules.

Women squat along the sidewalks selling vegetables and fruit, which are laid out in front of them on plastic sheets. Craving fresh vegetables and fruit after days at sea, I buy a few things from each woman. Plump ginger, magenta sweet potatoes, green beans, summer squash, parsley tied neatly into a tiny bouquet, spring onions, lady finger bananas, lime green starfruit, and brown mottled grapefruit. Over half of these women have eyes clouded over by cataracts, a very common ailment in the Caribbean.

A local warns me to be careful with my money. Absent-mindedly, I pull out a Ziploc from my backpack, which holds 200 Eastern Caribbean dollars—the equivalent of $75. A plump woman with salt and pepper hair says sternly, "Put that away! Don't show your money!"

Quickly returning it to my rucksack, I head to a grocery store filled with Christmas shoppers. After finding a loaf of freshly baked whole wheat bread, I stare in confusion over a cluster of unrecognizable frozen objects in the meat section. I settle for a bag of frozen shrimp from Malaysia, the only familiar thing I recognize.

Going from port to port, from anchorage to anchorage,

from one marina to another marina, I have found that we live in the truth of places. The artificial worlds of hotels where the grass is always green, where the flower beds dazzle, and where the birds chirp away almost on cue are something we rarely experience. Instead, we encounter the world on the other side of the gate. In this version, the birds sound a little different. And here, the real world creeps in with its iron-barred windows, its broken-down cars, and its dirt and filth. Thankfully, we can always escape this reality and taxi to a mall, restaurant, movie, or deserted beach.

I return to the dock at dusk, my arms lengthened like rubber stretch toys as I carry two large brightly colored Tunisian bags filled with groceries. The evening breeze is alive with the sounds of a child screeching, dogs barking, insects droning, a live reggae band playing nearby, and couples laughing. I motor back to the quiet, calm world of our sailboat, where the only sound is the water lapping against the sides of the boat and the lines creaking in the breeze. And the soundlessness of Lee playing a game on his computer.

It feels unusually empty this Christmas. I wish so much that I was with my family because Christmas Day doesn't feel the same without them. I'm not sure if I can endure another Christmas missing them like this. I'll be calling them later from an internet café that has pay phones, but the empty feelings I have will remain. Lee, on the other hand, seems unfazed by missing the holiday with his family.

The day after Christmas, the small beachside A-frame building overlooking the ocean is packed with swimsuit-clad kiteboarders lounging in the comfortable ladder-back cane chairs. We're now on friendly terms with the stern, standoffish, mousy-haired woman who takes orders for breakfast and lunch. While Lee sits in a corner reading John Irving's book on Vincent Van Gogh that he found in the book exchange cubby, I catch up on emails from my sons while feeling sad and lonely.

16

Saba and St. Vincent

It's been two years now since Lee and I first sailed past the small island of Saba—back when we were on the way from St. Martin to Barbuda and Antigua. At that time, we decided to bypass it after noticing its forbidding, almost vertical rocky bluffs. It looked like a mountaintop jutting straight out of the sea with no access areas or anchorages. If mooring balls were even available, where were they?

Today on our approach to this potentially active volcano with an elevation of 2,865 feet, the bright afternoon sunlight helps me locate a mooring ball. We're the only sailboat here. Like giraffes, craning our necks upward, we peer at the alarming perpendicular slopes above. Directly ahead is the "Ladder," nicknamed for its twisting, curling, snaking eight hundred steps that lead up the mountainside to a former customs house and then onward to a small village called The Bottom. The sailing guide warns that the steps shouldn't be attempted on a rainy day unless you're up for a rapid and possibly fatal plunge into the sea.

Unable to secure the dinghy in this location, we motor over rough, teeth-rattling seas to Fort Bay, an area that reminds me of Flores in the Azores. This tiny, no-nonsense port has a noisy electricity generating plant that blasts hot air at people as they walk past. There's one restaurant, three dive shops, and a lovely two-story white cottage with green shutters that houses the Saba Conservation Society. Its sparkling clean public restroom actually has liquid soap, paper towels, and toilet paper—things that are often plundered on the other Caribbean islands.

Having found a local guide named Donna, we're taken on a driving tour of Saba. Her car is almost vertical as it creeps up the severely inclined concrete road from Fort Bay, and I'm silently thanking myself that we didn't do the walking tour. As we slowly ascend the mountain, the landscape changes from a rather barren moonlike landscape into one of beautiful lush green meadows. At The Bottom, which is Saba's capital town, our guide points out three churches, one of which dates from the sixteenth century. A one-lane cobblestone street intersects this lovely village of stone walls covered with flowering vines, white picket fences, and pristine, green-shuttered white cottages with terracotta roofs and gingerbread detailing. She waves to everyone we pass in this hamlet of only five hundred people.

St. John's, a residential area on the island's windward side, perches beneath a peak named Mount Scenery. Our last stop is Willard's Hotel, which sits on a precipice overlooking the sea. This is the sister hotel of the four-star Willard's in Washington, DC.

The following day, we hike the Sandy Cruz trail, which has gorgeous views of Saba's leeward coastline and its secondary rainforest. Switchbacks take us through misty gorges and lush mossy areas brimming with fuchsia trees, palms, orchids growing on tree trunks, wild raspberries, prickly pear cactus, white begonias, and black-eyed Susans. Many of its mountain mahogany trees were unfortunately destroyed in a recent hurricane.

We end our journey at the Tropics Café, where we meet Jan, a Canadian, from the Conservation Society, his long-legged girlfriend from Denmark, Bob and his French girlfriend from Saba Divers, and Jim and Joanna, the owners of Julianna's Restaurant. Joanna, plump with massive, pancake-shaped breasts, flirts with Lee while winking and patting the seat next to her. I sit with an Englishman, formerly an advertising executive, who is now a photographer and web designer here. "There is one of everything in Saba," he tells me. I'm not sure what that means.

Four days later, we are scolded by the harbormaster. We were under the mistaken impression that signing in at the Conservation Society and paying our mooring fee was a quaint and quirky Saba-like way of checking into the country.

After an energizing cup of strong coffee in Fort Bay, we hitch a ride up the steep concrete road with a student from the island's medical school. It's mid-afternoon when we're dropped off at the summit trail, and most of the hikers are leaving as we're arriving. It's 5:30 p.m. when we reach the first summit outlook. The top of the mountain is shrouded in cloud cover as we trudge along a dirt path, which is now slippery, thick, gooey mud. This well-marked hiking trail meanders through a secondary rainforest covered with giant leafy elephant ears. At the peak is the Elfin Forest Reserve. I'm secretly hoping to see an elf but don't mention this to Lee.

We pull ourselves up a precipitous path with the help of a thick, moss-encrusted rope. By 6 p.m., we reach the fog-covered summit of Mount Scenery. Surrounding us are sheer drop-offs into the rainforest below. Our shoes encrusted in mud, our shorts splattered with dirt, our T-shirts soaked in sweat, we start our descent while being serenaded by birds and tree frogs. By 7 p.m., we can just make out the trail thanks to the reflection of light from the cloud cover. The numerous steps leading to the main road meander past The Bottom, the medical school, tied-up barking dogs, lit-up houses, and a closed restaurant.

A gentle breeze filled with flower smells cools us down as we admire the Southern Cross and the two Pointer Stars. Fort Bay hums with the sounds from the electric plant, which warms us with big puffs of air as we walk past. Using our headlamps to help us locate the dinghy in the now-darkened port, we find it coated with dust from the stone-crushing plant on the hillside above. I wash the dinghy with salt water as Lee pulls up the anchor. Back home, we congratulate ourselves on being stubborn and crazy enough to visit Saba, an island that only the most adventurous sailors visit.

―――――

After two weeks in Saba, we sail south past St. Kitts and Nevis to Vieux Fort in St. Lucia, where my son Alex, now twenty-one, and his girlfriend, Marie, are arriving at the airport. Alex is in his last year at Trinity College, and Marie is working in Hartford. They're going to be with us for two weeks. This is their initiation into sailing. At least they're being eased into it gently. Their return trip to the tiny airport in Vieux Fort, St. Lucia, however, may be another thing entirely.

Ahead of us, St. Vincent's mountains loom mysteriously

underneath a large bank of dark clouds. This island still echoes with the disturbing memories of the hot, molten lava that poured over the sides of La Soufrière in 1979.

Lee motors into the first viable anchorage at the southern foot of the volcano's steep mountainside covered with palm trees. We tuck into salad and vegetables from Vieux Fort as the long shadows from the setting sun envelop us. Unexpectedly, a loud clunking sound emerges from the rear. Have we hit ground? Has the anchor dragged? Are we being visited by pirates? Then we see three children, bobbing up and down in a small wooden fishing boat with a peeling red interior. They stare up at me expectantly.

"Are you okay? What are you up to? Are you selling fruit?" I ask hopefully. Then I add, "How old are you, my dear? And what's your name? Oh, and by the way, are these nice boys your brothers?"

Janet, who I discover is thirteen years old, pulls a football-sized greenish-yellow papaya from underneath the seat and holds it up for me to inspect.

"So what do you want for this lovely papaya?" I ask.

"Whatever you think," she answers after an extended pause.

I swivel my head toward Lee, hoping he'll answer. I see his blank-looking face.

"Okay," I say. "How about ten ECC?" This stands for the East Caribbean dollar which has an exchange rate of $1 US to 2.70 ECC.

"Sure!" Janet chirps happily. Then I ask her and her brothers Teron, age ten, and Jerod, age twelve, to find a coconut and a bunch of lady finger bananas for tomorrow's breakfast.

At 9 a.m., there's a knock on the port side. Janet has a grey T-shirt draped over her head for protection from the gentle morning rain. Teron, tiny for his age and wearing an inside-out red-and-white-striped T-shirt, holds a tired-looking coconut that has probably been decaying on the ground for months. I watch as he slams a machete against it. Totally dried up inside, the coconut slips out of his hands into the water. They continue their search, and I hear a loud twacking sound in the distance. Periodically, Jerod rows back to our boat to make sure we are still here. I suspect we're the entertainment of the day.

Later, as Teron slams his machete against the sides of two perfect coconuts, I ask him, "Have the other boaters bought fruit from you?"

"No," all three kids answer brightly. I wonder how *anyone* could resist these charming creatures.

Alex has been acting a little strange, so Lee and I decide to confront him about his unusual comings and goings. In the early mornings, he slips off the end of the boat like a feline and wades across the shallow water to the shore, where he vanishes into the underbrush. He guiltily confesses that he gave a young kid 20 ECCs if he could round up some pot. So Lee and I, in an adult way, decide that Alex should smoke pot out in the open instead of sneaking around.

Marijuana grows profusely on the northern end of this untamed and magnificent island. I ask the two fishermen who pull alongside us in a canoe teeming with fish, fruit, and vegetables where the mysterious boatloads of people are going in the early morning hours. Leaving the village at sunrise, they head northward across the bay. Then at sunset, they return.

One of the fishermen answers, "Oh they beez going to work on the plantations, mon."

"We could smell those plantations during our sail along the coast. Is marijuana legal here?" Lee asks.

"No! It's illegal. The US government takes local police in helicopters to the plantations, and they destroy the crops."

"What happens to the owners?"

"They get very, very stiff fines," the fisherman responds.

"Is the marijuana transported in powerboats to the other islands?"

"Yes, mon, they eeze taken to Antigua and Barbados . . . that is, if they don't get caught. The coast guard is looking out for them!"

The northern swells bring two days of pelting rain and turbulent waters. A red plastic bucket collects rainwater on our cabin floor as Alex and Maria laze on the salon sofa reading books from our collection. Feeling slightly befogged from the boat's constant jouncing, Lee and I putter about the boat in a disorganized manner.

Two days later, Alex and Maria pull up the anchor, and we leave a becalmed bay during a short let-up in the rain. Out in the deeper waters, the skies clear overhead. I glimpse back at the anchorage, now in the distance, to see a huge stationary black rain cloud draped over it like a big wet cloak.

With all this humidity, my hair—an entity of its own—shape-shifts into different forms. Today it takes on a slightly electrocuted look. During my last visit to San Francisco, Sally took me to her favorite hairdresser for some hair rescue. Tall and good-looking with spiked blond hair and a neck tattoo, her male stylist laughed over my inability to control my mop. "Oh my, that's fun. High maintenance hair and a boat," he said.

In Turkey, after my hair was dyed an eggplant shade and then cut into something similar to a flying saucer, Lee said, "I like this punk color. And your weird haircut. Just think . . . there are no limits for you now. You can even have green hair if you want."

I have to admit it was freeing.

Greeting us as we motor into beautiful Cumberland Bay is a fisherman with dreadlocks gathered together like one big pineapple on the side of his head. I'm so mesmerized by his hair that I space out while he talks. The engine sounds make it even harder for me to understand his lingo, and, smiling vacantly, I purchase four overpriced red snappers. A few more fishermen follow us into the bay and tie our stern lines around a palm tree. The water brims with squid and fish as egrets spin across the sky and bird chatter fills the late afternoon air.

———

One of our main goals in St. Vincent is to scale the summit of the active 4,049-foot-high La Soufrière and peer down into the crater rim. It's one of the Windward Islands' most exciting hikes. This volcano has erupted five times since 1718. Nowadays, there is a volcano warning system in place.

In his book *The Windward Islands*, Chris Doyle says, "The wind often blows a gale at the top. You have to be careful not to get blown down into the crater, which is a sheer thousand-foot drop with no handrail." According to him, the best way to climb the volcano is to start from the windward eastern side, which is less steep than the western side.

The driver of a minibus pulls up in a swirl of surliness and a plume of loud rock music. With our picnic lunches, our water bottles, and our windbreakers, we squeeze into the back seats of this van bound for Georgetown, which sits at the mountain's base. Along the way, it frequently slams to a stop to pick up an astounding total of twenty-eight people, and somehow, everyone fits into this physically impossible space.

We're squeezed five across in the back, and I've given up on any sense of personal body space or underarm odor. Or seatbelts. The bus blasts down narrow roads that wind their way through tiny villages, then, tires squealing and screeching, we round hairpin curves as if we're in a Mad Max race. Maria looks pale. Lee's eyes are closed as if he's meditating, and Alex stares straight ahead with a glazed expression as calypso and reggae music blare from the speakers. I study the two hair-netted elderly ladies in front of me. How can they do this at their age? The bus suddenly grinds to a stop, and three skinny, long-legged girls chewing bubblegum depart in a cloud of perfume.

Everyone stares straight ahead as the bus careens along sheer cliffs with no guard rails and passes cars in the middle of curves. Grasping the seat ahead of me, I wonder if risking my life for the fifty-cent fare was a good decision.

We disembark at the trailhead and wander over to a tiny police station where we're directed to our guide, Rufus, a forty-ish Rasta man with braided hair who looks eighteen and wears black shorts, a flashy red soccer top, and brand-new American tennis shoes. As we follow him into the dense, lush rainforest along mossy trails, he calls Lee "Pa" and me "Ma" and treats us both as if we're slightly decrepit, holding out his hand to us every time we ford a stream or balance across slippery river rocks. Thankfully, he drops this nonsense when he realizes how fit we are.

There are sheer thousand-foot drop-offs on both sides of a trail that has no guardrails. If anything goes awry, medical help would be lacking. At greater heights, as we view the ocean far below, I'm beginning to feel heat coming through my shoes from the earth. When we reach the bleak, ash-strewn summit of La Soufrière, its caldera is hidden under a thick mist that momentarily swirls upward, revealing rust-colored crater walls, a grassy floor, a small lake, and fumaroles emitting steam and volcanic gases. We back away from the edge as the wind suddenly shifts and threatens to push us into the caldera.

Rufus has realized, after noticing Alex's vain attempts to smoke joints surreptitiously, that we're okay with marijuana. On our descent, two burly men with long dreads and brandishing large machetes approach us, and I start feeling uneasy as I realize there are no witnesses within miles and miles. Then they politely introduce themselves. Rufus mentions that they have just returned from harvesting their crops. After removing their backpacks, they unveil a large bundle of several ten-pound wheels of densely packed hydro.

"These are my friends, mon. Do you want some pot?" Rufus asks.

Lee quickly negotiates an exchange and hands over $200 for approximately a pound of densely packed buds.

Before our departure for the boat, Rufus mentions that he had to use his AK-47 during a marijuana run to Barbados. Intercepted at daybreak by the Coast Guard, he eluded capture during a high-speed boat chase. After this foray into his past, Rufus gives Alex housewifely tips on how to make cannabis tea.

A large chunk of the cannabis is condensed by Alex into a fine, creamy tea mixture. Apprehensively, I take tiny sips of the tea. Nothing happens for what seems like a long time, and then suddenly, I'm slammed with a host of highly unpleasant physical sensations. Like a ventriloquist, I've thrown my wee, frail, squeaky little voice to the far end of the boat. In this woozy and paranoid state, I stammer, "I feel yucky. How loooong is this going to last? When is this going to be over?"

This is my first—and probably last—experience with cannabis tea. But for everyone else, it becomes a daily treat. Inertia slowly creeps in, and the boat is a mess. Feeling annoyed, I wash the dishes, fix the meals, and tidy up while everyone lounges around.

We motor past a large natural stone arch into beautiful Wallilabou Bay on the northwest coast of the island, the principal location for the *Pirates of the Caribbean* movies. We gaze out at a hillside brimming with coconut trees and shiny-leafed banana plants. In the foreground sits a Disney-made movie set. A village called Port Royal overlooks the long, curved black-sand beach.

On our arrival, we high-five the boat boys and bring our fists to our hearts while looking into their dark brown eyes and saying, "Brother love, sister love."

We inspect the memorabilia left behind on a long wooden pier that was built for the movie series. It was also the scene of numerous simulated hangings in the movie. According to the boat boys, we are currently anchored in the exact spot where Johnny Depp's boat was moored.

The wind grabs pieces of my rice cake and tosses crumbs around the galley, then lifts my cotton napkin into the air and ruthlessly slams it into a corner. The monohull behind us rocks back and forth here in Admiralty Bay off the island of Bequia in the famous Caribbean Christmas winds. We're anchored off Princess Margaret Beach, where soaring seagulls dive-bomb the dinghies as they dash about in a bay filled with charter boats out of St. Vincent, St. Lucia, and Martinique.

Bequia, which means "island of the clouds" in the ancient Arawak language, is part of St. Vincent and the Grenadines. Whaling is still allowed on this island. Using only hand-thrown harpoons from open sailboats, the locals are permitted to kill four humpback whales per year. Thankfully the limit isn't always met.

Bequia's small shops display locally made crafts, including hand-dyed batiks. Here we discover a treat that is rare in the Caribbean: ice cream. The homemade ice cream shop and the Gingerbread Hotel become a regular destination for all of us. We avoid the indoor market where the Rastafarians hassle and scramble your brain until all you want to do is hand them all your money to make them back off.

The four of us, wearing T-shirts drenched in perspiration, trudge up a steep, curvy, relentlessly sunny road that connects Admiralty Bay to Friendship Bay and eventually leads to the famed Moonhole on the western end of the island. Maxi buses and jeeps zip past, covering us with billows of dust. It's hot. *We're too dumb to get out of the afternoon sun*, I think as we plod on. A man yells as we walk past his lean-to bar, "White assholes!" Luckily Lee has a hearing problem. What he hears is, "Have a great day!"

The famed Moonhole house perches like a bird getting ready to take flight from the steep cliff overhang. This rounded home and its offshoots, all made of rock and concrete, were designed by Tom Johnston in the late 1950s and early 1960s. There isn't a single angle anywhere—just pure curves inside and out.

A massive, natural rock arch named Moonhole, accessible only by foot or boat, was the inspiration behind these homes.

Bedrooms, living rooms, and decks are integrated around preexisting native trees. During the '60s, Moonhole became the place to go for older Americans.

Tom Johnston's son Mark and his wife, Pauline, give us a private tour. Mark, his legs thin as twigs, his body stooped over a cane, mentions his background. "I was very angry when, as an only child, I was removed from my high school environment and plopped down in this strange place. My parents couldn't deal with my bad behavior, so I was shipped off to school in Barbados. Dad was an extremely difficult man."

Pauline, a pretty blond with long curly hair and blue eyes, looks depressed. Like her husband. The drab grey stone pathways blend with Mark's dull pewter-colored clothing. The red, orange, and yellow flowers in the planters on the patio bring little relief from this gloom.

Our tour ends at the bar, where we're treated to icy cold drinks. Mark points to a seat off by itself for people in a bad mood. For someone in a terrible mood, there's a seat facing the wall. Three large pet turtles wander by like mini prehistoric dinosaurs. Pauline, now lying in a hammock, is pushed back and forth by one scratching its back on the hammock's underside.

Alex, Maria, Lee, and I, needing some relief, jump at the first opportunity to squeeze into a taxi with two German tourists.

We are now moored in Salt Whistle Bay in tiny Mayreau, an island of 271 people and part of the Tobago Cays Marine Park, which includes five tiny uninhabited islands and the four-kilometer-long Horseshoe Reef. Owned by St. Vincent and the Grenadines, these cays have been identified as a regionally significant ecosystem.

Mostly flat, the white-sand isles are covered by palm trees, low vegetation, and occasional rock outcroppings. They look as if they're floating on the surface of the crystal-clear aqua water. We anchor the dinghy far away from the reefs and bob about in the peaceful morning breeze as we put on our snorkel gear. After reading that snorkeling conditions are dicey in the strong currents around the reef shelves, we swim to the protected areas where turtles usually feed. Alex and Maria each hold on to a turtle's back, disappearing with them into the depths until the turtles figure out how to ditch these unwelcome human interlopers. While braving the more challenging snorkeling areas, Maria is suddenly swept away by a swift current. Fortunately—after a panicked search for her—she reappears. She's worn out and unnerved, but okay.

In Grenada, we search for the Molinere Underwater Sculpture Park, the world's first aquatic park and one of the top 25 Wonders of the World according to *National Geographic*. The famed British artist Jason deCaires Taylor created these incredible sculptures, which are designed to eventually develop into artificial coral reefs. Several young boys, followed by goats, wander slowly along the white-sand beach where we stand looking perplexed. Realizing we're in search of the park, they stop. "The park is a hundred feet that way," they tell us.

Engrossed with cracking fresh sea urchins on the rocky edge of the beach, the boys look up when we wade out of the water, clutching our snorkels and fins. They offer us some briny, creamy morsels, a delicacy that would cost hundreds of dollars in a fine sushi restaurant.

By midday, we're on our way to the Seven Falls Park in a totally inappropriate rental van. Rocking and rolling along dirt roads past banana and coconut plantations, the car scrapes and jounces over rocks and ruts while the tires balance precariously along narrow ledges. Lee pulls over several times to let me out to direct him. "Make a very sharp turn to the left for just a few nanoseconds! Wait! Stop! You're about to go into a deep hole. Whoa! You just missed denting the car on a large rock!"

Without the expertise of a seasoned guide, we venture into the rainforest where we quickly lose all sense of direction. Having misplaced the path, we scale near-vertical hillsides while griping and clawing at roots. Lee, stoned and laughing merrily, wanders unsteadily along a cliff's edge, so I grab his arm and haul him away with a strength I didn't know I possessed. Eventually, we locate each of the seven waterfalls, where we bob about in the cool fresh waters until darkness descends and we have to guess our way back to the rental car.

We have a relaxed, low-key day at the old-school, unpretentious Westerhall Rum Distillery located in St. David. The weathered stone buildings, a few of which are in ruins, were built in the 1700s and are nestled within a beautiful deep green undulating landscape bordered by hot pink bougainvillea, lemon-yellow hibiscus plants, and crumbling stone walls. Wandering past old waterwheels, we visit the museum and the tasting room, where we sample deliciously spicy hand-crafted rum internationally known among connoisseurs. Later, Lee and I will both regret not buying a case.

Under furious, darkening skies, Lee and I triple reef the mainsail and furl the jib as the bow pitches and slams into ten- to fifteen-foot waves in the aggressively rough seas between Grenada and St. Lucia. Periodically, Alex stumbles from his perch on the salon bench to vomit into the sink while Maria, lying on a bed below, becomes airborne each time the boat plunges into a trough.

Forging ahead past St. Vincent, flying fish hammer themselves against the sides of the boat or fling and flop themselves onto the bow and the cockpit with each massive wave. These torpedo-shaped fish have long fins that look like wings that allow them to glide for long distances up to four feet above the water's surface. They're a delicacy throughout the Caribbean, but I can't get past the foul odor. After Lee and I toss these extremely slippery, rotten-smelling fish overboard, our hands reek for hours.

At 2:30 p.m., we limp into Vieux Fort. After Alex and Marie toss their mildewed, wrinkled clothing into suitcases, we rush to the airport, where they nearly miss their 4 p.m. flight. There's no time for long goodbyes, just quick hugs and kisses.

After they leave, sadness washes over me for days on end. Just before the college spring semester starts, I call the financial aid office at Trinity College to find out if they can cover any of the $6,000 I'm being charged for Alex's spring term.

"Mrs. Fredell, we hadn't heard from you. Yes, that's all covered in Alex's financial aid package," a woman says. "You need to call the dean of students as soon as possible to finalize the financial aid terms."

Oh geez, I almost dropped the ball. I immediately call the dean.

"Didn't you know?" the woman in the office says. "Alex dropped out of all his classes in December. Mrs. Fredell, is he planning on coming back?"

"Excuse me, what?"

17

Curaçao Heart and Soul

The gentle rain makes clicking noises on the black plastic garbage bags in the cockpit as I prepare for a damp shopping excursion to Willemstad, in Curaçao. Numerous stray dogs bark in a chorus of discontent as I stroll past them on my way to the taxi. I lunch at a Dutch restaurant overlooking the Schottegat, a natural one-mile-long inlet that divides Willemstad in half. While I gaze at the lovely view from the veranda, the sky suddenly opens up and spritzes me in the face, forcing me inside where every table is occupied. All by myself on the upstairs balcony, I write postcards to my family until the rain eases.

Curaçao lies thirty-seven miles north of Venezuela. Its first inhabitants were the Arawak and Caquetio Amerindians. It was acquired by Spain in 1499 and then taken over by the Netherlands in 1634. Only twenty-eight years later, it became a center for the Atlantic slave trade. The African slaves who remained were put to work on the local plantations. Eventually, Sephardic Jews from Iberia began migrating here and, as a consequence, helped to enliven the local economy and culture.

I'd really like to meet the descendants of the original Africans who settled here long ago. These people, I believe, are perhaps the heart and soul of Curaçao. From my vantage point, I can't discern if these two divergent cultures from Africa and the Netherlands intermingle with each other. The descendants of the African slaves literally ooze with warmth and love. For instance, the woman who drove me to the city charged me only three guilder ($1.70), which barely covered her gas expense. After giving her an extra five guilders ($2.80), she smiled, saying, "God bless you! I'll see you again . . . you'll be back riding with me."

Memorizing her face, her square-shaped blue glasses, and the miniature Raggedy Anne doll hanging from her rearview mirror, I promised myself that I would use her again.

In Willemstad, the architecture is mostly Dutch. The streets throb with heavily perfumed women in sparkly T-shirts and tight jeans. Men's heads are shaved in unusual designs, and most young girls have tiny multicolored beads woven into their black braids. Good-looking blond Dutch giants keep their distance as I walk past them on the sidewalk.

In the main department store, I'm assaulted with perfume odors, dyed clothing smells, and dust. I sneeze and cough my way through the narrow aisles stacked with brightly colored plastic from China. The quote "dollar stores are the work of the devil" runs through my head while "Auld Lang Syne" plays from overhead speakers on this late July day.

Unable to find bamboo cutting boards, I wait impatiently in line for thirty minutes to purchase two thin $4 plastic cutting boards displaying a picture of a happy Chinese house-wife. Plastic has shown up everywhere on our travels. It has washed up on beaches from the Caribbean to Turkey to South and Central America. In the Mediterranean, I was shocked to see a plastic island. Nothing is safe from the onslaught of this, especially the creatures of the sea who innocently ingest it and perish.

Zigzagging through town, often losing my sense of direction, I revisit some areas several times in my confused state of mind. I notice that sidewalk holes are filled with kitty litter, apparently a cheap and convenient solution.

Lee, usually unbridled in his enthusiasm toward strangers, behaves like he's running for mayor. Everywhere we go, smiling broadly, he greets and shakes the hands of all the waiters at a restaurant in town. Laughing and shaking my head in resignation, I stand in the background, patiently waiting while he does his spiel.

————

Early one morning, a small boat making a lovely *ting, ting* sound, packed with preschool children wearing yellow blazers, glides past. Multicolored beads and bows adorn the girls' braids. Three prim teachers sit at the bow overlooking their charges. The boat suddenly loops back as I stand on the bottom step taking pictures. I realize the skipper is trying to fish up a blue cushion in the heavy breezes and fast current. I jump into the dinghy, pluck up the cushion, and hand it over to the captain while the teachers and children clap. On my return, Lee stands at the stern clapping too.

Boats almost touch each other in this tightly packed bay. While attaching laundry to the safety lines with clothespins, I feel eyes on me. When I do cat pose on the foredeck, my rear end salutes our neighbors. When I sneeze, everyone grabs a handkerchief. I notice that Lee is especially attuned to the comings and goings of the attractive blond divorcée nearby.

Late in the afternoon, a loud and clunky Dutch catamaran anchors next to us. It's a bit too close. While we're sleeping, the wind shifts to the southwest, moving us even closer. Intuiting something amiss, we dash into the cockpit to the sight of a dozen nudists standing in the howling wind with expressions that say *do something!* We shorten our anchor chain by twenty feet and return to bed. At four in the morning, we awaken to a loud bang. Throwing on foul weather gear, we rush out into the blinding rain. The nudists, now dressed in yellow rain slickers, are trying to shorten their chain. At 7 a.m., shrieking voices jolt us awake. They are now only two feet off our starboard side. Having pulled up the anchor only partway, their chain is now directly under our boat. Lee, realizing that the captain is clueless, springs into action as two dinghies rush our way. One positions itself between our two boats while the other shuttles Lee to the Dutch boat, where he takes over at the helm.

Lee is currently advertising our Grand Circle of the Caribbean tour on our website for the coming fall and winter seasons and sending emails to prospective charter customers. Our plan is to sail to Bonaire, then to Cuba, then on to Mexico. From Isla Mujeres, we'll explore the Yucatan coast, ending up in Honduras and Belize, and after that, Panama and Colombia. If we can fund it, we'll go through the Panama Canal and sail around the world. If not, we'll stay in the Caribbean.

Today when I indicate some dissatisfaction with the lack of attention I get from him when paying customers are on board, Lee remarks, "This is a floating condominium! It needs people, and I need to pay attention to them."

"I just wish you didn't ignore me when charter customers are on the boat. I realize that we need to be professional during the charters, but can't we find a happy medium where we both feel satisfied? It's hard for me to put our relationship on the back burner for a week to two weeks. And anyway, it'll make people feel happy to see us in love."

Lee's face darkens. "You're breaking my balls, woman!"

His insistence on having a professional relationship is hard for me to accept. Why does it have to be all or nothing? Can't we find a middle ground? And anyway, the pictures of us in our ads portray us as a loving couple. It would be more authentic to show this from time to time during a charter. When our friends are on board, it's different. We're the loving, happy couple, and they enjoy seeing this. All I want is a little interaction. A hug before we go to sleep, a little peck on the cheek. Instead, he turns his back to me in bed. I don't feel appreciated for the important role I play during charters.

Now, at a large international anchorage in Curaçao, I catch a shuttle van designated for sailors. It drops us off at the large American-style grocery store in town. I have the mindset that I need to buy super large quantities of everything, for who knows when there'll be another grocery store with so many wonderful things. After filling the cart to the top, I notice that the sailors waiting to board the van outside have only two to three small bags. As my four bulging bags are loaded into the rear of the van I remind myself that I should downsize next time—I don't need to stock up as if we're going on a three-week passage.

The sailors on the van tease me mercilessly. An Irish couple suggests that everyone on the van come over to my boat for dinner to help us slog through the food before it goes off.

My hands are shaking after doing the "morning net" (radio broadcast) with Lee. Before we go on, I punch my fists into the air a few times while taking deep breaths. When it's my turn to speak on the VHF to an audience of over two hundred sailors, Lee, holding a death grip on the mic, forgets to hand it to me. I have to forcefully wrench it from him while he nervously pushes my script underneath the computer keyboard. Script and mic finally in my hands, I hope my voice doesn't crack because I'm very shy when it comes to speaking in public. I surprise myself with how well I do.

In the evening, our Australian friends, Kasey and Giselle, and Dennis, an American single-hander, join us for dinner. A single-hander is a sailor who is alone. Using a high test rum and disregarding the bright red label warning "Not to be used for flambé," Lee lights the banana rum dessert, and a ball of flames detonates. Running into the cockpit, he waits until the flames die down.

"Lee, what are you doing over there?" our neighbors yell across the water.

Before Kasey and Dennis leave for their respective mono-hulls, Lee decides this is the perfect moment to declare, "You're living in a fancy hotel, Wendy. You need to live on a monohull for a while, so you'll appreciate this catamaran."

Not in agreement, I consent, however, to join Kasey and his wife Giselle for a day sail while their preteen son replaces me as first mate. Glancing around their boat *Monkey Feet*, I realize that monohulls are actually quite pleasant. In fact, I almost prefer it because of the way it elegantly slices through the water. But I keep this to myself.

Now back on our vessel after the day's sail, I hear

strange clanking and grinding sounds and shout, "Turn off the generator, Lee!" It immediately sputters to a standstill. The galley instantly becomes a makeshift workshop with old towels draped over the seats to protect them from the greasy pumps, belts, pipes, and fittings that will be placed on them. Lee, now covered with black grease, is dripping with sweat. As I brush past him, black grease transfers itself to my T-shirt.

Five days into our sail to Curaçao, Lee's head had adjusted to being upside-down inside the cavity where the generator resides. For three years now, this damn generator has acted up and, on occasion, even spewed pink gunk onto anyone nearby. I've been hovering close these past few days like an operating room nurse, handing Lee phillips head screwdrivers, wrenches, numerous glasses of water, and clean rags to prevent sweat from running into his eyes.

I'm hatching a plan with our new friend Greg, who is anchored next to us in Curaçao. I'm organizing a surprise birthday party for Lee, and Greg has agreed to help me plan it. The morning of the party, I announce to Lee that I need some time alone. "Oh, by the way, we have to be on time for happy hour this afternoon," I mention. "We're invited for dinner on *Tara* afterward."

During the day, after shopping for the party and then discreetly depositing everything off at Greg's boat, Lee says on my return, "I'm feeling so lonely." I chuckle to myself because Lee has no idea what's in store for him that evening. He's usually so self-confident, and this little secret project has really thrown him.

The usual happy hour on land is a total bust because everyone is hiding on Greg's boat. We remain for a while with the few stragglers who have shown up, then motor toward the boat *Tara*. I had announced that we were invited to have a drink there. Halfway to *Tara*, Lee turns off the dinghy's motor.

"I'm depressed," he admits. "It's the generator and all the emails I have to write. And it's your unfriendliness today too. It's—"

Before he can finish, I break in with, "Oh, I'm so sorry, honey! Let's just keep heading to *Tara*. You'll feel much better soon."

The dinghy is gone, however. No one's on board. Lee whines, "Now this really depresses me. We're invited over for dinner, and they're not even here!"

"Oh, they must be over at Greg's. He's having an open house. Why don't we check it out?"

"Now I'm even more depressed! We weren't invited to Greg's party."

"No, that's not true. When he mentioned it to me I said we had another commitment."

Looking glum, Lee cuts the motor about twenty feet from Greg's boat, to which seven dinghies are attached. We drift and drift. Will we ever get there?

Finally, after a lot of prodding from me, we pull up to the boat's stern as sixteen heads pop up amid shouts of "Happy Birthday, Lee!" He looks overjoyed.

———

Now anchored off Bonaire, the sailor anchored next to us, the former financial director of the Hughes Corporation, dinghies over early one morning. Knocking fervently on the side of our boat, he yells, "Wendy, Wendy! Armageddon has just happened!! The stock market has suddenly dropped hundreds of points. I hope you've got cash! Hop in. I'll show you what just happened on my computer."

It's September 29, 2008, and the stock market has crashed due to a combination of things such as an unregulated market, consumer debt, exploitative lending, and the rapid decline of home prices. After seeing evidence of the stock market disaster on my friend's computer, I realize it's way too late to save my funds, and I decide not to fret over something over which I have little control.

As an escape from reality, I spend the rest of the afternoon skin diving while Lee naps in the hammock on the bow. Looking at fish puts everything into perspective. The spotted burrfish doesn't give a damn that Iceland is bankrupt or that Japan has high inflation or that the Feds didn't bail out Lehman Brothers or that deregulation and subprime mortgages fucked everything up. The filefish just rolls its nonjudgmental yellow-rimmed eyes at me as I hang upside-down, watching him while I hold on to a concrete mooring block.

We race all week in the Bonaire Regatta, which helps us forget, temporarily, the global meltdown. We have two couples crewing for us, two boys ages seven and five, and a dog named Sparky, who adds her own form of zen relaxation. In the galley on the first day, Giselle, Patty, and I chop and dice ingredients for potato salad and white bean salad while snacking on my homemade banana bread.

We win in our category, narrowly beating the *Alert*, skippered by a Hugh Hefner wannabe and crewed by fifteen Dallas Cheerleader types in eye-popping white bikinis.

Tropical Storm Omar, now a hurricane, is heading toward the Virgin Islands, five hundred miles to our north. Swells and building west winds bear down on us. The clouds, no longer white, are the color of lead.

We unhook from our mooring and motor toward the marina, where there's only one space big enough for our large catamaran. Tied alongside *MushiMushi*, the skipper of this ramshackle Chinese junk advises us to tie spring lines to his boat as a precaution. In return, he wants us to make sure his lines are holding while he's gone. Lee, shrugging his shoulders, looks over at me. The Chinese junk is evidently my project, I realize. If the skipper had been a pretty female sailor, I'm sure that Lee would have taken on the project.

———

The constant rain is giving me time to reflect on the slow process of transformation that is taking place within me. It expresses itself in my clothes and my jewelry. My shelves are now filled with rainbow-colored clothing. My jewelry is no longer understated. I now wear exotic, funky necklaces and earrings. In Curaçao, I re-covered the salon couch, changing its pale turquoise fabric to a dynamic bright blue. To go with this new look, a seamstress in town made eight pillows striped in reds, yellows, mustards, and bright aqua blue.

And I'm no longer holding back with people, I interact with them in a truly loving and affectionate way. In the past, afraid to let the real me come forth, I ventured timidly out into the world. I will no longer allow anyone to rob me of my inner light, and I will no longer hold back from letting it touch everyone around me.

A therapist said to me when I was in my mid-thirties, "You have a lot of baggage!"

I am now consciously dropping that baggage into the sea, forgiving all the people in my life who have brought me pain. This doesn't mean, however, that my life will be perfect.

Sadly, it's becoming more and more obvious that Lee and I have some relationship issues. I really wish that things were perfect between us, but it's almost impossible to have perfection when you live at sea with very little outside interaction. When we have our spats, I feel like a flower whose bright color has started to fade.

We'll both be tested again. Soon.

18

The Real Cuba

We're now anchored off Cayo Sur, an islet within the Isla de Aves island group located north of Venezuela. Isla de Aves means "island of the birds." These flat, scrubby, sandy cays, some of which are sprinkled with a few palm trees, could actually be classified as rocks. During hurricanes, they are often totally submerged. Hundreds of booby birds, seabirds, and herons perch in the dense forty-foot-high mangroves that thrive in these salty coastal waters populated with large green turtles.

Registering in Venezuela could involve being held up at gunpoint and robbed, so we've decided to hide out here. If the Coast Guard on Isla Larga catches us we're prepared to say, "We're on our way, just stopping here to rest."

Awakening to big white puffy clouds, blue skies, and a soft cooling breeze, I reflect on how wonderful it is to be away from technology and the complications of land life. After breakfast, we motor to an area where the mangrove leaves are as large as a man's fist. We drift close to a light grey booby bird whose orange-red webbed feet are coiled tightly around a branch. Its long beak is a beautiful shade of powder blue, and his indigo eyes circle curiously as I stand at the dinghy's bow. When I lean in closer, the bird startles and takes off.

The pelicans are dying, their decomposing bodies washing up on the white sandy beaches. One lands on the bow, where it remains overnight, barely moving. Remembering the dying eels in the waters off Bonaire, I'm deeply saddened to see its lifeless body the next morning. What is killing these creatures?

Lee sleeps peacefully below. The soft morning light dances across his face. There's a tiny crumb on his cheek, and his eyebrows are all tussled up from his nightlong interaction with a feather pillow. I like the way the hairs on his arm glow, and I love that spot of red, the size of a grain of sand, under his eye.

The flimsy scientific research center on a nearby, tiny island looks like something Robinson Crusoe would have cobbled together from whatever was on hand. Over to the right is a minuscule airport runway where small aircraft ferry scientists to and from Venezuela.

Dead coral is piled up off of Elbert Cay, forming a natural breakwater. In the deeper waters, beyond the breakers, there are more clumps of dead coral where fish dart about through holes, arches, tunnels, and intricate passageways. Indigo-colored parrotfish with bright iridescent blue and green patterns swim beneath us as we snorkel. While Lee heads further out, I swim to the breakwater, where a twenty-foot shark follows me. Lee has told me, "If a shark ever approaches you, look big. Bring your fists up to the sides of your chest, puff yourself out, and look fierce. Sharks go after the fragile, wounded fish. They don't go after the strong, healthy ones. They're scavengers." Not wanting to chance it, I swim back to the boat like an Olympian.

We're now parked next to a Dutch monohull off Los Roques, where giant mosquitos land on my arms then pause a second before drawing blood—which gives me time to whack them. Our new neighbors are Errrrnooo, who rolls the r's and the o's in his name, and Frida, his wife, a latter-day sex goddess. There she sits, nude underneath a thin sarong with her legs up on a table in a provocative way. While Lee works on deck, Frida entertains him with different hedonistic poses.

I make an effort to communicate with her, attempting to ferret out information. Something. *Anything.* Just to get some conversation going. Realizing that she might prefer male company, I give up and gaily wave good riddance to her the next morning when she and her husband leave for Grenada.

Lee impulsively decides to clean the rusty second-hand spear gun he purchased from a sailor in Turkey. For two years it has remained untouched in its bright yellow bag. Now he oils it, tunes it, files it, and does whatever else is needed to get it to function. I watch as he shoots it four hours later. Rancid yellow oil splatters all over the cockpit, showering the underside of the canvas awning. He continues fooling around with it obsessively. As I step into the galley, I hear a loud popping sound directly behind me. The spear has embedded itself into the fiberglass to the right of the salon door. Fifteen minutes later, after dislodging it, Lee packs it up and puts it away, never to be seen again.

We plan to visit Cuba before it becomes legalized for Americans. One of the most unique destinations in the world, it offers the rare opportunity to see a culture that has stood still for more than fifty years. Having learned from sailors that the Cubans are extremely friendly and that the beaches are gorgeous, we're told we can visit only certain anchorages on the mainland. Anywhere else is off-limits. We're also told to stock up on cooking oil, toilet paper, soap, shampoo, pencils, notebooks, coloring books, and toys because these are in short supply and make great gifts for the locals.

Our plan is to sail to Jamaica for a few days before continuing on to Cuba. Patrick, a documentary filmmaker, and his Dutch wife, Hettie, a hospice nurse, will join us along with a couple from Oregon, Marleen and Bruce.

A Cuban woman, a current resident of Bonaire, drives me to the grocery store the day before we leave. "Buy food!" she says. "Lots of food! Three hurricanes have decimated Cuba, and there's nothing to eat. Raul Castro has asked everyone to plant greens."

We leave rain-soaked Bonaire for an overnight to Curaçao, where Lee, Bruce, and Patrick load more provisions and two new two-hundred-pound batteries onto the boat by a pulley system. My last job before leaving this island is to arrange a money transfer to my youngest son. Unable to get internet on the boat, I locate a resort where I'm offered a table close to workers who are currently operating an electric saw and a jackhammer. Unfortunately, my bank account is closed due to fraudulent activity originating from an ATM machine in Trinidad.

Day two. Hurricane season officially ended yesterday, November 30th. According to statistics, hurricanes generally don't occur after this date. After sailing past Aruba, now lit up by cruise ships, we head northward for the six-day passage to Cuba. The seas are rapidly becoming more and more

confused as Aruba's lights fade in the distance under deteriorating skies. Since our passengers have booked flights from
Havana to Bonaire, we must forge ahead no matter what.

Inky storm clouds frame the horizon as my Croatian flip-
flops keep flipping over, causing me to lose my balance while
I prepare dinner. Both Marleen and Hettie, limp and sickly,
languidly sip water and suck on Saltines in the cockpit while
the rest of us dine on delicious French stew with homemade
garlic croutons.

The waves, at their peak, are fifteen feet tall, and the winds
are over thirty knots as we enter a tropical depression that is
quickly deteriorating into a tropical storm. Dark clouds race
overhead as cold rain pelts my face. I stumble back into the
salon just before we crash down a trench.

Suddenly overcome with nausea, I disappear below.
Hettie, now recovered, chats with the men in the cockpit.
Marleen is still indisposed. She has not left her room except
to go to the bathroom, and her only diet has been Saltines. If
I weren't so ill myself, I'd join her to commiserate.

I stagger into the captain's head, trying to avoid the four-
teen large Chinese multicolored shopping bags with cheap
untrustworthy zippers that are lined up like soldiers in the
hallway. Several have fallen over, spilling canned beans, rice,
cereal, long-life milk, and Ceres juice from South Africa.
Rolling back and forth across the floor, they turn a simple
trip to the bathroom into an obstacle course. I'm too nause-
ated to pick them up. Five dozen eggs, in a wicker basket at
the foot of our bed, are in imminent danger of being ruined.
This is surely hell, I think wearily as I lie on my bed in our
airless cabin that has taken on the odor of a men's locker
room. In my underwear, feeling hot, smelly, and miserable in
the stale air, my bruised and sore arms spread out like angel

wings. The tiny wall fan, humming, blows a gentle breeze across my face while I stare at the ceiling.

Feeling better a few hours later, I slip out of bed and groggily step on the eggs. Then, dazed from too little sleep, I take my turn on watch and make a few bad decisions because of my ignorance over the difference between a line squall and a regular squall. Angry black monster clouds are approaching fast. Quickly pulling the dry laundry off the lines, I toss it into the salon before the first drops of rain start. The mainsail, on a beam reach, suddenly moves to the middle of the cockpit and I wrench the mainsheet lines to hold the sail in place. The preventer line suddenly slips in the thirty-five-knot winds, releasing the mainsheets, which move dangerously side to side. The jib simultaneously jerks over to the starboard side, heading us in the opposite direction. What the hell? I release the port lines and then pull the main over to the starboard side. Just as I'm completing this last maneuver, the men, looking apprehensive, appear on deck. The dreaded self-jibe had just happened. Under my watch.

On this moonless night, squalls are coming through like an endless string of obsidian beads. The gale force winds are now up to forty-six knots and our speed is currently seventeen knots. The boat pounds hard into the twenty-five-foot waves, causing the sea to slam against the starboard side while rooster tails shoot high into the air along the stern. The jib and main, reefed all the way, resemble handkerchiefs. Unable to get a weather report on the SSB (Single Sideband Radio) Lee asks, "What the F is going on?" A dark cloud of fear moves over me as he says this.

Since it's impossible to stand up without holding on to something, cooking dinner from scratch is almost impossible.

I microwave Hettie's delicious Moroccan couscous with chicken, vegetables, and herbs.

"All hands on deck!" jerks me out of a deep sleep. With dread, I slip on my foul weather gear and rubber boots, then buckle up my harness before heading up the slippery salon steps. I force myself into the cockpit. Over screaming winds, horizontal rain, and constant lightning strikes, Lee yells that we had an unexpected jibe that broke the preventer. "We need to lash the preventer to the mast, then reef the main," he says.

Lee and Patrick, attached to the lifeline, head toward the port and starboard winches in the menacing blackness highlighted by white foam from the thirty-foot waves. They grab the preventer as it swings about with great force above their heads. Bruce, at the helm, lowers the mainsail while Lee and Patrick, struggling to avoid falling into the sea, tie lines to secure the main and the boom.

Day three. The food in the refrigerator is starting to mold. No one feels like cooking or eating. The fresh chicken I bought is beginning to smell. I wish the freezer worked. Five sets of hands have rearranged everything in the refrigerator and I can't find a thing. The new salon cushions are stained with salt water and the stack of dirty china rattles loudly in the sink with each wave.

In the confused seas, I can see the eastern coast of Jamaica as the sun peeks out from a line of clouds dotting the horizon. The winds have calmed. Bruce and Marlene, who is still in the throes of nausea, have decided to abort the journey. Marlene has spent the entire trip in her cabin. Skinny to begin with, she looks even thinner and slightly green.

A butterfly, its wings outlined in grey with iridescent soft pink and cream dots in the center, lands on my arm as I sit relaxing in the cockpit. Its tail, like a tiny tuft of silky hair, drags softly across my arm. Each one moves individually, feeling my skin, my essence. Thirty minutes later, still on my arm, it shrinks into itself while its life seeps away until it's a tiny shadow of itself.

————

The narrow entrance into the enormous Cienfuegos Bay is unremarkable. I was hoping for something more dynamic, more arresting. Not rows of shabby, dirty beige-grey buildings displaying faded and peeling murals of Che Guevara and Fidel Castro. As we motor deeper into the bay, massive Venezuelan oil tankers sit idly at anchor while fishermen in tiny homemade styrofoam boats paddle by, waving at us.

Since Cuba is on the United States DO NOT VISIT list, our passports can't be stamped. In lieu of that, an official document will be slipped discreetly inside our passports so we won't feel like illegal aliens. Sailors encourage us to bring euros, not US dollars, and to stow all credit cards. We can exchange our euros for Cuban Convertible Pesos, a currency reserved for tourists. Cubans use a different currency called the Cuban Peso, and they shop in dispiritingly understocked marketplaces while tourists buy groceries, clothing, and souvenirs in upscale shops that offer sophisticated European goods.

On our arrival, a bartender from the marina brings us "Welcome to Cuba" mojitos. Not long after that, five ruggedly handsome men wearing combat boots and intimidating black uniforms stomp onto our boat for the official boat inspection. The sixth officer brings a drug-sniffing dog. After stealing glances at these somber men, I watch Lee become his irresistible, charismatic self. Patrick and Hettie, feeling restless, leave for a walk.

"You lika beer?" Lee asks them in pigeon English, believing they'll understand him better.

After a few moments of hesitation and furtive looks, the men say in unison, "Yes!"

While Lee is passing out Heinekens, another official, wearing a crisp white uniform and a white cap enters the salon. "Ohhhhh, this is veeeerrry expensive beer in Cuba!" he says as Lee hands him one.

While we sit together talking and laughing, a man in a dark green uniform from the Department of Agriculture boards the boat. I take him on a tour of the refrigerator, the non-working empty freezer, and the space in the cockpit where I store root vegetables. Holding up a perfect, grapefruit-sized yellow onion, he stares at it as if it were the Hope Diamond. My heart breaks as he says, "This is nice! Veeerrry nice!"

The boat is inspected: every single cabinet, the bilge, even the tiny closet crammed with foul weather gear, rubber boots, and wetsuits. Sections of the floor are pulled up for a quick once-over with vintage Russian flashlights. Amazingly they forget to check the cavernous spaces under the beds, where we could easily stow several freedom-seeking Cubans. The VHF unit is a concern, however. Now wrapped and taped securely, an officer stashes it into a small portside cabinet which he seals with tape and labels with a red-lettered Forbidden! sign. This is because the government fears that sailors will give their VHFs to people to help them organize an escape. Since the only boats allowed in Cuba are government-sanctioned tourist boats, fishing boats, and Coast Guard boats, it would be next to impossible to make a break for it.

Before they turn to go, Lee offers our new friends pretzels. Turning them over and over gently in their large hands, each man studies their construction. "These are veeerrry American," someone comments.

I fill eight Ziplocs with pretzels and Dutch Speculaas cookies for each man to share with family members. Then I hug them before they step off the boat with their goodie bags.

Before we can leave our marina's high-security compound, our backpacks are inspected by a young woman in a tight mini skirt, black fishnet stockings, and high heels. Lee, Patrick, Hettie, and I board a horse-drawn carriage for our first visit to Cienfuegos. As we stroll slowly down the city sidewalks, people stare at us unabashedly.

Sensing an undefinable mysterious presence in the air, the Cuban time warp grabs me and sweeps me into a world where everything has stood still since the mid-fifties. What catches my attention the most while exploring the city is the cars. The four-door Chevrolets, Buicks, and Fords from that era all look lovingly cared for. Broken-down vintage cars with hoods propped up and heads inspecting engines are a common sight.

During our wanderings, I learn quickly what the expectations are if we want to photograph locals. First, we need to ask their permission. Then we show them the photograph. Satisfied or not, they hold out their hands for money. This is always followed by a request to hold and inspect our digital cameras and our flip-top cell phones. Children, on the other hand, are thrilled with a few caramels.

Our first dinner in Cuba is in a private residence recommended by the harbormaster. Facing us as we walk through the front door is a massive *Pieta* the size of something you'd see in a museum. There are no menus here, just the meal du jour, which is absolutely delicious. Ropa Vieja is a lightly boiled shredded meat cooked in a delicious sauce with bell peppers, onions, bay leaves, cumin, and other spices, served with black beans and rice. Since very few Cubans can afford to eat out or even buy basic groceries, every table on the large outdoor patio is filled solely with tourists.

Images of Che and Fidel are displayed everywhere: on murals, baseball caps, and T-shirts celebrating the fiftieth anniversary of the Revolution of 1956.

Julio, the harbormaster, is a handsome, dark-haired man who becomes our friend and visits us often during our two-week stay. On one of his visits, we give him a bag of clothing, soap, shampoo, ballpoint pens, food, and Advil for his frequent headaches. After scurrying around the boat looking for more gifts, I decide to give Julio's daughter my beloved pair of jeans from Italy that have become too tight.

After Lee takes his photos, Julio hides the 8x10 glossies under his jacket before leaving. During the night, he returns for his gifts and sticks them into a large black garbage bag. We watch him carry it down the dark dock, pretending to pick up trash along the way. Cubans aren't allowed to accept gifts from tourists—not even a photo or headache medicine, which is impossible to find.

Later, Julio tells me that his fifteen-year-old daughter loves her new jeans so much that she plans to wear them to a New Year's Eve party. "How much money do people make a month in the US?" he asks. His face falls when we tell him a general (and rather low) figure. Julio lives on $20 a month, and I wonder how he survives.

"Doctors make as much money as taxi drivers. There's only money for food, nothing else," he says. There are no private enterprises in Cuba. Everything is run by the government. Taxis, restaurants, tour agencies, hotels, and all markets.

Cubans often approach me whenever I'm alone window

shopping or meandering about. Glancing nervously in every direction to make sure no one hears them, long-withheld anger erupts from great hidden depths. "I hate Fidel Castro!" I hear this over and over again while here.

They also stare at me and even laugh at me sometimes. My natural corkscrew curls, a source of great interest, are often touched when I walk past people on the sidewalks.

Begging is a full-time occupation in Cuba. Women holding infants beg on the streets for diapers and milk, grabbing people by their arms and pleading as they walk by. Others say, "Soap, soap, please! Un peso por favor! Pencils!" When I remove my sunglasses to clean them someone will inevitably approach me saying, "Nice! Very nice! You give me?"

Young women wearing skirts that barely cover their butts dangle on the arms of mostly European men in government-owned hotel lobbies. In town, I watch people as they slink down side streets, stop in front of doors, look both ways, knock, and then disappear into their secret pursuits.

The bartender down the street from the marina is the local egg vendor. He hides a very large wooden bowl of brown eggs on a shelf underneath the bar and sells them to people who come in for a beer. People in the neighborhood sell lettuce from battered cardboard boxes in their living rooms. Everyone is selling or bartering something.

Trucks unload cabbage and red beans every morning at the outdoor markets. When I question strangers about where I can buy certain foods, they take me on elaborate journeys through streets and alleys until I'm face-to-face with someone in a one-room apartment or a tiny house where sellable food is hidden in wicker baskets behind sofas. Transactions are fast, and I pay with the sought-after Cuban Convertible Pesos.

I watch people rounding up chickens that run wild through the dusty streets. They drag them shrieking and struggling into their homes, where they are strangled. Then, sitting on three-legged stools, these same people display and sell the cut-up chicken parts on small battered tables in the alleyways behind their homes.

Our food stocks running low, Pedro, a handsome, boyish Cuban who waits outside the entrance to our marina in his horse-drawn carriage, drives sailors into town for shopping trips to the outdoor markets. We clomp along, my rear end aching from the hard seat, on a lovely seaside road bordered by declining mansions built by the French in the late 1800s. The streets of the city are alive with people. Pedro pulls up alongside a *mercado* for Cubans only and says in a scheming tone, "Wait here." I hand him my Cuban Convertible Pesos in exchange for his black market Cuban Pesos.

He returns, then motions for me to follow him. It's all very undercover. The locals in the ancient, dirty market watch as Pedro holds up fruit and vegetables and I nod yes or no. He places two bright-red tomatoes, a pineapple, some lady finger bananas, two coconuts, a green papaya the size of a football, leeks, green beans, and cabbage into my large straw bag. Feeling like a spoiled American, I can't help but notice that the Cubans have only a few items in their shopping bags.

As Pedro helps me into the carriage, his dehydrated horse suddenly falls over onto its side, its rear legs curled onto the wooden halter connecting it to the cart. "Has the horse died?" I ask, devastated. I've already witnessed the deaths of pelicans in Los Roques and moray eels in Bonaire due to blights.

A crowd quickly forms. Pedro disconnects the lines to the horse and then someone lends him a knife, which he uses to cut the rest of the lines. The horse's eyes are closed. Teenage boys gawk at the unfolding scene while laughing and pointing at Pedro, who has become a source of ridicule. After everything is removed, releasing the horse, I'm horrified to see Pedro whip it. Unsteadily, it moves into a standing position, and I maneuver myself closer, gently patting its head, ears, and neck. Pedro puts the harness back on the horse's head onto a spot where the hair has worn away, leaving a patch of raw skin that is rubbed and irritated by the tight, unforgiving leather. Then everything is reconnected with small pieces of string that Pedro has knotted together. He motions for me to climb into the carriage just as I nervously glance around for another taxi.

Before we leave Cienfuegos for Havana with Hettie and Patrick, I give Julio the rest of my Cuban Pesos, which amount to around $10—half his monthly salary.

In Havana, it's very common for people to rent out rooms in their apartments or homes to tourists. You never know what awaits, though. Toilets that rock back and forth and cockroaches hiding in bedside drawers or behind beds. Luckily our room is decent, and we have everything we need but soap.

While Lee, Patrick, Hettie, and I are wandering along Havana's upscale walking streets one late afternoon, an attractive young Cuban couple walking in front of us turns around to chat. We're invited to a party nearby, and everyone is game. Except me: I smell a rat. We follow them up a flight of timeworn dark wooden steps into a small second-floor apartment filled with young men and women and loud, pulsating Cuban music. We're offered rum, then sit on a couch and chat with the people next to us. After one very strong rum drink, I begin to worry as we're paired up with dancers. A man grabs me and pulls me into a full-body dance while pushing his crotch against me. I glance over nervously at my purse on the couch containing my passport and all my Cuban Convertible Pesos. I push him away then tap on Lee's shoulder. "You can stay here. I'm leaving. I've got very bad vibes about these people. We're being set up for something you'll regret later."

Grabbing my purse, I leave while everyone in the room glares at me. Lee and our friends catch up with me on the sidewalk minutes later and make it clear that they wanted to stay a little longer. I look at them as if they're unhinged. "Are you nuts? Are you out of your minds?" I ask in utter amazement over their apparent naivete.

Hettie and Patrick now gone, I go on a solo walking excursion while Lee works on boat projects. People sitting on stools in front of their homes motion for me to stop as I walk by. "Do you have a T-shirt or some food?" A maintenance man for a well-kept one-story peacock-blue bungalow with white trim grabs me by the arm and drags me across its attractive tiled floors for a tour of a house that's worlds apart from its neighbors. Then he begs me to send him a package of clothing and food when I return to the States, and I mention that I may not travel home for awhile. "No problem. It's okay. I wait for your package!" Then he adds, "I hate Castro!"

————

There's nothing quite like freedom, I realize after being in Cuba for two months. I took it for granted until I lived here. This lack of freedom in Cuba is oppressive, suffocating, and heavy. People live a life of humiliation and tedium as they wait in line for everything. And there's the mind control factor. They have to monitor *everything* they say. Very little outside information reaches them. I've read, however, that some entrepreneurial young Cubans have figured out how to get internet access, and they're quickly spreading information to others.

I see so much soul, so much feeling, so much yearning in the eyes of the people I meet. All of which are expressed through their music, which fills the air. Music is the one thing that can't be taken from these people. Sometimes I wonder if Cuban babies are born with maracas wrapped in their fists.

Trinidad, a beautiful colonial town with neo-baroque buildings and cobblestone streets on its main square, lies in central Cuba. During my solitary wanderings through the town, I come across six men playing music in an empty lot behind an abandoned house. I sit on a crumbling section of a wall to listen to them play and sing. Suddenly they stop and look at me. "What's your name?" they ask. Then they add it to their their lyrical, mesmerizing songs.

In Trinidad, I stop momentarily in front of a door to adjust my backpack. A thin bug-eyed older lady with dyed auburn hair and a prominent nose opens the door, grabs me with amazing force, then pulls me into her house, which is a well-furnished middle-class place. She introduces me to a toothless smiling elderly couple with jutting chins. A rack of gaudy homemade jewelry is suddenly thrust at me while a necklace is quickly draped around my neck. Then a funky straw hat and a homemade shawl are positioned on my head and shoulders. Next, I'm placed in front of a mirror so that I can admire my ridiculous self. Wondering how in the hell I'm going to get out of there, I glance down at my watch in fake alarm. "Oh my gosh! I'm late. I've got to catch a bus! Sorry, I have to run!" I race out the door slinging the hat, the jewelry, and the shawl onto the sofa. The next day, in my wanderings, I see the same auburn-haired woman, who is now wearing ratty clothing and begging in the streets.

Next to our boat, two men sit on the dock, their legs dangling over the side, fishing for small snappers. I have some extra clothing that I'd like to share. "Would your wives like some clothing?"

One of the men answers in halting English, "You need go Trinidad for clothing!"

"I meant that I have clothes for your wife."

"Oh no! That's not my problem! *Eets* your problem!"

———

There's a part of me that wants to go home. Right now. This very second. I'm feeling suffocated by Cuba's prison-like environment. But I'm not sure where home is anymore.

One night I feel a little sick, so Lee gives me a shot of rum to help settle my stomach. I retire early and wake up at 1 a.m. to a dark, empty boat. Checking the head to see if Lee is there, I notice blood on the floor and what looks like a clumsy attempt to repair a wound.

I go upstairs expecting to find him fast asleep on the couch. There are some blood spots on the floor, but no Lee. He isn't in the cockpit, nor is he lying on the trampoline. I start to panic. My voice shaking, I yell, "Lee! Where are you?" No answer. My world suddenly feels dark and empty, as if a bright light has been extinguished.

Something draws me back to the trampoline, where the Peruvian hammock is tied between two stays. I reach underneath the green tarp covering it and touch Lee's warm, soft, handsome face.

"Lee, I thought you fell off the boat!"

"It's okay honey," Lee says softly. "I've been here for about an hour." Then he sees the tears on my face. "Oh no! I'm so sorry I made you worry. You must really love me!"

His hug is one of the best I've ever experienced in my life. My heart is filled with joy because, as of late, our relationship has been a little strained. My feelings for Lee are still as strong as ever, even with our occasional misunderstandings. Happily, I can tell he feels the same.

Suddenly, I glance down at Lee's foot, which is wrapped like a mummy in white gauze. "What did you do to yourself?" I ask.

"Oh it's *nothing*," he says with a smile. "Just a little boo boo."

19

Living the Dream

Lee, sans underpants, helps our last Cuban charter of six Americans disembark with their rolling suitcases onto the pier in Trinidad. A carry-on-size dark green suitcase accidentally falls into the murky water, where it floats away daintily into the morning light. For a moment, we're totally transfixed and glued in place until one of our female guests leaps into action and rips off her jeans, revealing a dark brown thong. Simultaneously, Lee, preparing to dive in, rips off his baggy, oil-stained shorts, forgetting that he's wearing nothing underneath. In front of a rowdy, laughing crowd of Cubans, the smug marina manager hands Lee a long aluminum boat hook.

We remain for the night at the end of the pier, adjacent to a thatched hut where the local harbormaster has his office. During the evening, when I head for the bathroom, I'm horrified to find a large grey rat crouching behind the toilet. As it races down the hallway, its long pink tail, bald except for a few wiry hairs, trails behind. He disappears into the bowels of the boat, never to be seen again. But he smells.

We're back in Cienfuegos to check out of Cuba. The rat has a name now: Hernandez. He prowls the boat while we sleep and takes teeny bites out of each plump red tomato in the galley. There are alarming-looking circles of smelly wetness on the salon seats I recently had reupholstered in Curaçao. My pretty kitchen towel has been partially pulled into a hole under the sink. All the Q-tips in the guest bathroom have disappeared, along with my collection of sea beans. The cans of food stored under the salon seats have teeth marks on their labels, and there's a funky smell there, reminiscent of a Barnum and Bailey Circus.

We have no tools for ridding ourselves of the rat. It has dawned on me that our sail to Isla Mujeres in Mexico will be extremely unpleasant with Hernandez on board. I fill a pail halfway with water, place a sheet of newspaper on top, and lightly tape it to the bucket. On this, I place small pieces of Swiss cheese and bread. Then I put the bucket next to the table in the cockpit. I place more cheese on the edge of the tabletop. During the night, Hernandez does exactly what I imagined he would do—but he doesn't drown.

My mission, on this last day in Cienfuegos, is to buy fresh produce and locate a rat trap. Before leaving for town, Lee and I have a contest. The one who draws the best picture of a rat wins a hug. Lee's looks like a cross between a dog and a cat with a Mickey Mouse head. Mine actually looks better, except for the big grin on its face.

From the harbormaster, I learn that *trampa para ratas* means rat trap. Carrying the drawings of Hernandez in my hand, I locate a horse-drawn taxi on the long, wide Waterside

Avenue. After showing a driver our illustrations, he folds over laughing while speaking rapidly to the other drivers.

Today most of the stores are closed. My taxi driver, resourceful as ever, pulls up to a group of people walking down the sidewalks. "Where can this gringo get a rat trap?" he asks them. They study me with curiosity, then snicker. On my own, I wander into the most upscale hotel in Cienfuegos and ask a receptionist for advice. I slump away as she giggles.

So we're stuck with Hernandez. While we sleep, he enjoys all the free amenities of the boat—especially the guava and the papaya, which I absentmindedly leave on the counter-top. After depositing turds under the salon seats and the galley sink, he relaxes in the plastic bowls on the counter and then explores the wooden ledge behind the salon seats. Apparently craving more adventure, he squeezes himself into a hole in the panel where the navigational wiring is located. Then he moves further into the walls behind the refrigerator. During the day, Hernandez's domain is the port forward cabin, where he leaves behind half-chewed Q-tips and teeth-marked brown sea beans on the beds.

At 3 a.m., I hear scampering back and forth from stern to the bow. What fun Hernandez is having! Every time I open a cabinet, I expect him to jump out at me. I imagine him as super-sized, well-fed, and perhaps slightly sadistic. He speaks English with a heavy accent and wears basketball shoes and a Las Vegas–era Elvis white belt with sparkles.

As part of the checking out process, five policemen and a dog on a leash climb aboard. Using vintage flashlights, they inspect cabinets, the bilge, the closets, and lift up sections of the floor. We're approved. When I ask them if they would please arrest Hernandez they stare at me blankly.

We stop along Cuba's coast near Cayo Largo, with its white-sand beaches and transparent azure-blue water. On this cloudless day, the sunset is followed by a green flash, which is an optical phenomenon that happens just before the sun disappears below the horizon. The emerald color lasts only a second or two.

We've anchored near a lobster hotel well known to the local fishermen, who have happily shared its exact coordinates with Lee. All lobsters in Cuba belong to Fidel. Illegally catching eight lobsters with a gaff hook and a gloved hand, Lee tosses each one into the dinghy, where they climb over each other and scoot forward by furling and unfurling their tails. The most enormous one, after putting up a brave fight, hurries away while staring at us with disdain. I feel like a lobster mass murderer. Lee, however, is reveling in his role of hunter-gatherer.

The mess. The confusion. The dirty pots. The spills. Black lobster effluent on the cockpit's white fiberglass. Lobsters desperately searching for freedom. Nasal *err err err* sounds fill the air. Our cockpit has become death row for lobsters. Horrified by it all, I down a strong rum drink to dull my feelings of remorse as Lee throws the lobsters, one by one, into a large pot of boiling water.

We're running low on food. My last shopping trip to a real grocery store was fifty days ago. Trinidad's tourist markets have kept us supplied with fresh cabbage, onions, lettuce, tomatoes, green peppers, pineapples, and guavas. They're gone now. We have one quart of milk left. The thick-skinned greenish-yellow oranges that I purchased from a man on the dock have more seeds than pulp and are inedible.

We anchor off Cayo Rico and dinghy through a spectacular secret canal. The only footprints on the white beach are from our sandals, a heron, and a crab. A tiny brown bird bounces about in a clump of dried seagrass like a Mexican jumping bean and leads us to a thatch-roof cottage with hurricane damage. It was once a day spot for tourists from upscale hotels on Cayo Largo.

We move on to Cayo Cantiles, known as the island of the monkeys. The Ministry of Science, Technology, and Environment has an experimental station here run by three young males. As we dinghy across the transparent sky-blue water on this hot, breezeless day a bearded man flags us over to an area where we can land. Welcoming us, he shakes our hands and leads us across a powdery white sandy beach where we step over chunks of dead coral covered in algae, abandoned flip-flops, plastic bottles, and other debris that has washed ashore. Entering the front hallway of the researchers' cottage, we follow him down a hallway past a room empty except for three shabby foam mattresses with no sheets or pillows. The minuscule kitchen has a tiny counter and a stove where a slightly battered aluminum pot simmers and fills the air with the delicious smells of beans and rice and some kind of meat.

An alpha monkey perches atop a fenced-in area where around fifty monkeys spend their lives. The youngest worker, who looks to be in his thirties, hits a gong hanging from a tree and then pours a container of pellets into the monkeys' feeding trough. Sprawling on a concrete pallet nearby is the men's food source: a massive crocodile captured from a nearby lagoon. The muzzle and tail are tied up to a metal stake while its rear legs are tied to its body. When we follow the men on a pathway into the heart of the island, one of them points out the scat left by a giant rat called a hutia, a mammal the size of a small dog. Hutias nest in trees or in rock crevices and are hunted for food in Cuba. I'm relieved to hear that they usually only come out in the early mornings or late afternoons. We walk carefully across sharp, pointed, volcanic grey rocks to a lagoon bordered by thick reddish material that smells of sulphur.

Back at the cottage, Lee and I are offered a bowl of stew. We politely decline when we learn that the meat is from a hutia. We return with gifts in the late afternoon: a bottle of Club Havana rum, three sought-after Cuban Convertible Pesos, a bar of soap, and our last beer.

With great caution the next morning, we enter a narrow passageway between wave-breaking reefs that stretch for about two miles in all directions. Now twenty-two miles to the west of Cayo Cantiles, we anchor, nerves frayed, in a meadow of turtlegrass, which thrives in shallow, sandy, or muddy areas. After Lee fails to find lobsters in the reefs, I cheer him up with delicious spinach fettuccine with creamed canned chicken, sun-dried tomatoes, onion, canned mush-rooms, and spices. Here we wait, unprotected and rocking about dizzily in twenty-knot winds, for the cold front to move away before we set sail for Cayo Matias, Puerto Rico, only five miles from here.

Newly anchored in a different cove, I remove dead bugs from the ceiling, mold from the walls, and fling rat drop-pings like spitballs into the sea. Then I cook oatmeal with dried cranberries and improvise a pesto from dried-out basil leaves, garlic cloves, and olive oil. I can't help but chuckle over our highly eccentric lifestyle. Suddenly, hearing a sound in the cockpit, I glance over at a blackbird, which has landed on a cockpit cushion. It wanders over to the window to peer at me as I stand motionless at the sink.

The water swishes and swirls against the boat as twenty-knot winds ruffle the lines and the canvas bimini. The Indian light fixture with dangling colored beads clinks in the breeze that flows through the open windows. Today I journal about doing strange things in weird places. My life was a little bizarre before, but this is over the top. Here we are, living the dream with a large rat off of a deserted island while we explore the Cuban Canarreos Archipelago illegally.

The galley feels foreign in the mornings, as if it belongs to someone else. Namely Hernandez. Now I'm the visitor. *May I come in? I'll just sit on the edge of the salon sofa since I don't want to interfere with your life, Hernandez.*

Today under the galley sink, I find shredded newspapers, gnawed plastic garbage bags, and pieces of labels ripped from canned goods. A row of small teeth marks decorate a bar of kitchen soap, and the basil leaves have bite marks.

———

In the black of night, the pitching, rolling waves splash over the starboard side, causing the bow to swing sideways during our sail to Isla Mujeres. To distract myself, I turn my thoughts to Hernandez's nocturnal activities. Is he rolled up like a ball somewhere feeling off-kilter like me? Is he cowering under the sink or gnawing on the navigation system wires? Does he wonder what the hell is going on?

My eyes are closing independently of my own will. It's four in the morning, and I'm munching on peanut butter crackers and squares of cheddar cheese while trying to stay awake. My brother once said, "You'll never fall asleep if you're eating." That's not true.

My inner self yells, "No! Don't do it!" as I lie down on the sofa for just a moment. Twenty minutes later, I awaken with a start then force myself to leave my cozy refuge to peer at the horizon for lights from fishing boats, sailboats, and ships.

In the boisterous winds and heavy seas, one of the lazy jacks catches as we try to reef the mainsail under a bright red sunrise. Lazy jacks are networks of lines to help with sail handling as you reduce the area of the sail. This is a very serious situation because the block that slides up and down the mast won't budge, which prevents us from lowering the sail. In these conditions, the sail can be heavily damaged. I winch Lee forty feet up the mast in the bosun's chair while the winds and crashing waves whip him about, slamming him against the mast while he tries to untie the lazy jacks. The sail releases and we reef it to the lowest point to create stability.

The winds were supposed to be favorable for this passage to Mexico. Instead, they're coming head on so we're forced to return to Cuba as a large storm brews in the area and increases the height of the seas. Inside the boat, books are falling off the shelves and drawers are opening and slamming shut as if a poltergeist is on board.

Bleary-eyed, shivering, and dazed, we motor into a bay along Cuba's Guanahacabibes Peninsula to wait out the front. Riotous waves wash over the cockpit at the bay's entrance, and rain pummels our foul weather gear. As we make our way deeper into the bay's recesses, the turbulence of the seas slowly abates.

As I lower the anchor, a boy on a bike yells at us from a deserted beachside logging road. Long expanses of trees and palmettos line the bay's mostly deserted coastline. When I peer through my binoculars, I spot three men who are also staring at us through binoculars. Fearful of retribution for not checking in, we cannot leave the boat. Sitting at the helm under a heavy bank of leaden clouds, I suddenly want to go home. Again.

We've been off the grid for twelve days now. The goings on of the world are a mystery. Anything could have happened during the time we've been incommunicado. That aspect always makes me feel uneasy. The Global Star phone, an umbilical cord to my family and the world, has disconnected from our satellite service, so I can't call them. It's a pain to call them anyway because Lee, ever vigilant, stands nearby pointing to his watch while saying, "Remember, this call is two dollars a minute!" I really want to call Alex to see how he's doing, but I can't endure Lee's time obsession with calls on the Global Star system. It's so frustrating. And unfortunately, there are no internet cafés nearby.

Downstairs, the sink in the port head makes its usual loud gurgling sounds while the salon windows create shadow lines and grids that move up and down on the sofa with the waves on this long journey to Mexico. The sea air brushes past my face in a soft tickle as we slowly, slowly edge our way toward land.

All we have right now is our own small world that also includes an interesting rat. *What will Hernandez do next?* I often wonder. To revitalize myself, I write a children's story about his evolution as a rat. I've realized lately that he's quite the efficiency expert. The corner of the dishwashing liquid bottle has been nibbled away, which speeds up pouring. And he has trained me to put away all leftovers and wash dishes immediately after meals.

Now docked at the Paraiso Marina in Isla Mujeres, we hemorrhage money to the Immigration people, the customs people, the port captain, the owner of the marina, the agriculture official, and the sanitation person. And everyone needs a tip.

This minuscule bay is packed with sailboats, motorboats, and a fascinating floating island made of recycled plastic upon which rests a tiny house. Fish, sweat, flower, earth, and marijuana smells fill the senses. Under deep blue skies, our flag undulates like a hula dancer in the brisk breeze as the early morning sun creates light and shadow patterns on the salon table. As the local fishing boats make preparations to leave for the day, a man in an oversized straw hat fixes a fishing net spread out on his wooden boat. Mopeds with parents clutching toddlers to their chests, vans packed with tourists, and golf carts zip past on the nearby bayside road.

Lee and I meander down the uneven sidewalks of Isla Mujeres past gaudy shops. Once in a while, I pause to check out hand-woven rugs, silver necklaces, and exotic clothes in store windows. We buy freshly squeezed orange juice at a small farmers market, then corn tortillas from a lady who cooks them on a small stove at the entrance.

Like street urchins, we dig into plates piled with yummy breakfast food while watching salespeople lure, prod, and seduce potential customers who look upscale and well-off. Not trailer trash like us. After stuffing ourselves with scrambled eggs, cold waffles, a weird green cheesy tortilla dish, delicious pastries, and fresh squeezed orange juice, we waddle off to inspect the town on our own.

Lee tells the lovely, buxom tour guide that he's interested in buying a condominium. Unwilling to be part of his shenanigans, I escape and wander over to lounge on the beach which has narrowed to a thin strip of sand after the recent hurricane.

Lee receives an All You Can Drink coupon for the resort's

bar, plus dinner for two at its fanciest restaurant. At the bar, I worriedly glance over at Lee, who is beginning to slur his words. I head to the restroom, and upon my return, Lee is lovingly cupping a young woman's face in his hands while purring, "You are such a beautiful woman."

Suddenly imbued with supernatural strength, I wrench his T-shirt in my right hand and drag him away while saying, "We're leaving! Now!" I want to drag him by his hair, but don't.

I propel him past a kind man standing on the dock who, smiling broadly, says "Hello, mama!" which I return with my most evil smile. I'm not sadistic by nature, but I have to admit that I'm actually enjoying this whole thing on some level.

I watch, in a detached way, as Lee stumbles clumsily into the dinghy. Then, at top speed, I drive his sorry ass back to the boat where, instead of slowing down gradually, I slam to an abrupt halt, causing him to fall forward into a drunken heap.

This powerful aspect of myself that has been dormant for way too long is finally emerging. It's the side of me that can no longer ignore or put up with things that don't support me emotionally. It's absolutely thrilling to watch my own inner evolution. Finally, I'm removing the rose-colored glasses that in the past helped me make up pleasant stories about situations that were anything but affirming.

But it's much more than that. I think this voyage with Lee has actually helped me to become a warrior woman who doesn't need rescuing, who stands up for herself in disaffirming situations, who has integrity, and who treats others with love and dignity.

This is the last we see or hear from Hernandez. I imagine him being lured off the boat by the good food smells from land and a cute lady rat.

20

A Close Call in Honduras

Our next stop is Roatan, Honduras. It's hard not to notice the heartbreaking poverty on this Americanized island. In spite of this, people generally seem to be happy. Applebee's and Wendy's have recently joined Roatan's numerous fast-food vendors. After lunch at Applebee's, I ask for the check in my lousy Spanish. The waiter, brows furrowed, looking concerned, brings over a worried-looking manager who asks in English, "Is everything all right?"

Within a few days, our new charter will arrive. As usual, the water maker, the generator, and the starboard engine have sputtered out. This doesn't surprise me in the least. Boats are sadistic.

While Lee is focused on checking the engines and the generator, I'll be cleaning the toilets, the sinks, and the bilge and washing black mildew from the interior walls. This is just part of living on a boat. I find it rewarding to see the boat all clean and spotless. And since the cabins and the heads on a boat are very small compared to the rooms in a house, the work goes quickly. Then, when our guests arrive, we'll be the perfect professional hosts. And if there is a system failure no one will know because Lee has figured out how to improvise.

Finished with our duties, we relax on the couch. Turning toward Lee, I say, "It's sort of sad that we can't be a couple when we have visitors. Our guests would enjoy being with people who love each other. You have it all wrong."

"What's a couple anyway? I don't see myself as part of a couple," Lee answers heartlessly.

"What did you just say, Lee? Where did that come from? I'm stunned! If I had known that you felt that way, I would have wondered about the wisdom of my staying on the boat with you. I stupidly thought we were an actual couple."

What the hell is going on with him? After being clobbered over the head with that insensitive, mean, unfeeling statement I'm not sure anymore about Lee. How can I entrust my heart to a man who is so insensitive?

A while back, when I declared to his cousin Sally that I was in love with him, she snapped back, "What's love anyway!" At the time, I felt enormously irritated with her comment. In retrospect, maybe she was trying to warn me. I should have removed my rose-colored glasses at that juncture, but unfortunately, I stubbornly kept them on.

Feeling a twinge in my heart, I realize that I don't want to put my relationship with Lee on hold during charters. All along, I've wanted and needed the sweet combination of fulfilling my role as a hostess and fulfilling my role as a loving partner. Sadly, Lee and I don't share the same values.

David and his friend Anne are waiting for me at the airport. Their first evening on board, when Anne comes into the salon dressed for our evening out, Lee exclaims, "You look incredibly beautiful!"

I feel as if my heart has just been stabbed. Again. I wish Lee would say those same words to me. He did in the beginning of our relationship. Quite often. What has happened? What am I doing here?

During their charter, I spent a lot of time avoiding Dave's advances while feeling depressed over Lee's confusing behavior. For instance, on our last tour of the island in the dinghy, he suggested that I stand up to give everyone more legroom during an outing to Oakville. My legs spread out and firmly planted on the solid hull, I kept a firm grip on the painter as Lee brought the dinghy to a plane. Unfortunately, he stopped abruptly to point out something to Anne, and I was propelled through the air into the water. Fully dressed.

Anne, a longtime friend of Lee's, comments one evening while he sleeps below, "You're very different from Lee's past girlfriends. He has never had a relationship that has lasted more than five years." Then she adds thoughtfully, "I think he's already turned the corner into a long-term relationship with you. I've noticed, however, that you push each other's buttons. There's a certain tension in your relationship, which I think is actually good. You force each other to grow in the areas where you need to grow the most."

Nodding in agreement, I mention how hurt I was when Lee complimented her the first evening.

"He likes to needle you and get a rise out of you," she says. "He seems much happier and more confident than he was before. He's changed a lot since you've been together."

Soon after this conversation, she explains to Lee, in my presence, that women often misread his attentions and compliments and think that he's coming onto them.

Then she adds in front of Lee, "Wendy, when he acts like a shithead, back off and give him some space. Leave the boat for a day or two."

The fire of truth now lit, I realize that my childhood notion that I wasn't good enough to be loved becomes reactivated during the moments when Lee flirts in front of me. In a spiritual sense, perhaps I've picked Lee specifically to help me evolve and grow in this area.

After David and Anne return to the States, we drop anchor in a popular harbor north of Roatan. In the early morning hours, an earthquake of 7.1 magnitude strikes Honduras 10 kilometers below the sea and 64 kilometers northeast of Roatan. Sounding like a train speeding down a track, it feels as if we've rammed into a brick wall. A tsunami watch is now in effect for Honduras, Belize, and Guatemala. My biggest worry is that the world's second-largest coral reef, which is near the Honduran mainland, has been damaged.

The Fantasy Island Resort in Honduras always welcomes sailors. And their money. The resort's back porch overlooking the water will be my internet hangout spot during the next two or three weeks.

Within a very short period of time, we've met quite a few interesting sailors. Such as Chris and Laura, who specialize in approach-avoidance; Stan the stockbroker; Don the hang glider; Dennis, the world's messiest boater; and Leo, a young Honduran who's boat-sitting a massive catamaran belonging to an American expat living in Costa Rica. Leo is famous for throwing all-night parties and inducing hangovers in the entire neighborhood. The other night, he fired a gun—or perhaps it was just a flare—and woke us from a deep sleep. Wishing I was somewhere else, I throw out a suggestion to Lee. "Hey, why don't we head to the Rio Dulce in Guatemala."

The dead silence is followed by a terse "No."

I stare at him in disbelief. We used to work together on our individual goals and interests. But this is no longer the partnership we had in the beginning.

Who is this man? I wonder. He certainly isn't the same person who lured me away from Beaufort, the person who wanted us to be a loving couple. It's very hard nowadays not to focus on our slowly disintegrating relationship.

———

Fantasy Island is a melange of creatures: deer, monkeys, peacocks, agouti, ducks, and geese. The peacocks strut past me, dragging their beautifully colored tails across the grass while the agoutis wander by in slow motion after realizing that I'm not Queen Elizabeth, who, according to local legend, adores agouti stew.

One day as I stroll down the sidewalk to the resort, a mother duck and her four ducklings waddle toward me and plop down on the sandy path in a half circle in front of me, blocking my way. They all look rather traumatized, with their ruffled, bedraggled feathers, so I sit cross-legged facing them and ask the mother, "So what's up?"

She looks at me pleadingly as if trying to say, "Would you please save us? We're getting awfully beat up at night. The agoutis have already eaten two of my babies. Help!"

Sadly there's nothing I can do. I can't bring them onto the boat, and there's no animal rescue center on the island. I checked.

———

Today I'm scuba diving with Jamie, a local dive instructor who runs a live-aboard dive boat. I need a break from Lee, who has been grotty and moody for over a week now. I've decided to take care of myself and do my own thing—regardless of Lee. I'm going to treat him with the same thoughtlessness he's extending to me. Using this new approach is empowering.

Jamie, along with two other scuba instructors, meet me in the early afternoon. At a depth of sixty feet, Jamie unexpectedly hands me his mouthpiece so that I can try nitrox, an enriched mixture of gas and oxygen that allows divers to stay underwater for longer periods. I remove my mouthpiece but hold my breath instead of slowly blowing out bubbles. Consequently, my mouthpiece starts to free run with lots and lots of bubbles coming out. I panic. In my confused state, I believe that water is rushing into it and that if I place it into my mouth I will breathe in water.

Breaking every diving rule, I take off for the surface, eighty feet above, while holding my breath. My partner Jamie, thankfully, grabs my fin and pulls me close to him then shoves his mouthpiece into my mouth. I calm down immediately. Without his help, my lungs would have filled up with air like a balloon and then ruptured. Bubbles of gas would get caught in my body and cause severe pain. If I was lucky enough to survive that, I would have to be placed in a hyperbaric chamber to reproduce the sea's hyperbaric conditions. In scuba diving, you must never hold your breath and you must always make a slow ascent to the surface.

Fantasy Island is beginning to depress us. It's time to relocate to Guatemala's heat and humidity and the cow town of

Fronteras, a place without paved streets or sidewalks, where trucks rumble by and pedestrians have to jump out of the way to avoid being hit.

The check-out process in Coxen Bay is exasperating. The harbormaster, in a tizzy and possibly suffering from something personal, tells me in a growly voice to come back the next day. I arrive to locked doors, both there and at the customs office. There is no explanatory signage posted at either place.

On the third day, the harbormaster's female assistant chirps, "Come back on Monday!"

On Monday, keeping my anger in check, I explain to a different assistant that the customs office is still closed. This round-eyed bird-like woman with oily black hair drawn back into a tight ponytail says in perfect English, "I told you to go to customs at two p.m."

How did I miss that? I don't even remember this woman. I would have remembered her! At 2 p.m., I wait for what seems like hours for the harbormaster to do something. Suddenly, I sense some activity coming from his office. He's actually typing up a Zarpe, which is an outbound or inbound clearance document that needs to be presented when entering or leaving a Spanish-speaking country. Lee has always taken care of this detail in the past, but now he wants me to take over the job. So I'm learning as I go.

Even if we're officially checked out of Honduras, we've decided to overnight here. Needing to rest before our next passage, we motor to a small anchorage off of Roatan where heavy rains have left mud puddles on the dirt road leading to the main village. The local stores and restaurants are now closed for the rainy season, and only a few die-hard sailors remain anchored here. By late afternoon, as a thick grey mist settles around us, the warning buoy nearby disappears under the dark shroud.

Earlier today, during an argument, Lee said angrily, "You're having a meltdown!"

No, I muttered to myself, *I'm not a child having a tantrum. I'm an adult having a slightly psychotic moment because you are driving me crazy.*

Then, quickly changing the subject, he talks enthusiastically about our future together. "We'll live near the sea! Somewhere where the kiteboarding is great."

"Hmmm . . . " I said under my breath. "I'm not so sure about that, Lee."

I'm itching to leave the boat. I can't wait to pack my suitcase and head north for the month of August to see my family and my newest grandchild, who is now eight months old. Lee, on the opposite end of the spectrum, seems to have his feet lodged in quicksand. His energy is slow, sluggish, and dense.

———

We stay up until midnight discussing our relationship issues, which usually seem to circle back to me. Everything is usually my fault, from Lee's perspective. There's a saying, though, that if you only focus on what's wrong with your partner, you never have to look at yourself.

I don't have a problem admitting to Lee where I've failed as a partner at times. It's very freeing to do this. I just wish he could do the same. Truthfully, I still believe our relationship is worth the effort because there are so many good attributes inherent in our partnership. We have similar values, and we both have an adventurous streak. And, most important, we enjoy each other's company. At least we used to.

I walk away from our one-sided discussion feeling very dissatisfied.

We stop on the west coast of the Honduran island of Guanaja for a few days to anchor in a wild, wooly, windy anchorage. Overlooking us is an estate owned by a wealthy American who has a power plant on Roatan that charges fees the poor people can't afford.

A water taxi takes us to the Guanaja Settlement, a small town on the south side of Guanaja Cay. Red, our driver, suggests I bring a cushion to sit on, plus raincoats. We still arrive soaked from a bone-bruising journey through rough, choppy water.

Enveloped in strong sewage odors, we disembark onto a pier surrounded by bobbing trash. Guanaja's dilapidated dwellings on stilts overlook manmade canals that zigzag their way through the village. Speedboats, the main mode of transportation here, dart about, slicing their way through the continually agitated waters.

This settlement is mostly Seventh-day Adventist. Scripture messages cover the walls and the benches here. Red, a self-appointed guide, takes us past a combination police station and jail to lunch at a hole-in-the-wall where we have fragrant stewed chicken with fried plantains and coleslaw. Then he leads us to the old-fashioned Miller Hotel, where Lee and I catch up on long-neglected emails.

While catching up on correspondence, I overhear discussions about a plane and helicopter chase that took place over the skies of Guanaja last night. Two small planes landed on Guanaja's sister island around 2 a.m. to transfer a stash of cocaine from Panama to a second plane bound for the mainland of Honduras and then the US. A US Coast Guard plane and helicopter, along with a Honduran military helicopter, chased both planes directly over our anchorage. One escaped. The other one, newly loaded with drugs, was shot down while we slept through it all, unawares.

Utila is the last island in the Bay Island chain. As we near its main anchorage, I'm entertained by a conversation on the VHF between two women.

"I got cabbage, broccoli, potatoes, carrots, and one pound of chicken! It'll be jus' fine!"

"What kind of chips you got?"

"Doritos, Dora Delights, Franchises, Fritos."

"You got any yellow cheese? I got one pound of sugah."

"Gotta run out. Gotta go to work!"

"Rattan . . . the ratta . . . you read me Little Ratta? Loretta, you read me?"

In the evening, we visit Utila's main village, then, in an exquisitely romantic moment, we drift offshore in the dinghy under a star-filled sky and a becalmed sea lit up by glowworms. It's one of the most romantic moments I've experienced with Lee in our years together. *Maybe there's still hope for us. Maybe we can pull ourselves away from all the previous negativity and start anew*, I think wistfully.

Just as I find myself wondering if we'll ever leave for the Rio Dulce, Lee informs me that we're leaving—just in time for the arrival of a tropical wave. The seas are rough, it's raining, and the howler monkeys scream in the background as the trees and houses on Utila merge together in the distance. Undeterred, we plow ahead.

Ahead are the cloud-capped mountains of mainland Honduras. A tropical wave disturbance is brewing all along its coastline, so we have no other choice but to continue on. Dressed in our foul weather gear, we watch the rainstorm head our way. Lightning strikes all around as needle-sharp rain pelts our faces and the boat lurches and crashes through the confused waves. We power through it all, as we always do, and drip water all over the salon floor each time we come inside to check our course on the computer. The three sets of cockpit seats that Lee lashed together to prevent them from blowing off the boat, clamber down the steps of their own accord as if they too want to escape the storm.

Before dusk, exhausted after a sleepless night, we head through the narrow entrance of a deserted Honduran lagoon named Laguna El Diamante. In the darkness, we narrowly miss a reef off the starboard side and a massive rock off the port side. The lagoon is encircled by bright green shrubs and low palm trees and looks as if it was swirled with melted dark chocolate and toffee.

Now anchored snuggly in the lagoon's mud, Lee and I cover the sails and then curl up on the sofa together for an Audrey Hepburn movie and a steaming cup of hot chocolate.

Not long after our brief overnight visit to the lagoon, we're told that pirates had attacked a sailor and his daughter there. They were making their way to the Honduras Bay Islands from the Rio Dulce in Guatemala when foul weather forced them to seek refuge here, just like us. The man was killed, but his daughter survived by jumping into the water and hiding in the reeds along the shore.

Lee and I were lucky that the same fate didn't befall us on that dark rainy night. If we had known about that, we would never have taken a chance on stopping there.

21

The Rio Dulce

With both sails reefed under intense, grueling winds, we race toward Guatemala's Rio Dulce. The Honduran highlands, concealed behind dark grey clouds that hide its mysteries and God knows what else, loom ahead of us.

Guatemala will have its own challenges: specifically, mosquitos that can bore into your skin and deposit the botfly egg, which will then hatch into a parasitic worm. Plus unbearable heat and gun-toting bandits who will board your boat if you anchor anywhere other than at a secure marina. Amoebas, prolific in the river, can cause diarrhea violent enough to make you wish you were dead. We've even been advised to put all fabrics in plastic containers with small unopened packets of detergent to prevent mold.

"Deet will be your best friend in Guatemala!" a sailor warns us, and then adds, "The Mayans don't want the gringos there."

Sailors have mentioned the importance of "making it over the bar" at the river's entrance, which straddles the Garifuna town of Livingston. There is a shallow area at the mouth of the Rio Dulce and, if the tide is low, you risk getting stuck in "super mud." After boats make it over the bar, they announce on the VHF, "We made it over the bar! Woohoo!"

Making it over the bar was anticlimactic for us. There had been a lot of buildup beforehand from the sailors we'd talked to. The keel depths on monohulls can range from five feet up to eight feet, so sailboats with long keels get stuck quite often in the mud at the entrance to the Rio Dulce. Catamarans, which have a shallow draft, can easily enter the Rio Dulce with no issues.

There was nothing to it.

We motor through easily, then head up the Rio Dulce River toward the popular Monkey Bay Marina, where I reserved a slip for *Worldwide Traveler*. The hills of Honduras loom in the far distance.

Now situated at the marina's dock, we start preparations for our six-week, early fall visit to the US. I'm elated that I'll see my sons soon. It's been four years since I left Beaufort to live on the sea and almost a year since I've seen my sons. Thomas is CEO for an innovative tech startup in New York City and Markus is a Thin Film Design Engineer at Omega Optical in Brattleboro, Vermont. He was involved with the lens design of the Martian Land Rover and the Mars *Perseverance*. Alex works for Dell in Austin, Texas. They're all doing well in their respective professions.

Lee is dragging his feet a little and I'm not sure what's going on with him. I'm trying to ignore it. Meanwhile I'm excited over the prospect of seeing my family soon. I'll spend two weeks with Thomas and Markus in the Northeast. Then I'll join Lee at his brother Nick's house in Stamford, Connecticut, for a week. Following that, we'll be at his brother Jim's house in Miami before heading to Austin for a week with Alex. Finally, I'll visit my sisters Nancy in Atlanta and Joanne in Anniston.

I wouldn't be surprised if Lee returns to the marina much earlier than me since he has a low tolerance for staying in other people's homes.

————

Here in the States, I'm fascinated by a lipstick that makes your lips look temporarily bigger. It's way too expensive, so I settle for just imagining what my lips would look like if they were all puffy like an angel fish's. Lee's fascinated by the "As Seen On TV" products, especially an organizer made in China, which he buys as a replacement for my large string bag after witnessing me rooting through it mindlessly like a raccoon. The organizer, smelling like a petrochemical factory, is a thoughtful but repugnant gift, and I quietly tuck it away, never to be seen again.

I had forgotten how overwhelming the grocery stores are in the US with their abundance of food choices. I'm in awe of the range of options here. I've gotten used to mom-and-pop grocery stores that have very limited selections.

During this trip, I notice that Lee is more forgetful. His forgetfulness involves leaving things like wallets in taxi cabs. And I'm driving him crazy with my impulsive shopping. We're beginning to feel like traveling salesmen, living out of suitcases. And we're totally dependent on the whims of others. How do you tell your hosts that you're starving after six hours without eating?

We have some awesome moments with our individual families. Lee is now back on the boat. Having only two weeks left, I focus on my sons, my two grandchildren, and my sisters. My stay in the US has flown by way too quickly. After saying my final goodbyes, I extend open invitations for visits with us wherever we happen to be.

Back at the Monkey Bay Marina, an orderly line of ants, looking like tiny otherworldly metallic robots, march across my table as I write in my journal under the vaulted ceiling of a bamboo palapa. The entire structure rests on pilings rooted firmly in the slow-moving river and is bordered on all sides by tall, bright green rushes that sway continuously in the warm breezes. The long wooden walkway that connects it to the pier curves through a lush tropical garden of flowers: red bromeliads and white orchids flecked with purple. Sailors gather here for regular happy hour BBQs, or they simply come to lounge in the comfy wicker chairs. I find solace here among the sounds of parrots, howler monkeys, and small boats puttering up and down the greenish-brown water as I sit in my favorite chair with the red and green jungle-print cushion. The Guatemalan caretakers of this marina, a family with four young children, live in a small hut nearby.

This family-oriented marina is the smallest and quietest one on the Rio Dulce, which is one of the main reasons I chose it. I'm ready for a little peace and quiet after the daily parties in the Bay Islands of Honduras.

As I've gotten to know the sailors in Rio Dulce, I've changed my mind about wanting solitude. They're a wonderful group! And great fun to be with. Now I'm one of the first people to arrive at parties. I've totally embraced the sailing community here, and I hope the friendships I've made will be lifelong.

Lee, however, has a habit of lumbering over to the biweekly happy hour get-togethers late, just as the bug spray is being stowed into backpacks and the leftover hors d'oeuvres are being placed into Ziplocs. And that's okay. It's his choice. And everyone is happy to see him even if he is late.

Our neighbors to the right are physical therapists for the Florida State football team, and to our left is Jim, a purple-nosed former NASA scientist who was involved with the first lunar landing in 1969.

"What in the heck is Lee doing all night on the computer? He's way off the scale!" Jim scoffs one morning, hazel eyes narrowed and his huge greying afro bobbing up and down.

His wife, Kitty, short and round with light brown hair that sits like an upside-down bowl on the top of her head, smiles at me in a pitying way.

"Oh, he's working on the website, marketing our charters, doing email, probably looking up old female friends," I answer with a smirk on my face.

There's only one way to reach the nearby town of Fronteras and the restaurants that are scattered along the river's shore or hidden within the tributary's mangroves: by dinghy or water taxi. Fearful of having the dinghy stolen, we prefer to travel by taxi.

I ask John, the harbormaster at Monkey Bay Marina, how to locate the main grocery store since there's no signage.

"Walk down the main street," he says. "When you see two women selling chickens, turn right. Walk past a line of women also selling chickens. Then walk all the way to the end of the line. Back up two women. Turn left. You'll see the entrance ahead of you." To add to my confusion, this store is called "Cheek-ees" by the locals even though the actual store name is Tienda Reade.

With my groceries in hand, I edge myself carefully along the narrow, slanted five-foot-long board that connects us to the pier. I feel like a tightrope walker as I make my way across it to the boat.

Fronteras, a cowboy town, is just three short blocks situated along a dusty two-lane road. Growling, beat up-looking old trucks belch black smoke and are loaded with cattle staring sadly out through narrow slats. Or they're carrying propane or cardboard boxes filled with food supplies for the markets. Also inching along are chicken buses swaying back and forth violently over the bumpy road. These buses are packed with men in straw cowboy hats and women holding children or chickens on their laps. The locals look at us warily, as if we're freaks.

It's obvious that we're not welcome. Yet here we are, shopping daily and paying double for nearly everything because we're foreigners.

One day, after Lee narrowly avoids being hit by two vehicles, we stop for a late lunch at the Sundog Café, a popular hangout for expats. Inside, six American hippies sit on wooden bar stools drinking beer and smoking cigarettes. We sit at an odd-shaped rickety table covered with a red-and-white checkered tablecloth. More people pile in. One woman, Hispanic and married to an American, swats the bar dog with her napkin saying, "Get outta here, damn dog!"

Even in October, the Rio is very hot and humid. At 5 a.m., we tackle boat chores before the heat takes over, our T-shirts become drenched in sweat, and we become too physically exhausted to work. Unfortunately, the fall and winter rainy season has strangely shifted from this area to Guatemala City, and it's feared that the people in the nearby mountains will suffer economically because they will most likely lose their crops.

Lee wants to return to Roatan in a couple of weeks, so he

gets the boat ready for the long passage while I socialize with my friends. We usually go into town together for souvenir shopping and lunches at the tasty Guatemalan restaurants.

On the morning of our departure, all the sailors berthed at the marina show up to wave goodbye. Having realized that Lee and I are expert procrastinators, they smile with Cheshire cat grins as they line up along the dock to release our lines—even if we're not ready—at the exact time we promised to leave.

Lee and I have been getting along very well in Guatemala, and I'm hoping we can take that good energy with us. We've both been happy here, and I learned that socialization with other sailors is very necessary for me. There will be times when it's just the two of us, but when we're at an anchorage, I'm going to reach out to people and forge new friendships.

Everything is going wrong on our return passage to Roatan. The jib, having broken loose from the starboard and the port lines, thrashes about violently as the boat rocks back and forth like a mechanical bull in the confused seas. I'm having a hard time just getting my footing. One slip and I'm off the boat.

At the bow, as Lee is wrapping a line around the jib, his lower body suddenly breaks through the trampoline net, which is rotting away after five years of sun and sea exposure. Stuck, with his lower torso being pulled toward the angry water below, he manages to slowly haul himself back up to safety.

Once in Roatan, we'll sail down the coast from French Harbor and Coxin Hole in the north to Jonesville and Port Royal in the south—quite a dangerous passage. In the 1960s, an American author noted in her book *Roatan Odyssey* that she waited six weeks for a supply boat from the northern region because of the treacherous sea conditions. I hope our trip will be smoother than the one before.

We're doing well as a couple. I've understood that it works better for us to socialize more and avoid long periods of isolation. When it's just the two of us, it's easy to get on each other's nerves. I've always been a people person, and social interaction makes me happy. If I'm happy, Lee is happy.

———

In a gorgeous, crystal-clear lagoon, we rest for three days anchored off a small atoll. Naked, and loving every minute of being the only souls present, we explore numerous coral islands and reefs. On a distant, deserted island, a dilapidated abandoned shed with an orange roof looks strangely out of place. On the horizon, the lights of fishing boats flash and sparkle as the moon awakens to yet another night. Thankfully, I sleep more soundly than I have in months.

This is my Disney fantasy of our upcoming arrival in the San Blas: a group of exotically beautiful Panamanians with burnished brown skin, dressed in hula skirts, line up on a white sandy beach to wave at us as we sail into Cayos Holandeses. In reality, our welcoming committee is hideous weather.

Still slightly adrenalized from the challenging two-day passage from the Albuquerque Cays, which lie thirty-six miles southwest of the Colombian island of San Andres, we are now introduced to Panama's own version of Hades. On our approach, under threatening skies, the San Blas Islands in the foreground slowly disappear beneath a burgeoning mist that buries the island's palm trees under thick blankets of grey. Waves glimmer white as they crash loudly against the nearby reefs, and in the background, Panama's

mountain ranges illuminate themselves between the constant thunderclaps.

Heavy rain rapidly fills the five buckets I leave in the cockpit for clothes-washing purposes, and I'm feeling frustrated
over not having more containers for receiving these gifts
from the sky. If we had a proper rainwater collection system,
I suspect that we could have filled the boat's two water tanks
with this one rainfall.

We are the rain people, depressed, sulky, and waterlogged
from the nonstop winter showers. Adding to my growing cabin fever, the unrelenting twenty-knot winds make it
almost impossible to escape the boat. Looking down at the
dinghy as it bobs about like a plastic toy in the stirred-up
seas, I realize it would be crazy to attempt a short visit to the
handful of sailors anchored nearby. I wish we had stayed in
the Rio Dulce of Guatemala like all the other sailors.

A storm awakens us in the night. *How many times have I
staggered bleary-eyed out of bed because of storms?* I wonder. Putting on foul weather gear always brings a feeling of
dread for what's to come. Lee, on the other hand, becomes
dramatically energized in these instances. I wish we could
harness his energy to make electricity for the boat! Lee
prances about like Julius Caesar getting ready to fend off
Moorish adversaries. Loudly he stomps into our cabin just
as I'm putting on my navy blue bibbed pants and my wellies.
With a theatrical flourish, he opens the closet door, grabs his
jacket, races up the stairs, then hauls ass out into the rain,
lightning, and forty-knot winds to turn on the engines. Later,
hunched over while clinging on to the safety railings with a
small flashlight between my teeth, I pull up the anchor to
keep the boat from dragging into a coral reef. I yell out cuss
words, hating the discomfort of it all.

In the morning, cool winds charge through the anchorage as large ominous black clouds stampede toward us from the mainland. As we close all the windows and batten down everything on the deck, we're suddenly enveloped in darkness moments before the most spectacular lightning storm I've ever witnessed unleashes itself. Quickly we stuff our laptop computers, the GPS, and our cell phones into the microwave for protection since tall-masted catamarans are more prone to lightning strikes.

Safely ensconced indoors, we hear over the VHF that there was an armed robbery last night on a sailboat in Linton, Panama, which is not far from here. A man held a machete to a sailor's throat as his wife looked on and his accomplice took their passports, cash, $10,000 in US bonds, computers, and the GPS.

Having had no contact with my sons for weeks, I feel uneasy. *Was Alex offered a job at the tech company? How are Markus and Thomas? Markus works way too hard. So does Thomas. Is Thomas's startup going well? How are my grandchildren Tori and Annika? Susan is expecting her third child just before Christmas—how is she doing?* It crosses my mind that I have more questions lately than answers. The invisible cords to them are always intact, though, and I know that they can feel my loving thoughts.

Having no distractions other than the lousy weather, Lee focuses on me. He evaluates me like a researcher studying a petri dish, pointing out my shortcomings. I sigh heavily and go below to cheer myself up with Stuart Smalley's helpful affirmations. While sitting cross-legged on our bed, I decide to give Lee some slack, since there's nothing much to focus on other than reading. We're both feeling a little frustrated.

Isolation is bad for our relationship because Lee has

nothing better to do than focus on me. That focus does not make me want to cuddle up to him. Once we're in a new anchorage, there will be distractions and friendships. So for now, I'm going to sit tight and ignore him. Happily, writing fulfills me, and I can go to the port aft cabin and write my little heart out. And read. And dream.

22

The Most Famous Indian in Kuna Yala

Panama's hellish rainy season is over. We are presently anchored in the clearest, most beautiful aquamarine-colored water I've ever seen. The air is relaxed and smells of freshly washed linens drying on a clothesline. As I turn my face upward toward the sun, a soft breeze glides across my skin. Off our stern is an impressive view of the Cayos Limones, a small chain of islands in the San Blas archipelago where pelicans perch on the tops of palm trees. The water is so transparent it looks as if the fish are moving, in a dream-like way, along a ribbon of air.

This archipelago of 365 islands belongs to the Kuna Yala territory, which is an independent, self-governing country supported economically by Panama. Only about thirty-six of the islands are inhabited, and some of them are currently being reclaimed by the rising seas, forcing many of the Kuna natives to move to their mainland territory which is a narrow band of land extending along the northeast coast of Panama.

I'm intrigued by what I've heard about Kuna families, which are matrilineal. Women own all the huts, and when they marry, the men move in with them. The groom takes the last name of the bride, whose father holds authority over the groom. Women are the primary moneymakers because of their sought-after *mola* art, on which they work tirelessly along with cooking, watching children, and visiting nearby yachts to show off their handiwork.

I'm fascinated with the Kuna women. I can't stop staring at them here in this new anchorage in the Kuna Yala territory. They always dress in their traditional native costume: short, puffy-sleeved blouses upon which two ornate mola panels are set in the front and the back. Tied around their waists are mid-length cotton skirts which are rectangles of dark blue or dark green fabric ornamented with orange, mustard yellow, white, or lime green designs. Their black hair is covered by a square of red cotton edged with a bright yellow design, and wrapped around their calves and forearms are long strands of beads in orange, red, yellow, and black. These beads are called *winis*, and they protect the women from evil spirits. The married women always have a gold ring in their nose, and as part of their morning ritual, they draw a fine line from the base of their forehead to the end of their nose with Jaqua juice. The reddish-orange blush on their high cheekbones comes from the annatto fruit.

The Kuna men I've seen wear Western clothing and have an earthy, pungent smell from the daily grilling or smoking of fish and living close to the land. Their mornings are spent in the mountains of the Kuna territory, which stretches deep into Panama's jungles. Here they hunt and harvest bananas,

pineapple, limes, coconuts, cocoa, avocados, yucca, potatoes, and rice or make dugout canoes from the trees. In the
afternoons, they fish or sell their harvest to the village stores
or to the hundreds of sailors anchored throughout the archipelago. These men also supply Colombia with most of its
coconuts which are traded for goods.

I've learned that these Chibchan-speaking people are
descendants of the Carib Indians who once occupied the
Caribbean Islands. They don't have hypertension, they have
a long lifespan, and they rarely have cancer or cardiovas-
cular disease. You never see an overweight Kuna. The fat
in their diet comes mainly from coconuts, cocoa, fish, and
wild game.

————

In the sailors' boat journal, I read about a famous cross-dresser
here named Lisa, who makes some of the most sought-after
molas in Kuna Yala. She arrives at our anchorage on our second day. I recognize her in the distance in her suburban-sized
dugout canoe. Her *ulu*, made by her father from the mainland's massive cooba tree, has a bow that curves upward like
a miniature Viking boat.

Lisa, her face full and radiant, is wearing a straw hat with
fresh flowers woven into the band, a feminine light green
blouse, and dark brown running pants. She has an efferves-
cent personality, strongly sculpted cheekbones, dark brown
almond-shaped eyes framed by thin, drawn-on black eyebrows, straight black hair with toffee highlights, a slightly
flattened nose, and the high forehead of her Indian culture.
Her mother's and father's names are tattooed on the inside
of her lower right arm. Her body is muscular, her arms are

well-defined, and her hands are distinctly masculine. The youngest of the four boys in her family, Lisa was chosen by her parents to be the girl so that her mother's mola art could be carried on in the family.

"I no like being boy. I like being girl," Lisa explains to me. "My mother very happy that I carry on mola tradition and take care of her in old age."

Here, where homosexuality is totally accepted, many homosexual men dress as women and wear traditional female clothing. Their voices are feminine, and they often have young children in tow to appear even more womanly. Many of them are expert mola makers.

Lisa and her boat boy Alencia become regular fixtures. They always bring a bucket filled with her newest molas which she proudly places on the cockpit table for our view-ing. They often stay for lunch or for a day passage to a nearby island during which Lisa sits beside me at the helm and enter-tains me with stories about the various islands we sail past.

Venancia, Lisa's archrival, is gay but dresses in male cloth-ing. Long-faced with sunken cheeks and intense and enormous black eyes, he has seriously funky breath. He comes by to see me often. Venancia is considered to be the top mola artist in Kuna Yala according to the *New York Times*.

Lisa and Venancia live on neighboring islands but act as if they've never heard of one another. I love the little dra-mas that take place on our boat when they're both present and competing for my attention. It's as if they have tracking devices for each other's whereabouts because whenever one shows up, the other one appears. On rainy days, however, Venacia is the only one who visits me. His hair sodden and matted down, his clothes wringing-wet, I wrap him in thick towels and fix him coffee. Not having chemistry with him as

I do with Lisa, I find myself searching for words. Eventually, his trips become less and less frequent as it becomes evident that Lisa and I have a unique connection.

I have a strong antenna for things of the spirit, and the Kuna culture is a mystical, spiritually oriented society with which I resonate. I suspect that Lisa needs to vent her frustrations to an outsider about the increasing drug use among the young males on her island and her growing fears that the young girls are losing the desire to spend their lives making molas. We sit in the cockpit propped up with pillows and talk for hours while Lee reads or snoozes below and Alencia yawns with boredom.

"Girls most important in Kuna society. Boys not so special. God channels information to girls on how to make molas," Lisa says. The girls are taught this art starting at age seven.

Three weeks later, we've now anchored off the island of Tiadup in the Coco Banderos Cays. During our four months in Kuna Yala, we will visit almost every single island group, which will put us on the radar of just about every adult within twenty miles. At 7:30 a.m., while I'm dressing or having a second cup of coffee, a steady stream of women in dugout canoes peddling their textile art appear at the stern. Men occasionally show up selling fruit, vegetables, or fish. This continues throughout the day unless it's raining. They arrive during lunchtime, naps, conversations with Lee, or my attempts to accomplish something . . . *anything*. The American dollars I so carefully obtained at a Panama City ATM, the closest place for getting cash, are slipping away like sand through my fingers. I can't say no to these people, because I want to support them.

Lee seems oblivious to the fact that he needs to figure out a way to pitch in with expenses. Running low on cash due to our recent lack of charter customers, Lee keeps hitting up his two brothers and me for funds to tide him over until we have paying guests. We've been doing really well up until just now. His cousin Sally has funded him many times already, and I'm wondering how long her patience will last. And it doesn't help the situation that he still periodically leaves his wallet in taxis, or loses it while snorkeling.

One day, Lee astounds me as I'm washing up dishes in the galley. "Wendy, you need to pay rent on this boat!" he says.

Stunned, I stare at him open-mouthed. Then in a full-throated voice, I explode, "*You* should be paying *me* for all the hard work I do on this boat. The cooking, the cleaning, organizing most of the details for upcoming charters, and provisioning the boat myself, at my *own* expense. I could go on and on." This issue has been an ongoing problem for me because we haven't had charter customers for several months. Until things pick up, we're going to have to cut back on expenses.

And recently I've requested that he not join me on food runs (the few times that he does come along). Acting like a five-year-old, he'll approach me with his hands filled with packages of Oreos or candy, asking, "Can we get these?"

Against my wishes, Lee joins me on my provisioning jaunt to Panama City. In Carti, we climb into a dark green mud-covered van and slide into the seat behind the driver, who turns out to be a very talkative, friendly chauffeur. I turn to glance at the Kuna family squished behind us and realize they may have given up the comfortable mid-section seats for us. A girl with large, deep brown eyes sits there quietly, a small boy stares down at his feet, and the grandparents eye me cautiously. The woman's eyes convey that she's seen it all and is feeling jaded.

Lee leans over and mutters under his breath, "I'm not impressed."

With what, I wonder.

The fog is lifting as we approach the hills of Kuna Yala. Beyond are the flats of mainland Panama. The Kuna family is dropped off at a small concrete house. Outside, a weary woman with a postpregnancy belly and two yellow diaper pins attached to the front of her sarong awaits. The older couple hands the children to this blank-faced mother who shows no happiness at seeing them. An impassive preteen sits on a stool on the front stoop watching everyone while trying to catch glimpses of the gringos in the jeep. I smile at her unchanging face.

"Oh God," Lee sighs as he drops onto the plump quilt in our nice clean room at the Avila Hotel in an upscale part of the city.

I now have a collection of fifty molas. Many of my purchases are the direct result of Kuna women shaming me into buying them by throwing temper tantrums. After I say politely, "No, gracias," "No plata," or "No más dinero!" they throw their beautiful works of art onto the dusty ground in dramatic disgust. So I theatrically throw my purse onto the ground in similar mock disgust, which creates wild laughter. After that, I can actually bargain with them.

Occasionally, ulus are packed from bow to stern with adorable bright-eyed children. This is a marketing ploy to draw sailors in, warm their hearts, and break down all resistance. I hand out coloring books to the kids, who sit in the cockpit coloring while their mothers pull out stacks of molas, smelling of mold mixed with a gamey wood fire odor, from large bins that inevitably contain a few cockroaches that scurry away into the crevices of the boat.

No matter how many molas I've seen or bought, no matter how jaded I feel about them, there's always something unusual that requires closer inspection. I can't resist the mola glasses cases, the change purses, and the interesting beaded bracelets and necklaces made from shiny red and black seeds. Or the Kuna women who stare into my eyes saying over and over, "Nice mola, nice mola, nice mola." Hypnotized, I hand over $25 for a mola I don't need. "What just happened? Don't tell me I just bought another one," I mumble to Lee, who watches me with a smirk on his face. It's my money, and I'm determined to buy a few of these beautiful works of art.

————

After three months in the Kuna Yala Islands, I wake up in the mornings on tenterhooks, waiting for the usual clunk at the stern which signals someone's arrival by dugout. By daybreak, there are usually two canoes tied to the stern. I believe there's a sign on our boat, only visible to the locals, that says, "We're Suckers."

One day, a hobbit-sized man sticks his head into the forward port window where I'm catching a late afternoon nap on the bunk.

"Buenas tardes," he says.

Hiding my irritation, I ask in a controlled voice, "¿Qué pasa?"

"Fish!" he answers as I lean out the window to the sight of white crabs climbing over a fresh yellowfin tuna and a bright yellow Caribbean lobster in the bottom of his dugout. This man becomes my favorite source of fish.

Lee and I "adopt" Tiny Man and his family of seven Lilliputian kids. We tower over this couple who are a diminutive four feet in height. It's believed that the Kuna's evolutionary isolation in the jungle necessitated their smaller size. Interestingly, the Kunas also have the highest rate of albinism in the world. These "pale moon children," as they're known here, are seen as special, as natural leaders.

Yesterday, Tiny Man's entire family swarmed over every inch of the boat checking out bathrooms, cabins, and the bouncy trampoline until Lee rounded them up for photographs. My child-friendly American lunch of peanut butter and jelly sandwiches with potato chips and chocolate milk was met with quizzical looks. General restlessness followed by widespread pandemonium took over while Lee methodically printed out fifteen photographs.

Just before Tiny Man left with his wired-up family, I made his baby cry just by grinning at her. I've actually made a lot of babies cry in Kuna Yala. These somber people generally don't go around with big toothy American grins unless you do something unexpected like throwing your purse onto the ground. When I'm wandering through villages, people will, however, smile for my photographs because I pay them one "dolla" for each photo. Once, after forgetting to ask permission for a photo, I received a look that could kill followed by the rubbing of fingers together in the classic Mafioso sign.

Through word of mouth, we become the official gringo photographers for countless Kuna families who pull alongside in their dugouts with their children and line up on the bow of the boat for a portrait. Then they wait in the cockpit while Lee prints out their photos, a big status symbol in Kuna Yala. With great pride, they take these back to their huts where their portraits are hung on a fishing line that runs the length of the hut.

Sometimes they want us to be in the photos with them.

Others prefer for us to take their pictures while they sit in the cockpit or the salon, looking as if they own the boat. They always know exactly what size pictures they need. Large. The larger they are, the more status.

Lisa shows up one day with two *nuchus*, which are also called medicine dolls. *Is this a medicine doll outing? Do they take their dolls out on adventures?* I wonder. Their names are Ina Naidy and Mani Carpipillar. At the end of her visit, Lisa packs them away in her bag. Later, I discover that Lisa wanted to give them to us but was told by Ina and Mani that they were upset about something.

Every Kuna family has a group of sacred and loved medicine dolls. Some families have only a few. Lisa has fifty. Her deceased brother-in-law, once the top medicine man in the Kuna territory, carved them himself out of hardwood, then imparted spirits into them with a special ceremony during which he baptized each one with a name. The Kunas have these dolls for protection from evil spirits, for help with health problems, and to provide a link between the spirit world and the physical world. They believe that groups of malevolent spirits called *poni* wander the planet, bringing with them disease and illness.

Medicine dolls are small, free-standing figurines of different sizes carved out of wood into human or animal form. They are made by medicine men who use chants, herbs, and rituals to keep the spirits from the other world in line. It's extremely rare for an outsider to receive a living medicine doll. The ones sold in gift shops are usually made of lightweight balsa wood and have no living spirit.

Nuchus are actually angels and guardians. According to Lisa, they say "Go away!" to bad spirits. They can appear in your dreams, sometimes disguised as other things, but always wearing white like an angel. Dreams are extremely important in this culture. "Protection you when you have problem. Devil, bad spirits . . . they can't come boat. No enemy coming! Protection Wendy, protection Lee, protection boat."

During dreams, the medicine dolls often visit the people they're protecting, giving them personal messages or guidance meant for friends or for specific people in the village.

Two weeks later, Lisa arrives with Ina and Mani and two lovely handwoven ceremonial baskets. She hands the medicine dolls to me. "Ina, Mani ready be with you now. They happy! They want to live with you! They stand in baskets!"

Lisa has me write their names in pencil on the front of each doll.

After she leaves, Lee holds Ina while I hold Mani. They each radiate and hum with an energy presence. We place them across the room from each other and then move them together after sensing it would make them feel more at home. A large butterfly with beautiful gold-spotted turquoise wings suddenly attaches itself to the window right behind them.

As time gathers itself and unfolds, Lee and I respect more and more this new mystical presence in our lives. Strangely, I've noticed that whenever I write about the nuchus or the Kuna in my blog, my computer screen goes haywire every single time.

I'm wondering if Lisa sensed a dangerous situation on the horizon. Did she feel compelled to protect us with the nuchus? Ever since we first met her, Lisa has been an ever-present part of our lives. None of the other sailors have the close connection with her that we have. I feel very fortunate to have her as a friend and a guide. I dread having to say goodbye to her. If I could, I would take her with us, but her home is here in Kuna Yala. This is where she belongs.

23

In Rio Sidra

Lying beside an open window, breathing in the pungent odors of earth and jungle, a soft drizzle awakens me from a deep sleep. Wisps of fine white clouds, like bands of newly fallen snow, lounge along the mountain ridges of Panama in the distance. Directly across from us, the palm trees of Rio Sidra shimmer gold in the early morning light. A log, looking decidedly like a crocodile, drifts past in water muddied by a rain storm.

Male voices and children's laughter float our way from the island, intertwining themselves with the sounds of sea water lapping along the shoreline and the music of birds whistling to each other as they soar overhead. Fishermen in canoes powered by makeshift sails glide past silently in this deserted and somewhat unsettled anchorage.

When Lee and I pull up to the wharf in our dinghy, twelve naked, wildly rambunctious young boys high-five us. As we slowly meander along the hard-packed sandy streets of Rio Sidra past modest concrete dwellings painted bright yellow, pink, and turquoise, past rows and rows of huts interspersed with wooden shacks, they trail our every move on our search for Lisa's house. Looking like quintessential gringo sailors in our dark sunglasses and large hats, we are conspicuous among these people who don't even own sunglasses, much less sun hats.

Rio Sidra is buzzing with activity. This is the first day of a ChiCha celebration for a local girl who has started menstruation. Lisa has invited us as her guests. This is a long-standing tradition among the Kuna and is considered to be necessary for a girl's spiritual evolution. The parents are expected to supply the fish and the game and a drink named chicha that comes from cane juice that is cooked in large iron kettles two weeks ahead to allow for its proper fermentation into a rather foul-smelling, very potent dark ale. These puberty rituals are always held in the large thatched Casa de Congreso hut where the villagers dance and sing for days.

No one here owns a car or has electricity except for a few Kunas who have generators, a light or two, and tiny outdated TV sets. People generally go to bed when the darkness of night takes over, leaving the island in its own deep abiding silence.

Today the air pulsates with sounds, smoke, and presence. Smoked fish and Tule Masi, a porridge made of fish and plantains, waft their pleasant odors through the narrow sandy streets that have never seen a car. Smoke belches from a communal cooking hut as colorful laundry lifts itself upward into the gentle breeze.

Rio Sidra's palm leaf–covered huts are made from cane sticks or bamboo lashed to posts with a fibrous plant. Inside these earthen-floored dwellings are hammocks that hang from bamboo rafters. There is no furniture except for a few stools. The family medicine dolls stand in a small wooden box near the fireplace where logs smolder day and night and smell of autumn. In the dim light, women of all ages sit on stools working on molas whose essence is filled with the lives of these people.

"¿Donde esta Lisa's casa?" we ask a man who becomes our guide, leading us through the narrow passageways between huts and shacks, past young boys playing tag or blindfold, past a woman sitting on a stool sewing the tiny stitches for a mola, past a girl in traditional dress standing in her doorway who looks like she's just old enough to stand, past a child peeking out from behind a cloth door. Another girl, on seeing me walk past her home, runs out and gives me a big hug.

Lisa's wooden shack, which overlooks the water, shifts a little as we enter its cool interior imbued with autumnal smells from logs burning slowly in the fireplace. Lisa mentions that she'll have to move soon because it has become unstable. Ducking down, I glance up at the low ceiling which is covered with different brightly colored fabrics strung together. Her large collection of molas is neatly attached with laundry pins to the walls. We're offered plastic seats then are shown her family pictures that are so faded and worn that they're almost unrecognizable.

"You make these better?" Lisa asks Lee.

"I'll try," he answers.

Spending many sweaty hours making small miracles with Photoshop, Lee skillfully recreates hair where it had disappeared in Lisa's faded, crinkled photographs and brings out lines and form in photos washed out almost beyond recognition. Several of the people in her photographs, however, now look like they have black mops on their heads after Lee's heavy-handed doctoring techniques. Removing a man completely from the background of a photo, he instead brings Lisa's beloved parents to life again in her only remaining photo of them.

Lee prints out thirty-eight glossy photos for Lisa, and a stack of business cards. Word quickly spreads in Kuna Yala that we are not only photographers but also a photo and print shop. And free! A couple and their young daughter show up at 7:30 a.m. on our second day anchored off Lisa's island to request that we take photos of them. Running out of paper and printing ink, Lee is forced to say no. Disappointed, they paddle away listlessly. Until we can buy printing supplies in Panama City, Lee will have to turn away many, many more.

"Meet me at the ChiCha hut at 1 p.m.," Lisa instructs us on the second day.

We find her sitting on a large log outside the ChiCha hut with eight young men dressed like American teenage girls and wearing makeup. An albino woman sits next to Lisa. In an earlier conversation, she explained that albino people are able to view an eclipse of the sun or the moon and that God's son protects these special people who never fish or hunt, who must stay inside of the huts most of the time for protection.

Lisa, wearing traditional clothing, is allowed to enter the ChiCha hut, but instead chooses to remain outdoors with her friends. She encourages only Lee to enter the hut. Confused over my role, I perch on the log with Lisa and her buddies.

A line of men, two carrying lanterns and four wearing traditional dance costumes, enter the hut. Following them are six men in Western clothes who carry large gourds filled with fermented chicha. Peeking through the wooden slats of the Congreso hut, I notice that men and women sit segregated from each other on opposite sides of the hut in the dim light where they talk quietly with each other while enveloped in potent clouds of cigarette smoke and chicha fumes. This air of reserve decreases noticeably and quickly as both sexes leave to nip rum in a smaller hut and then return.

A crowd gathers outside. Two men and two women, with exaggerated energy, run out of the large hut holding food wrapped in banana leaves. The men place their food into two holes and then quickly cover them with sand while the women do the same. This is done with great excitement and happiness.

After much observation on my part, my take on this four-day-long mysterious ceremony is the following.

Day one: Party Time!

Day two: People rest and nurse their hangovers.

Day three: Party Day! Yippee!

Day four: The Big Deal. On this day, before a group of family members and friends, the celebrated girl's hair is cut short, after which she's dressed in a dark material that she'll wear for five days. In essence, the family of this girl has paid all the expenses for the food and twenty cases of rum, plus the dancers. In order for a girl to reach the much sought-after seventh heaven, this celebration of puberty must take place. I am honored that Lisa has included both of us in this sacred event. Lee doesn't have the same intimate connection that I have with Lisa and her culture, but he's happy to be included. I'm excited that we can both participate in something so extraordinary.

———

With a group of sailors, we board Lisa's ulu for an adventure to Rio Masargandi, where she leads us along a well-worn path to her parents' burial site. Burial sites can only be visited by outsiders if they're accompanied by a Kuna. When people die in Kuna Yala, they're first wrapped in their sleeping hammock. Then all the relatives sit in a circle around the body for several days, after which they place the body on the ground and cover it with clay soil which is formed into a mound. Following this, a grass roof is built over the body to shield it during the rainy season. Lastly, the relatives place the person's favorite plate and cup along with fresh flowers and woven palm leaves on top of the mound to ward off all evil spirits.

From the burial site, we follow Lisa up a steep mountain trail to a sacred waterfall where, according to legend, a mermaid lives. She informs us that if you jump off the high ledge into the water eight times you'll be healed of whatever ails you because the mermaid works together with the medicine men to heal people. Then pointing to a mountain in the far distance, she says that only the medicine men are allowed to go there.

While everyone swims and dives eight times into the pool below the waterfall, a woman in the group, anxious, tells me she has left her EpiPen in the dugout and wants me to accompany her to Lisa's canoe. Having a good sense of direction, I have the brilliant idea of off-trailing directly to the canoe instead of meandering along the switchbacks. So we scrape our way through the dense, low, tightly packed vegetation— an almost impassable terrain.

On our return, Lisa turns her disbelieving, saucer-sized eyes toward me. "You did what? You went right through jungle?"

She immediately removes her necklace, from which dangles a tiny medicine doll named Igua Yody, and places it around my neck. I wish someone had mentioned that the fer-de-lance snake frequents this area before I went dashing impulsively through the dense jungle. This pit viper is the most dangerous snake in all of Central and South America, and there is no antidote to its fatal bite.

A woman from Lisa's island recently dreamed that a female from Rio Sidra, only in her second month of pregnancy, is carrying a child destined to be a medicine man or medicine woman. This was verified by a medicine man from another island. According to Lisa, who has witnessed this occurrence before, when a woman gives birth to a medicine man or a medicine woman, either she or her husband dies. To prevent this, the local medicine man gives the woman special herbs to drink and potions that she can rub on her body for protection.

There's quite a stir here as this news filters down to everyone. Starting today at 4 p.m., the island will cloaked in silence for eight days. People will remain in their huts, and all dogs will be sent to the mainland or other islands. This is a significant event for the Kuna people. The child will be blessed during a celebration including musicians, dancers, and singers from other islands. They'll perform special ceremonial dances and every year after that, the dancers, singers, and musicians will return. This child, born with wisdom and knowledge, will not attend school. Instead, medicine men from many other islands will teach him or her traditional healing techniques and ceremonies. Unfortunately, having a medicine man or a medicine woman can be very expensive for a family. A single ceremony involving musicians, dancers, and singers can cost at least $1,000, so the people in the community help pay all the expenses.

When a woman is pregnant in Kuna Yala, she receives special herbs from a medicine man who can tell her the child's sex. Specific tonics are given if the child is sideways or feet-first, to help the baby turn. Midwives deliver all babies. When I ask Lisa if women experience complications during childbirth she answers, "No problem!"

In general, the Kunas believe in natural medicine for illness and only go to a hospital if it's absolutely necessary. If people are gravely ill and have to go there for surgery during which they die, they will not go to heaven. Instead, they go to purgatory.

Lisa adds, "The Kuna women no want Western man, Panama man, or Kuna man to see her body." In this culture, only female doctors are allowed to see a woman's body.

Before we leave Rio Sidra, Lisa asks me to be the official photographer of Rio Sidra's matriarchs. Lee also wants to take pictures of these women, but they turn their backs to him and pose only for me. The photographs I take that day sparkle with life, radiating the spirits of these amazing women.

After three weeks without an internet connection, I'm beginning to feel antsy. Every single day, I think of my sons and wonder how they are. Especially Alex, because he's still finding his way in the world. Three weeks soon become five weeks and I become increasingly unhappy over my lack of contact with them. I remind myself, once again, that I chose this life of adventure and, yes, there is a price to be paid. This may seem like a selfish endeavor to the outside world, but at this point in my wanderings, I feel that everything that has transpired was preordained. Especially my connection with Lisa.

24

Searching for Olo Waidili

Two weeks after having the medicine dolls Ina and Mani on board, Lisa pulls alongside in her ulu and joins us for breakfast. "You need offer Ina, Mani food every meal! Even snacks! They eat in spirit world," she says solemnly. "Their spirits leave if you no feed them."

Why didn't she tell me to feed them earlier? They've gone without eating for two weeks now.

"You good people," she reassures me. "Medicine man say it okay you have nuchus."

A week later, Lisa appears with more information about nuchu care. "You need wash them with special leaf from plant on Island Chichime! If you no bathe them . . . Ina, Mani . . . their spirits leave."

Oh no, they've probably bolted by now, I think. However, if they're still hanging out here, what's a good substitute for this plant from Chichime?

As if she had read my thoughts, Lisa points to the basil plant in the salon window. "This good! Nuchus like this. No soap in water, though."

Trying not to sound glib, I ask, "Are Ina and Mani still here?" Lisa promptly picks them up to evaluate their weight then says, "If light, no spirit. If heavy, spirit intact." Followed by, "They still here! Mani visit spirit friends other night Rio Sidra. He back now."

I don't ask, but I'm assuming that Mani just needed some space or wanted to visit a girlfriend, or perhaps wanted to kick up his wooden heels. I wonder what will happen when we go to the US for a visit. Do they go with us? What do we do in restaurants? Do we place them next to us? Is there an extra restaurant charge for nuchus? Or do we hire a nuchu sitter? But can we trust a sitter? What if the caregiver forgets to bathe them? When I mention these concerns, rather facetiously, to a sailor with zero sense of humor, she says, "Wendy, you need to see a psychiatrist."

Lisa shows me how to bathe the dolls in water infused with basil leaves. She washes Ina and Mani lovingly then pats them dry with a clean dishcloth. While she does this, her assistant Alencia is sent off to the island of Chichime to find the plant used for medicine doll bathing. Having no soil on board, I place the four-foot-high plant with intact roots into a bucket of water. When the leaves fall off, I'll store them in a Ziploc bag in the refrigerator.

A few days later, I casually mention to Lisa that we offer Ina and Mani rum at our sunset happy hour. Horrified, she says primly, "Noooo! Rum no good nuchus! Nuchu drink chicha only!"

But how do I make fermented sugar cane juice? In a large iron pot hung over a fire. Then, days later, I'll have to pour it into a large ceramic jug for the lengthy fermentation process. And I'll need to spit into it from time to time.

The dream life of the Kuna is a very important medium through which they receive messages from the spirit world. One afternoon while we're relaxing in the cockpit, Lisa mentions, "You dream of men in white, they medicine dolls. They no wear color. They wear white like angels. Sometimes they show people what heaven is like. They often visit in dreams. A woman on Rio Sidra dreamed about three men in a canoe. Bad spirits. A problem. She see men transform into devil animal. Maybe people who die in accident. Sometimes you see spirits when cooking. Sometimes they go into bedroom. Ina, Mani, they protect you."

The medicine men in Kuna Yala receive prophecies, knowings, and messages by smoking a special pipe and then going into a trance where they connect with the medicine dolls. These insights are shared at the village's weekly meetings, which we are invited to attend. When I ask Lisa how I can get messages from Ina and Mani, she gives me the following directions: Arrange to use a Kuna hut for five days. Bring a good supply of water, a hammock, and wood or coconut husks for the fire. Fast for five days, drinking only water or chicha. Ina and Mani will introduce themselves to you and will, from then on, bring messages to you from the spirit world.

Whenever I make mistakes with them, Lisa shows up in her ulu to let me know. She mentions that Ina and Mani come to her regularly in her dream state to tell her what I do wrong or what they need from me. Once in a while, Lisa picks them up to see if they weigh the same.

Out of deep respect for Lisa and her culture, I take care of the nuchus every single day, regardless of outside circumstances or other people's opinions of me. It has recently occurred to me, however, that now not only do I have to worry about my relationship with Lee, but I also have to worry about my relationship with the two medicine dolls.

———

It's 5 a.m., and I'm boarding a skiff for a three-day provisioning trip to Panama City. Lee stays behind to take care of Mani and Ina. From the very start of this trip, I have an odd feeling that I'm not alone.

The boat plows smoothly and steadily through the water while I squirm on a hard wooden bench, wishing I had a soft cushion. The young, handsome son of a local Indian chief drives the skiff, stopping periodically alongside other sailboats to pick up gringos. We're left at a long weathered dock where we're directed to the Carti airport, a one-story concrete structure with a cob floor, which is made from hard clay. After paying a $2 entrance fee, we mingle with Kuna women dressed in their national costume. I marvel over how exotic and magical my life has become and pinch myself to make sure this isn't just a dream. Outside, a row of women sitting on a long wooden bench swatting sandflies make room for me while smiling and staring at me with curiosity.

I'm pointed toward a mud-splattered and rusted white Land Cruiser that has a mountain of wicker baskets and packages tied to the roof rack. Alberto, our driver, heads down the defunct runway then onto a dirt road where we sway and jostle through the dense jungle until we come to a river bank where several jeeps wait in line to cross. Our overloaded jeep heaves and sways as it edges down a steep red mud embankment into a swiftly moving river that seeps into the jeep as we make our way across. Forgetting to lift up my shoes and my purse, cold brown water soaks both.

One and a half hours later, at the Kuna territory checkpoint, a man in military fatigues looks at my passport and then nods okay to the driver. I need a bathroom visit, but realize there'll be no stopping for another two hours. Since I'm the only gringo in the jeep, I feel shy about asking.

The Panamanian landscape reminds me of the green, rolling hills of southern Virginia. It's just more compressed, more contained. The last mountain we climbed had a view of the Kuna Yala Islands from the summit and Alberto stopped momentarily so I could take a picture. I desperately wanted to say, "Un momento, necesario me encuentro baño" but didn't after Alberto honked impatiently to hurry me along.

After driving through vast fields of reeds swaying in the wind against the backdrop of green rolling hills, the jeep, now empty, stops at Alberto's hilltop house. His wife is sweeping the front entrance with a straw broom. This airy, multiwindowed cottage is nestled in a rambling garden overflowing with tropical plants. A rooster with bright red feathers prances about as if he is a direct descendent of nobility. The cottage is practically empty except for one tired beige sofa and a rickety rattan table. Madonna statues grace the whitewashed window sills and ledges.

I feel like a highly esteemed guest when Alberto's wife serves me delicious roasted chicken and white rice covered in a savory sauce. As I *ooh* and *ahh* over every photo ever taken of his family, Alberto points to the rooster as it struts past the open door. "You just ate his brother!"

Hours go by. We move to the wooden rocking chairs on the front porch, where Alberto's many friends stop by to meet me. Totally clueless about what's going on but not wanting to break the spell, I'm wondering if I'll ever make it to the city. Alberto indicates it's time to leave. Feeling a little relieved, I lovingly hug him, his two kids, and his wife.

I double-check my seatbelt as Alberto speeds down hills that are nearly vertical. As the land flattens out, I have a panoramic view of Panama City in the distance. At the time-worn and rather ugly Hotel Marpariso, I give Alberto an extra big tip and a hug, then drag my overnight bag to my cheerless dull green room where I'm greeted by a supersized cockroach who motors past into a secret hiding place. In the tiny bathroom, a weary face stares back at me from the small red plastic wall mirror, and I wonder how I'll survive this awful place. There's not even a cell phone charging outlet, which presents another challenge. And yet, as I stand there observing my disappointing new digs and listening to a loud car honking from the street below, I suddenly have a very strong feeling that I'm not alone. There is a strong presence in the room.

The main reason for my visit to Panama City is to be checked by a famous orthopedic surgeon in the sports medicine section of the Pacifica Hospital. My right leg has been hurting when I walk. Five X-rays later, the Kuna radiologist shakes his head knowingly but says nothing. The doctor gives me a painful shot into my right hip, moves my leg in and out, and then puts it into multiple positions while I wince with pain. Diagnosis: arthritis, a groin strain, a possible tear. And hip replacement surgery down the road.

My direct debit Visa card is declined when I try to obtain cash for grocery shopping in the city's large American-style grocery stores and for future living expenses in San Blas. Amazingly, we lived on $200 last month by eating lobsters, fish, and crabs caught by the local fishermen, plus canned and dried food from our provisions. We desperately need cash, since there have been no ATMs on the islands we've visited so far. And after paying Alberto $80, I'm now down to $20.

Put on hold for long periods of time, I'm forced to listen to chirpy elevator music while waiting to talk to a customer representative at my US bank. After ten futile calls from a pay phone, I move my phoning operation to the mezzanine of the lovely Marriott Hotel, where I can recharge my phone while settled in a large, comfortable chair. My outlook suddenly becomes much more positive during the fifteen-minute wait to talk to a living person. A kind-hearted person answers and agrees to wire $1,000 in emergency funds to the US Embassy.

Roger, the former manager of the now defunct Panama Yacht Club, picks me up for a day of gathering together boat parts for Lee. I've been told this guy knows all the marina stores in Panama City and can locate any boat part we need.

After Roger demonstrates a convoluted trick to opening the passenger side door of his small beat-up white car, we speed away, dashboard Panamanian flags aflutter in the breeze from my open window.

Roger wonders, "Does the fan molest you?"

Laughing exuberantly, I explain the meaning of the word molest. Later he says, "The rain is having a war with the sun, and the sun is winning!"

Five enjoyable hours later, everything is checked off Lee's list, and I'm ready to return to the boat.

Upon my return to the boat with cash, five bags of groceries, and boat parts, Lisa appears in her dugout. Wearing stomped-down shoes, faded jeans, a feminine pink cotton top, and dangly earrings, she reports, "Lee no feed Ina,

Mani! Lee no bathe them! They no want to be on boat with Lee. They follow you Panama City!"

One afternoon, Lisa brings us a hand-carved wooden ulu decorated with what look like miniature Tibetan prayer flags from bow to stern.

"Nuchus need boat! Visit other spirits! They no go across ocean to visit other spirits without boat!"

Will they need a car next? I wonder.

A few days later she swings by again.

"Ina, Mani need female nuchu! Not for sex! For companionship."

"Where can I find one?" I ask, hoping she'll give me one of hers.

"You go islands Kuna Yala and find one. You be okay. No worry, Wendy," Lisa answers in her comforting way.

I suspect that Mani and Ina have been visiting spirit friends in Rio Sidra a little too often and probably need the calming, grounding influence of a female nuchu.

As we sail into the beautiful and remote Snug Harbor, Lee decides that this is the place where I will find a female nuchu. Our friend Arvid, a handsome and energetic young father of three who lives on the island of Playón Chico nearby, offers to help me find a female nuchu with a living spirit on his island.

Arvid, wearing the navy blue cap Lee gave him, picks me up for the ten-minute dinghy ride to Playón Chico. I've been instructed by Lisa to take Ina and Mani with me and I carry them in a cloth shoulder bag. Just as we pull up to Arvid's hut, almost hidden behind a row of coconut palms, three of his kids scamper along the dock yelling, "Wendy, Wendy, Wendy!"

Arvid's three-year-old daughter proudly shows me her plump blond-haired baby doll with pink mud-smeared cheeks. When we visited this bay four weeks ago, Lee and I spent hours teaching English words to Arvid, including numbers. At that time, we gave him two pairs of sunglasses to protect his eyes while fishing, fish hooks, weights, a fishing line, an English/Spanish dictionary, food for his family, and clothing for the kids. Arvid gave us his wife's freshly baked bread, newly picked fragrant limes, plantains, coconuts, and sweet-smelling leaves for Mani and Ina's baths.

This time, I'm treated as the guest of honor and offered a child-sized red plastic chair that's placed in the middle of a half-circle of fifteen family members who seem to be mesmerized by me. I'm the odd curly-haired gringo wearing black sunglasses, a wide-brimmed sailor's hat, shorts, a T-shirt, and sandals.

Feeling like the bearded lady in a freak show, my nose starts to itch. Excessively. While I discreetly scratch it, they watch me as if they have never seen anyone do this before. I try unsuccessfully to redirect all fifteen pairs of dark brown almond-shaped eyes to the baby boy whose black hair sticks straight up and who is wearing Arvid's large fishing glasses.

Arvid's teenage son approaches me. "How old are you?"

Like a seasoned politician trying to deflect a question, I answer, "You speak such good English!"

Undaunted, he asks my age again.

"Oh, you really don't want to know!" I answer, remembering Oscar Wilde's quote about how you should never trust a woman who tells you her age.

Arvid's father-in-law, smiling toothlessly except for two upper teeth, exclaims, "You nice person!"

Exquisitely moved by his kind remark, I smile up at him from my little red chair.

Arvid gives me a hand-carved wooden dog that looks

like an anteater, and then his wife brings me a suspiciously muddy-looking, watered-down cocoa drink in a faded blue plastic cup. Then she sits down on a stump in front of me and, placing my right foot on her knee, wraps a rust orange and black beaded bracelet above my ankle until it becomes a wide anklet. Assuming that I'm married, she wants to make me legit by drawing a line of henna down the bridge of my nose and piercing my nose with a small gold ring. Thankfully, a commotion in a nearby hut commands everyone's attention, and I quietly pour my drink into a clump of weeds and stand up to go.

Before leaving on our nuchu hunt, I present Arvid and his family with a five-pound bag of rice, several bags of dried beans, five bars of soap, a set of twin sheets, crayons, marking pens, a small notebook, baby shampoo, reading glasses, two rugs, and a towel. Arvid's wife, in the meantime, has painted Ina and Mani's cheeks orange-red from a special fruit found only in the mountains of Panama. Gently, I return them to my bag.

We take off on foot and visit almost every hut in Arvid's community. Stooping low as we enter each dwelling, the women dressed in simple cotton sarongs arise from resting in their hammocks in the soft light, or they stop stirring fish stew simmering in large iron pots balanced over fires that smell of autumn, or they put down the molas they're currently working on. The female nuchus I'm presented with are either too small or too big, or they're made from inferior balsa wood. Or worse, they're termite-ridden. Oddly, no one seems to wonder why a gringo is looking for a female nuchu, and everyone knows Ina and Mani's last names.

I'm enjoying this whole process of looking for the right female nuchu companion for Ina and Mani, and I am honored to meet these women in their homes. Some of the huts look very sturdy and erect while others look as if they could easily be pushed over. A few entrances have wooden doors. One hut has a sign that says "Do Not Enter!" It's here that I find a sweet-smelling newborn puppy with a huge belly and paws that smell of Fritos. Outside once again, a crowd of young boys of varying sizes line up for a photo. They love to see their image on my digital camera.

These women have such a powerful presence that I forget how tiny they are. They all want to help me to find the perfect female nuchu. Language isn't necessary. Our spirits converge as I absorb all the sounds, smells, and colors of each hut I enter.

Arvid and I end up where I wanted to be all along: at the medicine man's hut. His wife and two daughters hover invisibly in the background as we enter. Several beat-up aluminum cooking pots hang from the ceiling, and a tiny wooden shelf holds a stack of six plastic plates. Furry coconut husks, split in half, lay in a small pile on the hard-packed earthen floor. Snappers, brushed with coconut oil, are being grilled slowly over smoldering coconut husks while a delicious-smelling banana and fish porridge bubbles in a large iron pot. A colorful rooster struts past me followed by two hens, while an ant wanders by carrying a piece of green leaf on its back. I move my foot out of its way. I wrap my pink bandana around my neck as sweat drips down my chest.

The medicine man wears a 1950s-style hat, and his hairless chest is bare. His lower torso is wrapped in a thin blue-and-white-striped towel. He invites me to sit in a small white plastic chair while he and his wife and two daughters round up their female nuchus. Arvid reminds the medicine man, *"Espiritus vivande muoy importante!"* I lift Ina and

Mani from their bag and hand them to the medicine man who studies them for a minute and then says, "Ina, Mani living spirits!"

After viewing a parade of nuchus, I pick one that's visually and cosmetically pleasing, but the medicine man disapproves because it's not on the same level as Ina and Mani. He and his family decide that Olo Waidili, who has a nunlike air, will be the most compatible with Ina and Mani. Olo is a heavy, dark doll about ten inches tall with a prominent nose, deep hooded eyes, and a headdress like a nun's. She will definitely keep Mani and Ina in line—not to mention Lee and me.

"¿Cuánto cuesta?" I ask.

"Veinte dólares," the medicine man answers.

Not wishing to haggle with the most respected man in the village, I hand over a twenty dollar bill. As I do this the whole family lets out an *ahhhh* as if they're startled that someone would actually pay that for one of their nuchus.

On our way back to the boat, we stop for a quick visit with Arvid's wife. I ask her to tell me where she got the cream she put on Ina and Mani's cheeks, and she shows me an oval beige fruit the size of a walnut covered with small soft spikes. She opens it by pressing hard and inside is a sectioned interior lined with small orange balls. She takes one and squeezes it onto her finger. It has the consistency of a creamy blush, and she applies it to my face.

During the night, I dream that I swim around the boat several times naked, becoming one with rain drops on the water which I realize are tears. The gentle flow of the water pushes me to the end of the boat. It's luxurious being there in the union of fresh rainwater with the salty sea. I'm the secret mermaid of Snug Harbor, and I swish my tail and merge with the elements. Then I drag my long, heavy tail onto the rear steps, where I rinse off the salty water. As I sit there, the knowledge comes into my heart that Olo wants me to recover the lost goddess inside of me. Not only that, but she also wants me to connect with the little girl inside of me, the girl who played by herself in a gentle gurgling magical brook near my childhood home. It may sound weird, but I totally understand the connection that the Kuna have to their medicine dolls. For me, Ina and Mani are this silent but powerful presence on the boat. I don't know what it is, but I sense this power all around them. And when I eventually leave the sailing life, Ina and Mani will be constant reminders of my friend Lisa.

25

Sapzurro

Our Panama visas are expiring soon, so we'll need to sign out of the country, check into Colombia, sign out of it five minutes later, and then return to Panama. Sapzurro is a popular and relatively easy visa fix among international sailors. The name alone makes me want to visit the place because my imagination conjures up an exotic, moonlike, and barren landscape like Iceland's, or perhaps a South American version of Timbuktu.

We enter a tiny yet dramatic bay encircled by a pristine white sandy beach. The coconut palms lining the shore stand guard against the relentless pounding surf. This outpost sits at the base of cloud-cloaked mountains that rise tall and straight from the turbulent deep grey sea off the Colombian coast. Along the bay's western end, modest tin-roofed one- or two-story pastel-colored concrete cottages stretch along the shoreline. The 270 inhabitants of Sapzurro, mostly descendants of African slaves who were brought here by Spanish colonizers, have been joined over the years by a handful of American expats and Europeans.

There are only ten monohulls here in the anchorage, and all are stern-tied to palm trees. Like motorized rocking chairs they bob up and down in the harsh and unrelenting rolling surf. Our boat sways side to side, as catamarans do in conditions like this. Hopefully, we'll be able to tolerate this for our quick overnight.

This rather forlorn frontier town is carved out of an uninhabitable wild landscape. Feeling vaguely unsettled, we head into town, where we meet a heavyset bearded French baker wearing an inside-out faded blue polo shirt that stretches tautly over his belly. His stubby fingers point out a house for sale on a piece of land overlooking the bay. "That's a good buy! A great place to live!" he insists.

Out of politeness, Lee acts interested as I strain to hear their conversation over the sounds of a generator nearby and the pounding surf. Continuing, the Frenchman says, "That house has radar for the purpose of tracking the movement of the FARC. It helps the owners sleep better at night."

I already have insomnia; why would I want to add even more to my life? He goes on as if the radar was a major selling point. "Sapzurro was a stronghold of the FARC until 2004, when it was cleaned up. However, they're still in the area. But, if you mind your own business and go about your normal life, the FARC will leave you alone."

FARC stands for Fuerza Alternativa Revolucionaria del Común, also known as the People's Army. Formed during the Cold War, this guerrilla movement became involved in the Colombian armed conflict from 1964 to 2017. Eventually forced by the Colombian government to leave the territories it had seized, the FARC relocated to Colombia's jungles and mountains. They are recognized as a terrorist organization by most nations.

Parrots and birds chatter loudly under the pearl-grey sky as we clamber onto a skiff at 8 a.m. the next morning for the fifty-five-minute ride to the immigration office in Puerto Obaldía. Lee and I are both dazed from lack of sleep. This rural Panamanian community situated close to Colombia's border is where sailors prefer to check out of Panama. We briefly considered hiking the trail over the mountains to this port until we heard rumors of the FARC's presence on the steep mountainsides. Our guidebooks offer conflicting and confusing advice on the prudence or imprudence of taking these trails.

Joey, our young Colombian driver, is mustached and quite handsome in his bright red-and-white-striped polo shirt. He asks if we're prepared for a rough, wet trip. Wearing rain jackets and quick-dry expedition pants, our day packs enclosed in extra-large Ziplocs, Lee and I are ready for almost anything.

Within seconds, my teeth want to fly out of my mouth. The traditional, open boat shoots upward over a large wave and then bangs down hard into the dip. Eyeballs bulging, I inch my way to the stern to sit next to Joey, who seems to be having a whole different and far less jarring experience. I'm immediately directed back to my seat, which is taking the brunt of the choppy seas. Warm soothing water sprinkles over me intermittently between each cresting wave, and as we slam hard into the seemingly endless procession of large rollers, I yell out, "Shit! Fuck!"

There's no cushion on the hard wooden seat, and my abused bum throbs in discomfort. The only way to survive this ordeal, I realize, is to close my eyes and recall a vision I had in my early twenties. In this vision, I was floating down a river on my back, letting myself go with the flow, allowing it to take me wherever it wanted to take me. As I picture myself drifting down a river, my body starts to relax a little, and the waves and the hard pounding seem to soften.

The village of Obaldía is heavily guarded by stern military men wearing fatigues and carrying AK-47s. We check in with a haughty military man sitting behind a makeshift desk. Pursing his lips, he studies our passports for a few moments, then disdainfully hands them over to another soldier, who questions us with an air of superiority. Lee and I morph into our innocent, never-committed-a-crime-*ever* routine. Quickly removing his camera from the backpack, Lee photographs this handsome, square-jawed man. "Put that camera down! No pictures allowed!"

I'm stunned by his reaction.

Then, walking over to Lee, he demands to see his camera. Not concerned about what he'll find, we're more concerned that our favorite photographs will be erased accidentally. Thirty minutes later, the official matter-of-factly returns the camera without uttering a word. Lee speculates later that they were afraid we'd hand over the pictures to subversives, who would be able to see who's guarding the town.

In the next building, we meet with a Brylcreemed immigration official wearing a traditional Panamanian embroidered white shirt.

"Why didn't you bring your boat here? You left it in Colombia, and you're not even checked in there. How dare you! What you're doing is highly illegal. The Colombians could seize your boat if they wanted to!"

Shifting uncomfortably in my seat, feeling shameful, I glance down at my saltwater-infused pants, sandals, and raisin-like toes, and then back up at Lee to see how he's planning to handle this angry outburst.

"We were told by sailors who have checked out here that this anchorage is untenable and that Sapzurro is the only viable anchorage," Lee responds calmly. "If we had known how nice it is here, we would have anchored in your beautiful harbor."

The official continues scolding as he sullenly hands our passports to an official who puts two stamps in each passport.

Obaldía's one and only restaurant reeks of rotting fish and Lysol. Sitting outdoors at a red plastic table with matching chairs, my appetite vanishes as flies swarm over my fried fish. Lee and Joey, oblivious, continue eating while I leave on a futile search to see if there's anything redeemable about Obaldía.

After lunch, Joey motors straight to Capurganá, where we can check into and out of Colombia in one go. On our approach to this small fishing port, the town dock is teeming with activity. Hundreds of cases of beer are being unloaded from a rust bucket Colombian supply boat and then reloaded onto donkeys, the only mode of transportation here. Simultaneously, hundreds of cases of empty beer bottles are being loaded onto the boat, which sits alarmingly low in the water, almost level with the port holes.

In the middle of the town square that's mostly dirt, a horse chews lazily on a sparse clump of grass as roosters and chickens strut about, clucking and crowing. In this charmless place, my goal is to find the beauty amongst the squalor. I *ooh* and *ahh* over anything half attractive. A small flower bush. A young child. Even the sad-eyed brown dog lounging under a tree. As we wander toward a bright green parakeet perched on the seat of a red bike, a young boy, school bag slung over one shoulder, walks over to the bird, picks it up, and hands it to me. It was a magical moment for me.

Sticky and uncomfortable from the dried salt water on our skin, we amble along the muddy walkways until we locate the immigration office, where we check in and out.

Back at our anchorage, we swim vertically as if we're riding stationary bikes. This bay has both a strong current toward land and a strong undertow out to sea. Dripping wet, we head up a path toward what we hope will be a waterfall. A caramel-colored dog we call Perro joins us and soulfully leads us on an interesting journey—just not to the waterfall. Overriding Perro's assistance, we find a curvy path flanked by banana plants and sweet-smelling orange trees leading up the mountainside to a gorgeous waterfall cascading down the rocky hillside. As we do at every water-fall we visit, Lee and I baptize ourselves three times while Perro, curious, head tilted sideways, ears cocked, watches from the edge of the pool.

Early the next morning, we sail past the dramatic main-land of Panama and numerous wild and deserted craggy islands that resemble pointy drip castles. Perme, one of the most eastward and remote islands in the San Blas archi-pelago, appears mysteriously in the ghostly grey mist and welcomes us with torrential rain that pummels the boat.

The anchor slipping, we nearly crash into the decayed pilings of a dismantled old dock and I have to reanchor the boat as frigid rain drips down my neck and underneath my jacket. In this part of the Caribbean, winter howls loudly. I'm beginning to wish I was somewhere else.

At the break of dawn, we're standing alongside a short runway, watching a pilot bank low over El Porvenir, one of the more modern islands in Kuna Yala. He makes a sharp 180-degree turn and then heads over to where we stand among a group of tourists, all of whom flee from the swirling blades. Then, in a quick Harrison Ford maneuver, he turns the plane sideways to us. Our two dazed charter guests from Switzerland step off the plane as the blades come to a stop.

Hans Peter, a Mickey Mouse lookalike, and his wife Esther join us for a snorkel around a wreck about forty feet off of Dog Island. The pale aqua water blends with the sky. It's soon apparent that Hans Peter isn't used to swimming, so Lee places him on top of three water noodles and has him dip his face into the water while he paddles about. According to Esther, this is his very first time to swim in the ocean. Once in a while, losing his confidence, he flails his arms about until Lee calms him down by holding his hand.

I feel for him. For his fear. Suddenly he's like a child in a man's body, and I want to give him a big hug. I'm a little surprised that he can't swim because Holland's coastline is situated on the North Sea. The Dutch people I've met learned to swim at an early age.

———

Lisa and I have one last discussion before I leave Kuna Yala. "I ready to die. I say to our gods, 'You take me whenever you want.' I not afraid. I make many beautiful molas and meet many sailors. I work hard. I feel tired. I ready to see heaven. When God tell me, no more mola, no more sell gringos, no more work, I say, 'Okay, God, I come!'"

She explains that in her culture, the Kuna don't hold on to life the way we do in the West. They go gracefully when their time is up. It's a normal part of the life cycle. If someone dies in an accident like a gunshot wound, they don't go to heaven. However, if it's a natural accident—for instance, if you're hit by lightning—you go to heaven.

While discussing my coming departure from Kuna Yala, Lisa says, "Ina, Mani sad leaving Rio Sidra. But, it's okay. Ina, Mani new life! See new things! You show Ina, Mani new places!" Lisa points with two fingers at her eyes and then outward. "Ina, Mani see world! You invite them travel!" That's a tall order—and expensive. But I think I can do it.

Before we leave, Lisa gives me a Kuna bracelet. This one is yellow and orange. She says, "You no find this Panama City! Very rare! They no make this type now. My grandmother wear this, then my mother." I'm told to wear it on my left wrist. *Maybe the universe is telling me to relax on the time thing*, I think as I put my watch away. I hand wash the molas that smell of Kuna huts and fire and earth. These smells are now washed away forever. I've saved one, though, so that my grandchildren can smell the pungent odors as I tell them stories about the people of the San Blas Islands.

As we prepare to sail to the Cayman Islands, Lee looks at me in the large mirror in the captain's head and stares.

"How old are you right now?" he demands.

What? I wonder.

"Psychologically, I feel younger. A lot of my friends back home are ten years younger than me. Maybe it's my outlook on life. But physically, I feel my age. I have some aches and pains like a lot of people my age. But, I don't let that stop me. The most important thing is to maintain mobility. The Scandinavians are my role models because they never stop walking, and it keeps them flexible. I've been hiking trails since I was twelve years old, and I plan to do that for the rest of my life."

His eyes take in every detail while I wonder what's going on. "Look at your face. You'll never look as good as you look right now."

As I study my reflection, I agree. "Yes, of course, I'm growing older by the minute, and the wrinkles will deepen as my skin loses elasticity. But isn't it really about how a person feels? I have more energy and more zest for life than when I was younger. And anyway, why are you asking me that question?"

He looks down for a few seconds then mutters, "I was just wondering if you're a little delusional?"

"Hey, I hate to break up this scintillating discussion, but to be perfectly honest, I'd rather be swimming in the ocean. See ya later, alligator!"

As I walk away from Lee, I recognize that I've become more willful. I wonder if Lee will like this free-willed, self-assured person. It really doesn't matter, though, because I'm evolving, and I'm loving it. It's his problem if he has a negative reaction.

26

Colombia

I'm dreading the passage to Cartagena. Heavy rains have washed massive logs from Panama's rivers into the sea, and unfortunately, they're invisible in the darkness of night. Just as we're heading out, another sailor warns the sailing community on the VHF radio that undergoing a passage to Colombia from Panama is not a good idea and that we'd be wise to tuck in somewhere.

High winds and furious seas await us. We're passaging at the tail end of the period when you can safely sail eastward. The Christmas trades are howling with their steady northeast blow, which means wind on the nose. Add to that eight-foot waves and mounting seas. Anticipating that cooking will be difficult, I prepare split pea soup and cornbread for our grueling thirty-hour passage. Halfway to Cartagena, we hear an announcement on the SSB that a sailboat has struck a partially submerged container and is currently sinking off the Colombian coastline. Containers that go overboard are a big threat to sailors because they're impossible to detect as they bob about just below the ocean's surface. A flotilla of sailors, our friends, are trying to locate survivors in the rough seas and near-gale-force winds. After hours of searching, they locate the life raft and all the survivors.

Now closing in on the White City, we take the longer and more scenic route, sailing past dozens of sailboats tied to moorings, along beaches with thatched roof palapas, and fishermen who don't glance up as we silently glide nearby. A ship's captain suddenly hails us on the VHF to see where the hell we're headed. Horrified to see that we're on a collision course and wondering what happened to our brains, Lee radically alters our bearing.

These are some topics listed in the table of contents of my Colombian travel guide: cocaine; bandits; FARC; ELN, short for the National Liberation Party; *boleteo*, the guerrilla practice of taxing landowners in exchange for leaving them in peace; *burro*, a witch doctor or shaman; *burundanga*, a drug extracted from a plant that's used by thieves to render victims unconscious; and *desechables*, the "disposables" who are the homeless, the beggars, the street urchins, and the prostitutes. All of them are the objects of social cleansing by death squads called the "cleaners." The list goes on.

My skin glistens with sweat in the sticky tropical heat as I help Lee install mosquito nets on all the windows under the relentless sun. We're anchored off Club Nautico in downtown Cartagena, a small struggling marina that was once a viable and lively place with a bar, a restaurant, a social events calendar, and clean bathrooms. Rats have now made their home in the rubble.

Not wanting to have a tetanus shot, I'm obsessed with avoiding the rusty nails that protrude from the pier's warped boards. In the late afternoons, we brave happy hour amidst concrete debris. Sailors, still hungover from last night's binge, guzzle beer while remaining oblivious to the puddles of filthy runoff expanding around their sandals. An ashen-faced woman with dark hair named Candelaria is the owner of the marina. She spends most of the day staring blankly into the distance while sitting on a tired plastic chair perched in front of her office. Morose relatives occasionally sit with her.

Lee is currently having issues with communication, and I wonder if the universe is trying to tell him something. His computer was recently repaired by Felipe in the San Blas Islands, who set up Lee's Vista program in Spanish, a language he doesn't speak. All of Lee's cell phones have ended up in the ocean. The costly navigation charts are screwed up, and the Global Star phone doesn't work. Ironically, he always wants to teach communication skills to people on our charters. Yesterday, after the taxi dropped us at the marina and then sped off, Lee exclaimed, "Where's my wallet?"

The Colombian girls, stunningly beautiful, wear tight dresses and high heels. They sashay past in clouds of perfume as we wander about the city. Lee, fully engaged in the spectacle, insists on walking behind me. We're like two disconnected free-floating entities. Feeling jealous and insecure, I glance back to see his big, sexy, come-hither smile. So I wink and flirt with every single man I pass. Most of them flirt back.

At 3 a.m., a Chinese junk sporting pirate flags stops motoring back and forth in the anchorage while shooting off fireworks and playing loud salsa music. The noise of a nearby dinghy jostling about in the water, the gurgling sound in the port head, the faraway puttering of a motorboat, and the gentle rocking of our boat in the tiny baby waves lulls me to sleep.

We are now living on South American time, staying up with the moon and the constellations and sleeping late until we're jerked to attention by the disembodied voices on the morning net. The morning net (also called VHF) is a radio network that sailors use to communicate with each other.

Today, someone says on the VHF, "Sailing vessel *Patience*, sailing vessel *Patience*! This is sailing vessel *Jupiter Smile*!"

The *Patience* answers with, "Down one."

Everyone in the anchorage follows. That channel is unfortunately occupied by loud-voiced Colombian men. "Go to channel seventy-two."

So we all go to the same channel where two female sailors are discussing how to cook a lobster. "So you pull off the torso and toss it into the sea and then cook the tail? Right?"

Followed by a voice breaking in, "Does anyone know where I can buy mango chutney?"

Then, "Has anyone found a left black sandal?"

"Is anyone heading back to Panama? I need a ride."

This is the lifeline for the sailing community.

Every morning there's a roll call, and usually, twenty-five boats out of the hundred and fifty or so anchored here check in, although all the other boats are actually listening in. Estimating that there are at least two people per boat, I would guess that approximately three hundred people are paying attention.

The following morning, we turn on the net to hear the latest news and the introductions of each sailboat. As soon as there's a pause, I grab the VHF and announce, "Good morning, sailors! This is sailing vessel *Worldwide Traveler* checking in."

Suzie, the gaudiest flower in the anchorage, trumpets her horn this morning on the net in her typical peacock fashion.

How would we get along without Suzie? This morning she announces, "In the wee hours of the morning, I heard what sounded like a container being dropped onto our boat . . . or a hacksaw cutting through our dinghy chain . . . so I ran upstairs naked and saw a French boat that had drifted into our boat. Its owner didn't even apologize! Or say that I have nice boobs!" I love Suzie. She's always so entertaining.

We have a new English friend named Julian, who owns the *Tropicbird*. A storm of unruly sun-bleached hair and ruddy skin, he has untamable bushy eyebrows that move up and down when he speaks. Talking to him is like trying to communicate with a cat whose attention is captured by the next shiny thing.

Julian has an internal radar for knowing when we're immersed in boat projects. Whatever we're involved in is quickly aborted because he has a way of getting us off track. This morning, jolted by his sudden presence in the galley, I nervously dump my French press coffee into the sink instead of my mug. Deciding that I need a "healing," he seamlessly goes from placing his hands on my back to placing them on my head, then rapidly bends down and plants both hands across my feet to "ground" me.

He suggests that a group of us head to El Centro for some people-watching at Fidels. Julian introduces two chatty middle-aged English widows who have just chartered *Tropicbird* for a passage to Panama. Do the ladies know what they're getting into? That's a wild and wooly passage.

Mildred, plump with a softly wrinkled pink face and a heavy Cockney accent, ends each sentence with a charming yet irritating little cockatiel-like whistle. Dorothy, also plump and slightly wrinkled, has finer features. She escapes behind her oversized '60s-style glasses that magnify her chestnut brown eyes and her penciled-in black eyebrows. Sporting a pot-belly held up precariously by two birdlike legs, her bright red frizzy hair is her crowning glory. I chuckle to myself and decide that they're perfect for Julian. They'll give him a run for his money. Suddenly feeling tired, Lee and I finally release them all to the vapors of the Cartagena night and dinghy back to the tranquility of our boat.

Watching the *Tropicbird* fade into the distance, I breathe a deep sigh of relief. Days later we hear on the VHF net that Julian hit nasty weather along the way. There was major structural damage to the boat, but luckily everyone survived.

The dinghy is currently deflating due to a small rip in front. Duct tape can only do so much. I'm embarrassed to go anywhere in something resembling a giant grey bedroom slipper. Sensing my embarrassment, Lee purposely sends me out on missions. Shamefully pulling alongside nicely inflated dinghies, I feel like my twelve-year-old self suddenly—a shy, self-conscious girl forced to wear nerdy clothing picked out by her mother at B. Altman and Company.

Late one afternoon, I stop by the marina's office to pick up our washed and folded laundry. A hawk-faced woman in black pants, a taupe blouse, and patent leather heels stands in the middle of the room, speaking loudly in Spanish. Facing her is a contrite man who looks to be around thirty. Candelaria hovers in the background. Everyone seems to be in a trance, and, slowly realizing that an actual exorcism is underway, I quietly fade into the background and edge myself inaudibly into a seat.

Candelaria holds a lit candle over the man's head while the other woman continues reading from the Bible while stomping her foot forcefully. Candelaria and the man also stomp their feet. Half an hour later, the woman abruptly stops the ritual and looks over at me. "Do you need something?"

I pick up the laundry and skitter out the door.

———

In early October 2010, I fly to the States for a three-week visit with my sons. While kayaking in Maine with my eldest beneath a canopy of red and golden leaves, he stops rowing and turns to me. "So, Mom, how long will you be the flavor of the week in Lee's world?"

Thomas has a way of getting to the truth quickly.

Offended, I snap back defensively, "He actually really loves me. I'm much more than just the flavor of the week!" As I'm uttering these words, I immediately want to retract them because they don't ring true.

"Thomas, I'd like to rephrase that last sentence . . . that's an old tape. I'm beginning to rethink this whole thing with Lee. I'd like to believe that everything is wonderful in our relationship, but we've been having issues for a while. His shenanigans are annoying, and I'm getting tired of having to lend him money. I'm not sure how much longer I'll stay on the boat."

That conversation with Thomas gives me the nudge I needed to rethink everything. I decide to be even more watchful of him on my return to Cartagena. Just before I left for the States, a male friend gave me an unsettling warning. "I'd keep that man on a tight leash if I were you!"

Just days before my return, Lee emails that he's not sure if he'll be able to pick me up at the airport because he's down to his last Colombian peso. *What's new?* I think. He's there, however, waiting for me outside of Arrivals with his big goofy grin. Then he pulls me to him in a hug. "I wasn't sure if you would return to me!"

"Why did you say that? I'd never leave you in the lurch. What were you thinking? I missed your wonderful hugs and your boyish grin. And especially your companionship."

While we sip pinot noir under a dark magenta sunset, he fills me in on all the projects he completed. Then he delivers the infuriating news that Isabelle befriended him during my absence. A gorgeous Colombian lawyer, writer, and social activist, Isabelle regularly appears at the marina's happy hours and has made it known that she's looking for a permanent relationship with a sailor. Isa, Lee's affectionate nickname for her, needed help with computer issues, so he tutored her on the boat. *Naked,* I wonder? *Or perhaps wearing black stockings with a sexy black lace garter belt?*

Lee explains that after they had several dinners together in town, Lee invited Isa, her younger sister, and her niece on an all-day sailing adventure. Lee proudly shows me his digital pictures of her. It's obvious that Isa went to great lengths with her hair and her wardrobe. A rage envelops me.

Furious, I sputter, "I hate you, Lee! Not only did you hang out with another woman while I was gone, but you also almost failed to meet me at the airport because you used up most of your money on Isa!"

Not only do I want to flog this man, but I also want to leave him now. Immediately. And never see his sorry ass again.

Then I cool down. Somewhat. He promises me that nothing happened. "It was just a platonic relationship. I was lonely." How I wish I had bought that digital alarm clock I saw in the airline's in-flight magazine. The one that clandestinely videotapes bedroom activities.

Eventually, he admits that she got drunk one evening during dinner, and he had to carry her partway home after holding her while she vomited.

With a surge of jealousy, I say, "How do you think that makes me feel? I go away for a few weeks, and you immediately replace me with the marina flirt."

He answers, "Nothing happened, Wendy. I promise. She needed help with some computer issues."

"Yeah, right!" I say under my breath.

Then he adds, "It was totally platonic."

"Excuse me, Lee, I'm having a hard time believing you."

He seems startled by my reaction. What was he expecting? A namby-pamby response?

At the next happy hour, Isa presses her hands together saintlike and bows before me. "Namaste!" she says.

Namaste my foot! I turn and walk away in bruised silence.

The city has plans to demolish the marina so that a developer can build a more upscale one that will attract international mega yachts. Yesterday, Candelaria stood outside the mayor's home yelling profanities. Today, while I'm emailing my family from an internet café in town, there's a sudden commotion in the room. I look up to see Candelaria, who's yelling in the middle of the café at no one in particular.

"Would you please be quiet," a man nearby mutters under his breath.

On my return to the boat dock, John, the marina's manager and a Dr. Seuss lookalike in a multicolored striped stovepipe hat, informs me on my return from the coffee shop, "The marina will be bulldozed within a week."

After passing this news on to Lee, he looks surprised when I add offhandedly, "By the way, I'd like to wear a wedding ring so that women will stop hitting on you in front of me.

It's disrespectful, and it makes me feel bad." Despite the dissonance I feel between my heart and my common sense, I know that I need to take action. So I drop my gold earrings off at a jewelry store in Old Town with the instructions to melt the gold into a wedding band.

Looking stupefied after hearing this, Lee doesn't say a word.

In the midst of preparations for our passage to Panama with a Swiss couple who signed up for a last-minute charter, I contact the Carulla grocery store to have them deliver food to the main boat dock. A young girl wearing a green polo shirt meets me at the entrance to Club Nautico and then pushes her grocery-filled cart down a rock-strewn sidewalk through a makeshift blue plastic door that separates the crumbling world of Club Nautico from the world of Cartagena. Our charter guests, Esther and Per, arrive simultaneously, so I drop them all off at the boat before scooting off.

Esther, looking confused, asks, "Aren't you coming with us?"

"Oh, I have a quick errand," I answer giddily. "I'll be back in a couple of hours." If they only knew what a crazy, impulsive venture I'm embarking on. I'm on a mission to pick up my new wedding band in Old Town. *What a brilliant way to solve these ongoing issues*, I hope.

I bounce around like a pea in the back seat of a taxi bound for the Old Town Clock Tower. The warm, humid breeze rearranges my hair into cotton candy as I walk past natives selling handmade jewelry displayed on brightly colored blankets. I pass the Tourist Information booth, where no one speaks English, and a man selling fresh lemonade. "Lemonadah?" he asks.

I promise him I'll buy one on my way back.

At Mora's Jewelry Store, my beautiful gold wedding band awaits me. I pay one hundred US dollars and slip it onto my finger. Lee actually smiles when he sees it. "You need this, don't you?" he asks.

"Yes, I do," I say. "I need the feeling of security and solidity that comes with marriage. It says to the world that this is not some fly-by-the-seat-of-your-pants relationship." I don't really want to marry Lee. I just want to give the impression that we're married so that I'll feel safer in the relationship. Maybe the ladies will back off when they see the ring.

Will my hunger for Lee's love be satisfied with this wedding ring on my finger? Will the I'm-not-good-enough feelings subside? Will I stop obsessing about our relationship? Will it confirm to other women that he's off-limits? All of these questions are running through my head.

Before we leave Colombia for Panama I make a mental list of what I like here. The Old Town with the pastel-colored two-story buildings where deep pink bougainvillea spills over the iron balconies; the cheap, great restaurants; the spectacular night view of the city from the boat; the charming old-fashioned museums; the friendly locals; the women who walk down the street with bowls of fruit or pastries on their heads; the ancient trees that spread low over the city squares; the smell of ripe mangoes in the carts of street vendors; the dancers in brightly colored costumes who suddenly appear from nowhere and put on a show in a walking street or a park; the taxi drivers who love their city and want to share it with tourists; the brightly lit apartment-building-sized container ships leaving the harbor at night; the Colombian naval band welcoming tall ships from foreign navies; the Chinese junk anchored next to us that's spilling over with ebullient lively children, a squawking parrot, and a small, hyperactive dog. And where will you ever see women riding horses in high heels? I did, at a famous equestrian event in a lovely village five hours from here.

I'll miss the tight community of sailors in Cartagena who always had our back. But I won't miss the overwhelming heat. Since there were no breezes to cool us off, we spent a lot of time in front of the fan. Jumping into the dirty water at the marina wasn't an option.

It's a miracle that Lee didn't get whiplash in Cartegena. I have to admit that the highlight of my stay in Colombia was when Lee walked off a pier fully dressed while eyeballing a woman. I felt sorry for him, yet at the same time, wildly elated. Maybe one day soon, he'll read the book I gave him— *The Art of Being a Gentleman.*

27

Lost in the Jungle

I will learn that the Rio Chagres will reveal its mysteries layer by layer if we are observant.

Four parrots on a mission screech overhead before diving into the thick forest canopy. It's 6 a.m., and the tropical birds are calling out *qua, qua, qua* to each other while the howler monkeys roar across the treetops in their otherworldly way. The river is still as glass at this hour. I'm standing on the deck breathing in the fragrances of flowers and trees and earth while Lee sleeps below.

Preparing myself for yoga in the cockpit, I pull on my black yoga pants, a white T-shirt, and a bright orange bandana. Within five minutes, I'm down to my underwear. In this part of the world, the heat is already sweltering at this early hour. I've never experienced anything quite like it.

A gunshot sound early this morning stirred up the jungle's creatures, who reacted with noisy fear. It took a while for calm to return to the forest.

Anchored in the crook of the river, I'm greeted by a bee who stings me with bee-like unconcern. An hour later, another bee stings me inside the boat, and I yell, "Lock down!" With a vengeance, I slam shut the cockpit door and all the windows, waking up Lee. As I'm switching on the two indoor wall fans, it occurs to me that we're the invaders of their territory, so I can't blame them for being upset.

Late in the afternoon, the orchestra of the river revs up again as I do yoga moves on the foredeck. *Roar, roar! Chee ha! Chee ha! EE EE EE EEah! E ah! Buzz. Pop! Ke reep, ke reep, ke reep! Uh uh uh! Oh oh oh! Ah ah ah ah! Qua qua qua! Crump, crump, crump! Chip, chip, chip! Shake that thing! Shake that thing!*

I realize that they are continuing with their daily rituals as Lee and I continue with ours. I step outside for a moment and shout loudly in my best howler monkey voice. There's a moment of complete silence as the jungle's creatures puzzle over the alien sound and then resume their orchestration.

There's a sandbar at the entrance to the river. Yesterday, as we approached it with our hearts pumping, the seas calmed, and our entry was perfect as we breezed in on the wings of a large swell. I'm relieved to be here, just the two of us—except for a thirty-foot steel monohull farther up the river.

It's almost too hot to move on our second day here. The air is perfectly still, and the water reflects the trees, the sky, and the clouds in its large mirror. Lee spends the morning reading my copy of *Running with Scissors* while I do my morning prayers and yoga.

Lee wants to dinghy up a tributary that will hopefully lead to a waterfall, so he gathers supplies, including a machete and bug spray. Before we leave for our first jungle adventure

I go for a quick skinny dip while praying the crocodiles will stay away. It's only 7:45 a.m., and I'm already sweating profusely.

By late afternoon, we still haven't left for our adventure. Lee has spent the past half hour searching for his compass, which was put in a "special place." This compass will be an invaluable tool for helping us find the dinghy after our wanderings in the wilds. So our first mistake is not leaving by midday when the intense heat puts the crocs to sleep—and our second mistake is deciding to go without the compass, which we're unable to find.

I'm all suited up in cargo pants, white knee socks, a long-sleeve light blue fishing shirt with air vents, a wide-brimmed jungle hat, and hiking shoes. I'm worried that starting a jungle hike in the afternoon could be a huge mistake.

The dinghy creates its own delightful wind. While I fantasize about skipping the hike and just motoring up and down the river for the rest of the day so I can cool off, Lee directs the dinghy into a tributary with a wide opening. Large black vultures soar above as the passage narrows.

Unable to motor further because of the shallow water, Lee cuts the engine, and we both row until the creek becomes too shallow in places. We drift slowly under a thick leafy canopy toward a steep clay mound covered with massive exposed roots and deep green vines, a good place to tie up. Gulping at the sight of a jungle so dense that I can't see through it, I worry about stumbling upon a fer-de-lance snake hiding under a pile of leaves. I'm reminded of the many warnings about this deadly aggressive pit viper which has a lethal bite. Fer-de-lance give off a warning smell similar to feces, so I'll be sniffing the air obsessively.

We lose our way in the jungle. I question Lee several times,

"Didn't we pass that tree an hour ago?" While glancing down at a wild cat's scat I wonder, *Why didn't I get a prescription for anti-malarial medicine? Why did I assume that our long-sleeved shirts, long pants, and knee socks would be enough?* Hours later, we finally find our way back to the dinghy.

Based on yesterday's experience, I change my mind about wandering through the jungle with Lee. "I think it's better if I wait for you in the dinghy," I announce. "How long do you plan to be gone?" I'm usually happy to go on adventures, but this time something is holding me back.

"Oh, I'll be back soon!" Lee says as a tarantula walks across his foot.

For an hour, I meditate, take photos, do deep breathing exercises, and periodically push the dinghy away from a revolting stack of howler monkey poop on a tree trunk nearby. Where is Lee? Thirty minutes ago, I heard him hacking his way through the jungle with the machete I gave him for Christmas. I yell our secret code, "Coo wee!" No response. I can just make out his blue T-shirt and his face through the foliage, so I assume he's working his way over to this side of the creek. He'll appear soon, I'm sure.

I'm getting worried about Lee. It was 3:40 p.m. when he took off, and it's now 5:10 p.m. The jungle is closing into itself under the growing darkness while the creepy-sounding evening din is starting up. The howler monkeys scream with their otherworldly voices, and the parrots, always in pairs, are returning to their roosts. I yell out our code word, "Coo wee" in my loudest voice. Nothing. There is no sound of a machete chopping through the underbrush. I'm worried that something has happened to him.

Lee will surely return before the darkness sets in, I assure myself. But what if he doesn't? What if he roused a fer-de-lance as he was walking over piles of dead leaves or rocks? Or maybe he slipped and hit his head on a rock and was knocked unconscious.

My inner self pipes up and says, "Calm down. Breathe deeply. Stay in the present moment." This is a major jungle with dangerous critters. And spending the night in it without protection is a bad, bad idea. In addition to the snakes and crocodiles, there are wild cats, mosquitos carrying malaria and dengue fever, plants with sharp spines harboring aggressive ants, poisonous caterpillars, spiders, scorpions, killer bees, and bullet ants. Plus, monkeys and bats carrying rabies.

I've wandered through enough rainforests and jungles to know that you need to be out before sunset. In the jungles of the Kuna territory of Panama, I once wandered off the beaten track by mistake. When I was found, I had cuts all over my arms and legs, bug bites in every crevice, and an alarming rash covering my body. I've got to find Lee as soon as possible.

Thirty-five minutes have passed, and still there's no sign of Lee. My voice is hoarse from calling out to him. I need to motor out of the creek within fifteen minutes, no matter what, because the darkness will make it difficult for me to find our boat without a flashlight. Plus, I'm pretty blind without my glasses. My common sense tells me that if I spend the night in the creek, there will be two people in trouble instead of just one.

At 6 p.m., I unhook the line from the root of a tree. Once more, I yell out, "Coo wee," but only the howlers answer. Down the creek, parrots squawk as if they're having a terrible disagreement. The night is slowly revving up for its jungle critter orchestra.

I sit in the front of the dinghy, rowing as the shadows grow longer. Moving slowly over sunken trees, avoiding branches sticking up, I grab low tree limbs overhead and pull myself forward. River plants keep latching onto the dinghy as if they're trying to keep me there. A red-eyed crocodile lurks in the shallows. Every few minutes, I yell out to Lee. No answer.

Thirty minutes later, I'm finally out in the river. Praying that Lee's okay, I lift up the heavy 25 HP outboard motor and lower its blades into the water. I motor downriver toward our boat, which is a mile and a half away. The river is now cloaked in blackness, and I can barely see where I'm going.

Back at the boat, it feels weird and lonely, and I realize that my life would lose its color and vibrancy without Lee. In the distance, I hear a ship blowing its horn, followed by fireworks as it enters the Gatun Locks at the Panama Canal six miles away.

I say out loud, "Keep your head. Think straight," as I gather together and test all the flashlights on board. Almost all are low on power. Since Lee's battery collection is in one of his special hiding places, I'm unable to locate them. Into a bag, I toss three flashlights, bug spray, and the VHF hand-held. After checking the gas level in the dinghy, I estimate that there's enough fuel to get me back and forth to the spot where Lee disappeared. Putting on my headlamp, I head out into the dark night.

I motor over to the sailboat in the distance, hoping that someone can help me find Lee. There's a dim light inside, so I know someone is home.

A woman in her thirties comes out to the deck and introduces herself as Kim. "Hi! We were wondering about you guys. We watched you leave in the afternoon but never saw you return. Scott thought you may have found something really interesting."

I try to explain in a cracking voice what happened. "I can't find my boyfriend. He never returned from the jungle. I'm afraid he's been injured!"

Without a word, Scott and Kim immediately start preparing. They gather flashlights, a VHF, a pair of knee-high dark blue rubber boots, extra gas for the dinghy, and drinking water. I calm down just by watching them.

Kim stays behind to monitor the radio. I drive the dinghy while Scott sits in front, aiming the light along the bank of the river. In the distance, crocodile eyes move down the river like red beacons. Suddenly, I recognize the tributary we explored. "I think we're near the entrance to the creek where Lee disappeared. It's a nice open cut in the beginning then it immediately makes a wide turn to the left. There's a large tree to the right." Just as I say this we hear someone yelling off our right.

"It's Lee!" I shout.

Just past an entrance to a creek, we spot, in the dark of the night, a white shirt being waved from the end of a stick. Slowly pulling up to some large razor-edged tree roots, Lee, his face etched in worry, stands holding a yellow flower for me. His clothes are drenched in perspiration, and he looks exhausted after having trekked through the jungle for hours trying to find his way back to the river.

Without a compass and unable to locate the dinghy where I was waiting for him, he worked his way toward what he hoped was the river after seeing a small stream and remembering what his father said on a camping trip when he was a boy. "Put a leaf in the stream and see what direction it goes in. Follow that direction. It will lead you to the source."

This was a big lesson for both of us. It was foolish for Lee to take off alone into an unforgiving jungle without proper equipment such as a flashlight and the VHF handheld. And I should have been prepared on my end for any and all eventualities. Lee was actually lucky to survive in one of the world's most dangerous jungles.

Looking back at this, I realize that we were both ill-prepared and naive to take on the perilous Panamanian jungle that first afternoon when we wandered through the wet, rugged terrain without a compass or a VHF. The jungle was so impenetrable that we could barely make our way through it. Every time I stepped over a log or a pile of leaves, I prayed that a fer-de-lance wouldn't kill me with its lethal bite. I tied short lengths of white material around low limbs to help us find our way back to the creek where we left the dinghy. But we quickly got off track, and our only alternative was to head for the Chagres River. After many wrong turns, we finally reached the riverbank.

Climbing onto a large boulder overlooking the river, we could just make out our boat in the distance. Lee wanted to chance it and swim all the way back. On my end, I was praying that the crocodiles lounging along the shoreline were napping, since I didn't want my boyfriend to be a feast for crocodiles.

It was terrifying to watch Lee as he swam down the Chagres River toward our boat, now a spec in the distance. Soon losing sight of him, I prayed for his safety.

To my relief, I heard the unmistakable sound of the engines starting and the anchor chain being wrapped around the bollard. Not long afterward, he motored up the river. As soon as he came into view, I jumped into the cool water and swam to the boat. Grabbing the ladder off the stern, I climbed up the steps into Lee's waiting arms.

28

Dead Reckoning

It's early December 2010, less than a month after the jungle incident. We're sailing across the Caribbean Sea in a northeasterly direction to the Grand Cayman Islands. Under a sky partially obscured by clouds, the port engine, its fuel line broken, sputters out during this long, arduous crossing from Honduras. Diesel sloshes all over the port engine room as the boat bucks about in enormous waves. The only solution we can come up with is to remove the fuel with the wet/dry vacuum cleaner.

Seesawing violently with each new wave, I sit on the stern steps tethered to the boat while waiting for Lee to hand me a diesel-filled container. Knowing exactly how many seconds it takes for him to partially fill the bucket, I deliberately swing my body to the right as he, fiery-eyed with forearm hairs glistening with fuel, lifts each container methodically out of the chamber of horror while desperately trying not to slip in his oily crocks. Aching with remorse, I grip the slick container carefully, then swing to my left to pour the contents into the sea, the silent witness to my terrible crime.

My biggest fear is that this gallon-size bucket—the only one we have—will slip out of my hands into the water. My back, arms, and hands ache from the strain of the repetitive motion and the weight of the heavy load. *Don't give up*, I tell myself while fretting over how long this will take. It feels like forever.

My nerves are frayed from having to grab on to the railing to avoid being flung into the sea each time the boat pitches upward. At least I have fresh air to breathe. Not once does Lee complain about the toxic fumes he's forced to inhale for over two hours.

Unnoticed, we ghost into the Caymans' main harbor and then cool down with an early morning swim, during which Lee suggests we hitchhike to the airport in the late afternoon to pick up our crew for the upcoming passage to the Bahamas.

"Don't you think we should call a taxi instead?' I ask, horrified. "Aren't you tired? I don't feel like walking or hitchhiking at this point."

Lee, having gotten his way, thumbs a ride partway to the airport then we trudge, sweating profusely, the rest of the way. Embarrassingly late and looking sheepish, we arrive in a cloud of sour body odor. Lee's cousin Sally and her San Francisco friends Greg and Louise are leaning against a rock wall just outside Arrivals. Sally has been with us many times before, and this is Greg's second visit to the boat. This is the first time for Lousie. They all perk up at our approach.

Louise immediately strikes me as a take-charge kind of person. She's of medium height, slight of stature, with dark hair interspersed with grey.

Into the trunk of a large taxi, Lee crams their three large canvas backpacks, a load of heavy boat parts from West Marine, and his mail from the US. Over $50 later, the taxi driver dumps us off at an indecipherable location in the darkness.

Lee disappears down a sandy, grassy slope to the dock. Within moments, the dinghy, lit up by a flashlight, approaches. Sally, bewildered, asks Lee in a sharp tone, "Why is the dinghy motor uncovered?"

Lee looks at her tiredly. "It's having problems. I'm still missing some parts."

"Well," Sally grumbles. "We're not leaving the Caymans until that outboard is fixed."

While Lee is occupied with boat projects, I head out with our crew to locate fuel and parts for the outboard. A Jamaican lady driving an empty bus, possibly bored and perhaps needing some money, picks us up and immediately turns her bus into a taxi. Not quite understanding that we need fuel for the dinghy, she takes us instead to the Esso fuel depot and then a gas station that's closed. Eventually, she heads to the Harbor House Marina where we hand her $25 and relinquish her services with relief.

Captain Mike, a portly middle-aged man with froggy eyes, notices our plight and offers to drive us to Spott's Pier, where his fishing boat is docked. After organizing a fuel delivery for us on his VHF, he mentions that bad weather is heading our way. After recommending a safe anchorage on the lee side of the island, he promises, "I'll be back soon. Wait here for my return."

Lee's eyes sparkle when Mike reappears with a large bag of ice—a luxury—and a liter of Cognac. While we drink papaya and rum cocktails in the cockpit, Mike contentedly sips his Cognac on ice as Louise, at the wheel, motors past Seven Mile Beach off the island's west coast where the setting sun melts into a spectacular green flash.

Captain Mike, at the helm, carefully guides us through the numerous coral reefs off the North Sound. Having refused our invitation to dine with us on the boat and clutching his almost empty Cognac bottle, he departs at a defunct yacht club, a once members-only association overlooking Governor's Harbor beach. Closed down ages ago due to financial issues, this abandoned two-story structure is still standing, and the four Doric columns lining the front entrance are still intact.

Lee continues to tackle boat repairs while we take off in the rental to search for engine parts. Assuring us that she's an expert at driving in the left lane, Louise insists on taking the wheel. Greg, quickly growing anxious, frantically yells out instructions from the front passenger seat while Sally waves her arms excitedly from the back. Louise, noticeably flustered, bumps into a curb, smashing two tires. Flat tires now repaired, we make our way to the marine supply store.

The misbehaving Yamaha outboard engine takes up half the back seat of our car. Unable to shrink ourselves like Alice in Wonderland, Sally, Louise, and I pretzel ourselves around it. After Lee deposits it at the Yamaha dealer, we reanchor off Stingray City, where we wade through the transparent shallows and gaze at dozens of silky friendly stingrays that brush our legs as they gracefully glide past. Later, fending off unkempt roosters and chickens endeavoring to join us, we scarf down a meal at The Jerk, a small outdoor café within walking distance.

The only boat in our new bouncy anchorage is a super yacht, which Sally points out belongs to Paul Allen, the cofounder of Microsoft. While Lee prepares breakfast, the propane suddenly cuts out on the third pancake, so we add it to our day's growing project list. Frustrated, Lee collects the propane tank from a small cabinet on the bow. "The tank valve's linkage is broken. So we can't use the stove until it's repaired," he says gravely.

On our way to retrieve the Yamaha engine and parts for the propane's connector valve, we stop at a tiny post office in a village named Hell. We busy ourselves dashing off dozens of postcards with this unusual postmark. "Yes, we are indeed in Hell," Sally remarks as she writes "Love From Hell" on each card.

Having given up on crewing with us to the Bahamas, Sally, Louise, and Greg book an early morning return flight to the US, the day before their round-trip tickets expire.

Now alone with Lee, I spend Christmas Day on Grand Cayman Island checking out US-bound flights. I'm homesick for my family. It breaks my heart not to be with my sons today. Lee doesn't share my sentimentality about holidays, in particular Christmas. Feeling empty, lost, and lonely, I'm the only customer at the local Subway. A heavyset black woman with salt and pepper hair and friendly dark brown eyes looks at me with curiosity as she hands me a tuna fish sandwich. She mentions that she's having a celebration with her family later in the day, which only makes me feel sadder. I desperately want to call my sister to see if I can stay with her in Florida until I can find something to rent.

Originally, I believed I would always live on this boat with Lee, and the sound of water sloshing against the pontoons would be a steady background noise in my life. But of course, it hasn't always been smooth sailing, neither on the seas nor with us. In the very beginning of our journey, Lee said, "This isn't forever. It could all be over in the blink of an eye." In the dead silence that followed, rather taken aback, I wondered what he really meant. Suddenly feeling insecure about this new man in my life, I thought at the time, *Is he planning to leave me before I leave him?*

Just before booking a one-way ticket home, I have second thoughts and close down my computer after realizing how selfish it would be to land unannounced on my sister's doorstep on Christmas Day. I'd also promised Lee I would make the passage with him to the Bahamas. It will be a hair-raising journey because the trade winds are blowing east to west at this time of the year. But since Lee has charters booked for February through June there, we have no other choice. So, feeling conflicted, I return to a man who doesn't have a clue about how to celebrate Christmas or birthdays. "Presents are commercial nonsense," he said early on.

When I check out at the immigration and customs office near the cruise ship entry point, the woman helping me says in a sweet voice, "If I had known you were here, child, I would have invited you over for Christmas dinner!"

Inspired, I vow that next Christmas, *if* I'm still on the boat, I'll put a notice in the local paper: "We are two sailors, past our prime, who are feeling lonely this Christmas without our children and grandchildren in the States. Please invite us to share Christmas dinner with you. We'll do the dishes! And we're fun and entertaining."

Before we head out, I study the map intently, hoping to find an atoll or a tiny island along the way where we can find refuge. I've already packed up the Christmas decorations and the delicate angel wing shell that I found on a local beach.

Daybreak. The boat shudders violently, and the jib flaps furiously as we sail away from our safe haven under a pale, hostile sky. The increasing wind is causing the rigging to moan loudly, and in the far distance, a dark grey water spout appears to be heading our way.

Seasick, I lie on the sofa in the salon entertaining myself with the shifting shadows on the ceiling and the thought that the 360 degrees on a compass are divided into 12 sections like a clock. And that there are 365 days, 12 months, and 12 full moons in a year. Amazing!

I enjoy watching Jacques, a small stowaway lizard from Roatan, as he turns yellow with tiny dark brown dots from his perch on a ripe banana. Feeling guilty for not being able to help Lee, yet knowing I would be more of a liability than an advantage, I watch as he ambles by, shoulders hunched over, hollow-eyed and haggard after a full night on watch.

Two days later, feeling well enough to pitch in with watches, I groggily check the radar and the horizon for other vessels, then reset the flapping sails, and wind up the jib to keep it from smashing into the stay. After setting the timer for twenty minutes, I immediately pass out until the alarm startles me back into consciousness. Earl Gray tea, dark chocolate, solitaire, and sudoku no longer help me to stay alert nowadays. Not even the hair-raising story of an English friend who fell asleep during a passage and woke up next to a freighter the size of an apartment building.

The mainsheets unnerve me, and I've been afraid to handle them under these dangerous circumstances. During a close haul, there are mighty forces at play when the sail is fully extended in high winds. If you lose your concentration while taking a line off the winch, the mainsheets will whip around so savagely that the skin on your face, hands, or arms could be ripped off. Several months ago, after losing my grip, the mainsheets thrashed about uncontrollably and shredded my wrist, which soon became badly infected.

Infections at sea are to be avoided since they can quickly get out of control.

Day four. No longer feeling queasy, I'm on duty at the helm as we slowly glide past the six-mile-wide entrance to Cuba's Guantanamo Bay, which is lit up like a giant Christmas tree in the dark, moonless night. Several of our navigation lights are out, and Lee worries we'll be pulled over by the Marines.

Day five. The next morning during Lee's watch, I glance up from my book to a horrifying sight. We're on a collision course with a rocky cliff. As we draw closer and closer to it, Lee springs to the helm to alter course. We're now about 1,056 feet from landfall, and I can see, quite clearly, a white-roofed blue car speeding along the coastline road. For the next two hours, we continue sailing illegally along Cuba's southern coast. Only a handful of people are visible on the beautiful white-sand beaches bordered with coconut palms and hills and mountains.

As we sail close to Guantanamo Bay, whose entrance is brightly illuminated, I overhear a steady, monotonous voice on the VHF. In broken English, it warns, "Selant butt, Selant butt . . . Catamaran . . . you are forbidden to navigate in this area." Then a few minutes later, a little more adamantly, "Selant butt, Selant butt . . . Catamaran . . . you are in a restricted area! Please go six miles south off the coast."

Then, ten minutes later, "You *must* go to limit six miles off the coast. Prohibited. You can be arrested!" We both hear the same messages but remain strangely oblivious. As if the silent boat being addressed has nothing to do with us.

This hypnotic state we're in seems to absolve us from this clear and present danger. We're about a hundred feet from land in thirty feet of water so clear I can see a starfish on the bottom. A boy wearing a mask and snorkel, trailing a fishing line, swims alongside us. A teenage boy in a faded orange T-shirt waving wildly at us from the beach is soon joined by four naked boys who also wave wildly. We continue along in our silent, dreamy state, impervious to any danger. Part of me loves this glorious pushing against the limits—our lovely silent rebellion. After the Guardia calls once again in a much more strident tone on the VHF, Lee relents, moving the boat six miles from land into glass-smooth water.

Is my nomadic life at sea about to end? I ask myself, although I already know the answer. I think we both intuitively sense that our vagabond lifestyle is slowly coming to a close. Lately, I've felt that the spark has gone out of our relationship. That it has run its course. Neither of us seem as happy as we once were. We still care for each other, but we've both lost the spark that ignited us in the very beginning, and I don't believe that we can re-ignite it. We still have strong feelings for each other, but somehow that's not enough at this point. And the strong connection I have to my sons and my family of origin is reeling me in. The message of my "Enjoy the Journey" necklace is about enjoying the adventure and the experience. It's the doing, not the destination, that matters. Journeys always have a beginning and an ending.

Strangely, as if she intuited my thoughts about leaving the boat, Sally remarked to me before she left, "If you leave, there will be a long line of men wanting to have you on their boats." I know in my heart, however, that this vagabond lifestyle has irrevocably run its course.

I made a verbal commitment, however, to Lee to help with the Bahamas and the New England charters. Maybe I could leave the boat from time to time, then return refreshed and happy to see him. And perhaps we'll get along better, and he'll realize that he still loves me, I think wistfully. But during the long hours of doing nothing other than nauseously staring at the ceiling, I realized that whether or not Lee still loves me doesn't really matter. What matters is that I love myself.

———

I'm suddenly lifted into the air and flung like a rag doll across the salon into the dining table after a rogue wave slams into the boat off the southern coast of Cuba. I hobble over to the sofa, seasick and sore, and collapse onto it. Currently plaguing us are the metallic, tumultuous seas that are common in the northern West Indies.

The seas have finally calmed down as we approach the Turks and Caicos, a British Overseas Territory. Drooling, I watch Lee line-catch a mahi mahi, which will be my first real meal in days after a steady diet of toast and ginger ale for seasickness.

Lee's acting weird again. Just before we left Honduras, during a discussion of his future sailing plans with our friends, he said, "I will go here. I will go there." Not *we*. That saddened me, but honestly, I'm not surprised in the least. During our last three charters, I've felt as if I were invisible. In the infancy of our romance, I believed in the illusion that I would be the one to break Lee's pattern of five-year relationships, that I would be the woman he truly fell in love with. Instead, I'm currently staring at a live Ken Doll sitting directly across from me during lunch. Feeling needy and desperate for attention, I glance his way to make sure he's breathing. Unable to penetrate the dark veil of his sunglasses, I ask, "What's the matter?"

"I need to focus!" he mutters. "I don't want to get caught up in a conversation with you."

"Do you want me to leave the boat?"

Sighing loudly, he answers impatiently, "No. Of course not!" Then suddenly throwing his hands into the air, he spurts, "You're driving me crazy! I can't control you!"

I stare at him, my arms crossed, thinking, *Wow! What a Freudian slip.*

"Why on earth do you need to control me?"

The way a man controls things can be subtle or not so subtle. It can be glaringly obvious, or it can be almost imperceptible. My thoughts about our relationship are running wild, and I can't reign them in. They're like lines blowing in the wind, whipping manically against the stays.

In the early days of our relationship, Lee stated, "Remember that I love you, even in my dark, walled-off moments." I realize that I can't do this any longer.

And recently, Lee admitted, while we sipped wine in the glow of candlelight in the cockpit, "I've never talked so deeply to a woman before. Somehow you always manage to explore the depths with me." I felt a faint glimmer of hope, yet I realized simultaneously that there were parts of him that would always remain a mystery. And in me. Perhaps in all of us. Can we ever truly know another human being?

My body has been trying to tell me all along to reconnect with my own spirit. I haven't been able to hear this because I've never stopped long enough to breathe deeply, close my eyes, and connect with God. I was rushing like a wild animal through my life, expecting the world to deliver what I needed, yet running away from myself. Looking back over the past five and a half years, I wonder if I was asleep, just dreaming that I was on a boat. It was a dream where I was only partly present. I had abandoned not only my family and my friends, but I had also abandoned *myself*. And in

Lee's presence, I *still* felt all alone because I wasn't there to love myself. I wanted him to give me what I was unable to give myself. Until now. Right now.

Little things have started to irritate me. Silly things such as Lee clicking his spoon against the side of his bowl when he eats cereal. And his constant obsession with our website. I believe that I am slowly waking up from a spell that has been cast over me.

A lanky, grizzled fisherman with the misnomer White Man guides us into an anchorage in the British Turks and Caicos, where we tie up to a pier near the cruise dock. In the evening, Lee snuggles with me in bed. *Maybe everything's still okay*, I think hopefully. *Maybe he still loves me. Maybe we can retire from sailing and live in his idea of a dream home . . . a grey container. My antiques would look a little weird there, but we can work around that. I'll have a handyman cut out large windows because of my need for light.*

No, that's a horrible idea! I'll never be able to accept or endure Lee's version of how to live comfortably. It would be compromising all the things that I cherish. Bottom line: It's the right time to leave. As soon as we're docked at a port, I'm booking a flight to the States.

I awaken the next morning in the shadow of a thirteen-story Holland America ship and a warm hug from Lee. During breakfast, however, he's aloof again, as if a heavy curtain is drawn between us. The mood isn't exactly unfriendly, it's just that Lee isn't present. Who is he, anyway? I don't really know him after five years on his boat. Lee reels in my love, then snips the line and lets me go.

After hitchhiking a ride in the back of a rusty blue pickup truck, we do a quick walking tour of the sandy streets of Cockburn Town, where we buy pastries and freshly baked bread at a bakery and then pull on our wetsuits and dinghy out until the coastline is just a tiny speck in the distance. I'm always a little nervous about diving, but this time, I'm more anxious than usual because my dive equipment is brand new. Will the regulator and BCD work properly? The Buoyancy Control Device that my brother bought me on eBay inflated suddenly at twenty-five feet while we were diving a wreck in Croatia, and I was propelled to the surface as if wearing a jet pack.

Shivering from the cooler ocean temperatures in the Bahamas, I hover twenty feet over Lee as he descends. I wait patiently for my ears to equalize as I slowly edge my way down the rim of a cliff. Without looking up to see if I'm following him, Lee continues plunging downward, apparently forgetting that we're dive buddies. At eighty feet, I assume he'll level out, but he continues descending. At one hundred and twenty feet, where the water is dark and murky, a sharp, piercing pain wracks my ears and, in mounting fear, I slowly ascend to a level where my ears stop hurting. Lee never once looks up to see where I am.

———

After enduring five days of untenable seas and howling winds off Great Iguana Island, Crooked Island, and Cat Island in the Bahamas, I insist that we seek shelter at the Emerald Bay Marina on Great Exuma. I offer to pay since Lee has neither money nor credit cards.

After announcing our approach on the VHF, the dock fills with dozens of curious sailors who are anxious to see how we're going to navigate the marina's narrow passageway under the worst possible conditions. Just as we enter the tight rocky entrance, the port engine sputters out. After noticing Lee's struggle to keep the boat from veering sideways onto the rocks, a sailor named Corning speeds our way in his dinghy. He pushes our boat away and shadows us until we reach the quieter waters of the marina. Suddenly, all the sailors who are lined up along the docks watching us cease clapping and cheering as a strong wind gust propels us helplessly toward a concrete wall.

"Wendy, put down the daggerboards!" Lee yells from the helm. "*Now!*"

With Corning's help, we limp into a slip at the far end of the dock in a quiet area away from the hubbub of the marina and its constant socializing. This is fortuitous because I need some space to reflect on the ramifications of continuing or discontinuing my journey with Lee.

Corning and his wife, Tita, arrive for dinner our first night there. As usual, I let everyone do the talking while I listen. After Lars died, I realized, with horror, that there was no one to hide behind. Instinctively, I always knew that I needed to connect with the entertaining and interesting person within me. But how? Apparently, I haven't progressed very far, because I'm still hiding behind people.

In the morning, I take a long walk on one of the island's many sandy paths. As I wander past a fancy resort and young couples sunbathing on the beach, I say a little prayer: "Help me find someone I can confide in. Thank you."

Back at the marina, I run into Corning.

Feeling that he's a safe person to bear my soul to, I admit, "I want to leave Lee and the boat. I've never felt so good in my life, yet so bad at the same time. I think Lee and I have finally run the course of our relationship. And I'm missing my family so much." Corning looks at me with such tenderness and empathy that it's hard not to tear up. Then I add, "And if Lee knows what's up, he'll do his best to talk me into staying."

"You need a little outside support, Wendy. Would you mind if I share this with my wife? I know she'll want to support you too."

"I would love to have your support!" I say. "Thank you so much for being there for me."

The next day Lee and I run into Tita, who invites us for lunch with her and Corning. Thankfully, Lee decides not to join me. After we all share our most horrific, hair-raising sailing stories, as sailors always do, Corning leaves the two of us alone. Tita regards me with serious eyes. "We need to talk! About what's going on with you."

After admitting that I'm preparing to break up with Lee, she says, "Let us be your safety net. When we came to your boat the other night, I was stunned by you. You're gorgeous and absolutely adorable! I was more interested in you than Lee. Corning said you lit up the room with your smile."

Wow! I appreciate what she said. I know that I have a lot to offer, and I'm anxious to embark upon my own soul-filled journey. My ultimate goal is to light up rooms with loving energy and be a healing presence in the world.

The next morning, I have a surreptitious meeting with Tita and Corning on their boat *Blessed Spirit*. Corning says, "Our guest cottage in Maine has your name on it."

Then Tita reminds me, "We really want to support you! A boat can become a prison. You might as well be living in Alcatraz. You look out at the dazzling water all around and the land in the distance, but you're stuck on the boat. And you always have to leave the land, the flowers, the earth, the trees, and the people to go back to prison."

Until this moment, I hadn't been able to articulate that,

but now it hits me that she's absolutely right—I've been living in a jail with a gorgeous view.

"Tita, I don't know what awaits me, but I'm ready to take off."

"That's where trust steps in," she reminds me. "Trust in a good outcome, trust in everything working out. The universe abhors a vacuum. It will rush in and fill you with more love than you ever dreamed of."

Then she says something very similar to what Mary, the personal coach, said: "You will have the capacity one day to love the whole world. You're being initiated into being willful. You're supposed to be alone for the time being. Not forever, but just for a period of time. Promise me you'll leave Lee!"

So I promise her that I'll take a huge leap of faith and trust that everything is going to work out better than I could ever imagine.

When I first met Lee, all I could see was his enormous capacity to love. This was what I tapped into and fell in love with. Interestingly, it was me I fell in love with.

I recall a moment back in the Caymans when Sally took me aside one day and asked, "Why do you stay on the boat? You could crew on any boat! There are a lot of men out there who would be thrilled to have you join them."

"But I love Lee," I whimpered in a sappy voice.

"What is love really?" she blasted back, making every hair on my arm stand at alert. The next day, after watching me run, jump, and fetch for Lee, she unnerved me with, "Where's your brain, Wendy?"

I was insulted. She'd hit a nerve.

Now I realize that she had known the truth all along.

Absorbed and bewitched by Lee's magic spell, I was unable

to think or see clearly. He was the dashing, charming man who came to my rescue—the Peter Pan who spirited me away to Neverland, a utopia where we would always be young and free. The nickname he chose for me, Tiger Lily, was interestingly a character in the book *Peter and Wendy*.

While Lee works on our website at the marina, I quietly pack in the port cabin. I stash my clothing, souvenirs, journals, BCD and regulator, a small wooden Buddha, and my medicine dolls into four striped Guatemalan baskets that I hide under the twin beds. I'm surprised over how little I've acquired during all my years on the boat. While I gather up my belongings I listen for Lee's footsteps in the cockpit or the whine of an approaching dinghy. During these moments of my clandestine packing, I'm in fight or flight mode. The slightest noise makes me jump.

In the evening, suspecting that something's up, Lee follows me around like a lost puppy. Suddenly he wraps his arms around me. "Are you really staying with me?"

"Yes, I'm staying," I lie, while avoiding his eyes.

"Are you *sure* you're staying?"

Unexpectedly he grabs my hand as we head to a party at the marina, he whispers, "You are so beautiful! I love you very much."

Then ten minutes later, he says, "We need to fix the port engine in Freeport, as you know. I'm going to need to borrow money from you. Remember, we're in this together."

Once again, I'm the proverbial cash cow. Will he ever repay me for more than five years' worth of interest-free loans?

Continuing, he says, "We only have each other. It's just us, Wendy. No one else really cares about us."

Maybe that's true for you, I think. *But my family and my friends love me.*

Turning on the charm, he mentions all the fun things we're going to do in the Bahamas as he lovingly positions a flower behind my ear while I try not to meet his eyes.

Coincidentally, Lee's friend David emails me about a shift relationships go through after five years. "Many people break up at this time," he says. Not wanting to admit the truth, I write, "We're doing just fine. Thanks for the information, though!"

My young friend Kim, who helped rescue Lee in the Chagres River, confesses that she and her husband, together five years, were having major marital issues when we met on the river. Another friend comments, "Five years is a period when many sailors get sick and tired of being on a boat. It's often a time to quit the boating life."

Everyone is pointing out the truth to me in a delicate way, and I'm now paying attention.

Pulling up my sense of humor, which has been somewhat dormant lately, I imagine a discussion with Lee about our upcoming "divorce": "I'll take the four nuchus. You take the geckos, including the one still in diapers! And that tacky ceramic Mexican lizard of yours. We'll share the molas. You can keep the straw mats from Dominica, and I'll take the two handmade ChiCha baskets from Lisa. My shell collection, by the way, is nonnegotiable."

Corning and Tita, who know that I'll be leaving Lee in Freeport, Bahamas, wave goodbye from the dock as we edge out of the slip. I'm scared but excited about what's on the other side of the door I'm about to open.

My eyes are ringed with dark circles. I've been waking up several times during the night feeling as if small charges of electricity are coursing through me. Soon, I tell myself, the boat will cease to be my problem, and I will depart before the marina's yard smells and dust enter every crevice of the vessel. And before my wallet is emptied by Lee.

In Freeport, I want to catch a flight to Panama City, Florida, which is close to where my sister Nancy lives with her husband. They're already expecting me and have invited me to stay for as long as I need to. Not wanting to overstay their welcome, I'll make plans a week later to fly to Austin, where Alex lives. And if I like it there, I'll make Austin my permanent home.

It has taken over 24,000 nautical miles (which translates to 27,618 land miles), 50 countries, and 5.5 years on the open seas for me to discover the power and strength that live within me. It won't be easy to leave behind such a wonderfully adventurous life with a handsome lover—but I've discovered that I've been running away from myself. Even with Lee in my life, I've felt alone because I haven't been there to love myself. I've wanted *him* to give me what I couldn't give to myself. As this truth settles over me, I know the time has come for me to leave Lee. And love myself.

29

Moving On

Every page in my passport is filled with stamps. What will my future passport look like? I may choose, instead of international travel, to be a modern-day gypsy in a Klondike RV exploring the wilds of my country.

What sounds more feasible is to visit Thomas and his family in Sherborn, Massachusetts. While I'm there, I'll buy a brand new red Mini Cooper with a white roof. Then I'll take off for Vermont to see Markus and Jen. Finally, I'll drive to Austin, to see Alex and Tara. And who knows, I just may decide to settle there.

The sea will no longer watch me through the port cabin window, and it will no longer lull me to sleep as it crashes against the shallow reefs, sending waves to shore. Gone will be the soft breezes that swept through the window and stroked my face as I lay in a beam of silver moonlight, listening to the sounds of fish slapping their fins against the sides of the boat and dolphins coming up for air. Will I be able to reconnect in the future with that deeply profound silence of the sea filled with power, energy, and love that connected me to something much greater? Will I still have encounters with God in the dark secret places of my mind?

My decision to leave Lee, the boat, and my life on the sea is one of the most heart-wrenching choices I've ever made. I wanted to believe in the universal story: the one where you fall in love with Mr. Right and sail away with him into the sunset. I wanted it to last forever.

It would have been wonderful if Lee had truly loved me the way I wanted to be loved. I'd have continued sailing with him under those deep blue skies, a playground for clouds chasing each other to the ends of the earth.

This is the perfect time to leave, I tell myself. My first grandson's expected arrival is four weeks from now at the end of March, which is my birthday. I want to hold him in my arms and rock him to sleep. I want to be part of all the milestones in the lives of my grandchildren before they grow up and have lives of their own, and I want to spend more time with my sons and their wives.

I need to detach from Lee before he shape-shifts again into his irresistible, loving, charismatic self. Tonight, as I stare out at the moonlit sea while he works on the water maker, I think about all the times I've considered leaving him but didn't. Now is the perfect time. One thing I've learned is that you can sleep right next to someone but, at the same time, feel desperately alone.

———

We sit side by side eating breakfast, and Lee, perhaps sensing that something is up, quickly morphs into his bewitching self as he describes all the cool things we're going to do in Freeport while I nod along politely.

The next day is the last day of February, and I awaken to a beautiful baritone Bahamian voice on the VHF.

"Freedom Won, Freedom Won, Freedom Won!" Knowing, of course, that he's hailing another boat, I can't help noticing the irony.

Lee has trained me well: I'm an accomplished sailor now. Like a greyhound waiting for the bell to ring and the gate to open, I want to charge out of the stall before I change my mind about leaving.

"Are you okay?" Lee asks. He looks suspicious. "You seem so wired up."

I leave for the marina's office as soon as the boat is cleated to the dock with the excuse that I have to check something on the internet. I can feel Lee's eyes following me.

"Are you really staying with me?" he asks as I lift my leg over the boat's safety line.

"I just need to take care of something," I say casually over my shoulder.

As the boat is being readied for the haul-out I'm readying myself for my own version of hauling my ass out of here. As the boat is placed on large slings for lifting it out of the water, I'm whispering secretively to the receptionist at the marina office, "Please help me get a plane ticket to the US. I'm leaving a man I've been with for over five years, and I don't want him to know. He may come into the office at any moment, so I need for you to do this discreetly."

I know full well he'll try to seduce me into staying if he finds out. I don't want to have a long discussion with Lee, and I don't want to have to defend myself. It's best if he doesn't realize what's going on until the taxi arrives. I want a nice clean getaway.

Normally, I make my own flight arrangements, but I'm feeling too hyped up to think clearly. In response, she whispers in complicity, "Which airport do you want to fly into?"

In my state of utter confusion, I answer Ft. Lauderdale instead of Panama City, which is closer to my sister's house. Lee suddenly appears just as I'm handing her my passport. "Why don't you leave the boat for a while?" he suggests. "Go have a rest. Visit your family. It'll be good for you."

I say, "Yes, that's exactly what I'm doing."

I watch him as he paces about nervously, never removing his sunglasses. He senses that something is going on with me. Frustrated, I glance over at the receptionist with an uplifted eyebrow. After much dithering, Lee finally slips out the door. The receptionist has me booked. Taking a deep breath, I email my arrival plans to my sister Nancy.

In three hours, a taxi will pick me up for my late afternoon flight. Back on the boat, Lee is nowhere in sight. Sweating profusely, I dart below and fish out my two heavily stuffed duffle bags and my rucksack from beneath the port bed. Then I quickly stuff two medium-size suitcases with an eccentric mixture of souvenirs and exotic clothing, including the outfit I bought in Turkey that makes me feel like ABBA's dancing queen.

Lee finds me in the guest cabin where I've hidden my packed suitcases. Plucking up all my courage, I stammer, "I need to talk to you." He says nothing, so I continue: "I'm leaving, and I'm not coming back. I still love you, but I have to go. I can't give you what you really need. You told me not very long ago that you want to be with a woman who will boss you around, who will call all the shots. I can't be that person."

He looks at me with a mixture of sadness and consterna-
tion but doesn't say anything. I add, "I'm leaving you because
I'm not sure if you still love me." At that, he turns and leaves
the boat. Feeling deeply shattered, I pull myself together and
continue packing feverishly as sweat drips into my eyes.

I'm feeling fragile and depleted of energy after weeks of
tossing and turning in bed, mulling over how and when to
depart. The call to love myself is propelling me to leave now,
this red-hot moment, and I need to pay attention. Doing this
is an act of love for myself.

Queenie waits patiently in her taxi as I stuff the rest of
my underwear and socks into the crevices of my suitcases
in the guest cabin where I've hidden them. For some strange
reason, Lee photographs me during these final excruciating
moments. Then, carrying my tightly packed bag with lacy
underpants sticking out the sides, Lee walks down the gang-
plank to land. As I follow after him with my heavy backpack,
he stops and turns to take an unflattering photograph of me.
How odd. Maybe he does this so he'll remember how awful
I looked that day.

As I open the taxi door Lee says, "We need to talk."

"There's nothing more for me to say. You know in your
heart why I'm leaving you. It's too late now. I'm moving on
because I don't need you anymore." He looks crestfallen as
I utter this.

Just before I step into the taxi, Lee grabs me and pulls me
into his arms. Leaning me backward, he plants one of the
sexiest, most alluring kisses on me that I've ever experienced.
It's similar to the famous photograph of a sailor kissing a
nurse in New York City after the victory over Japan. After
five years with this man, his touch still electrifies me—and
for one brief instant, I don't want to leave. I want to call the

whole thing off, find our magic again, get back on that boat, and sail away with him.

The trip to the airport goes by in a blur. After a quick thank you to Queenie, I run to the check-in counter.

"What? The plane is a twelve-seater? Oh shit!" I say to the attendant.

Shaking his head sadly, he says, "Miss, you're only allowed to check two bags. You've got five, and they're all extremely heavy. You're going to have a massive extra luggage charge. Plus an overweight fee." I stare at him in horror while wondering how much money I'm going to have to pay.

Not knowing what else to do, I spill out the abbreviated version of my sad love story. Looking at my desperate face, he says, "There are three people on this plane with no luggage. I'm putting their names on your suitcases. Instead of owing $350, you'll owe only $100." I hug him. Then, as I turn toward the gate, he says, "Love yourself! Have fun with yourself!"

That's exactly what I needed to hear. My new journey—whatever it is—will begin with this simple request: "God, help me to love myself. I'm ready for all the walls to come down."

I need my family. I need hugs. I need birthday parties and holidays with the people I love. Maybe even a home where I can settle down, at least for awhile. Unless a new adventure turns up.

Before leaving the boat, I wanted to say to Lee, but didn't, that when he disappeared into himself, I didn't know how to reach him, that when he wouldn't speak to me from morning until night, I was forced to revisit a dark place I knew as a child—the fear of not being loved.

But now I've learned how to sit down with that *very* fear and allow myself to truly feel it. Loving *myself* is the antidote.

I'll always be grateful to Lee for bringing me to a place that encouraged me to grow, expand, and transform. He'd been my messenger. It was never about whether or not he loved me. It was *always* about loving myself.

————

There are times when I wake up at night in terror and wonder if I've led a good life, if I've loved as much as I could have. That terror comes from a tiny sensation behind my ear that tells me I've failed in small ways. Maybe I have. But I have succeeded in the big ways, and I know in my heart that's what counts.

Even now, all this time later, after all my experiences on the boat, I still haven't entirely solved the puzzle of who I am. I'd like to believe, though, that I have learned how to love and detach at the same time.

Maybe the *real* journey is just beginning: a mission of not running away from myself, of facing my fears head-on. Every single day, in every moment.

When I said goodbye to Lee, I realized that the love I had been looking for all my life on the outside had always been on the inside. The nickname Tiger Lily is made up of two opposites—strength and fragility—and I have both. And that's okay. I'm embracing both aspects of me. And I'm keeping my nickname.

Epilogue

I drive from Jacksonville to Blue Mountain Beach to stay with my friend Sally for a week. After a brief respite, I head for Texas. Along the way, I stop at a gas station near Houston, where the man at the counter asks, "Pretty lady, where are you going?"

"I'm moving to Austin," I tell him, while smiling broadly.

"Lucky Austin! Pretty lady going to Austin!"

Wow, perfect timing, I think. *I needed that little confidence boost.*

In Austin, I feel like a wild woman who has just left the jungle. I relearn how to wear heels, hold my stomach in, wear makeup, and act like a lady after being a tomboy for so many years. No longer a first mate, I feel somewhat lost in the beginning.

I am terrified of driving after so many years without a car. As I drive the Texas highways, I feel as if I am on a speeding bullet. There are so many things to get used to here in the States. Such as the endless pharmaceutical company ads on TV that bombard me with the horrific side effects of their medications.

I have to get used to a whole different lifestyle in Austin. I feast on tacos instead of newly caught mahi mahi and finally understand the slogan "Keep Austin Weird." I haven't been to any turtle racing events yet, but Alex and I visit the zany Cathedral of Junk, which was created in the backyard of a modest home in a quiet Austin suburb. It's a shrine to the Deity of Garbage. Brightly painted bashed-in garbage cans, worn-out garden tools painted in odd colors, old guitars with strings hanging out, randomly placed starfish, beat-up hubcaps, and hundreds and hundreds of cast-aside everyday objects are all assembled in an artistic, wild way by the artist who lives there.

I volunteer one afternoon a week at Pets Alive, where I play fetch with the dogs and raise some eyebrows with my unconventional descriptions about them for their website. My fun writeups help a number of dogs find loving homes. In the one about a cute little white terrier with beige coloring around his eyes, I describe him as being so good and easy to train that he could enter the priesthood for dogs. He was adopted the very next day.

I also volunteer three days a week at the Livestrong Organization, where I help cancer patients connect with the services they need. In Connecticut, I worked for the Susan G. Koman Foundation setting up golf clinics throughout the US and internationally for breast cancer awareness, so this job was a good fit for me.

My son Alex and his wife, Tara, are kind enough to offer me their comfy couch in their cozy place downtown on West 6th Street for a few weeks while I look for an apartment. Happily, I find a beautiful one overlooking a park and within walking distance of downtown.

No longer a wild boat woman, I exchange my Tevas and

my hiking boots for tennis shoes, and I now wear jeans instead of khaki boat shorts with lots of pockets for boat tools. I'm wearing makeup for the first time in years, and my hair is trimmed by an actual hairdresser instead of having it cut by Lee. The last time he trimmed my hair was a disaster. Looking worried, he said, "Don't worry. It'll grow out!"

I'm going to movies and eating ice cream (a luxury on a boat), and I'm thrilled over having internet whenever I want it.

I'm learning to be a little less open in general, except to my sons, my sisters, and my closest friends. I'm accustomed to being with sailors, who let it all hang out because they never know if they're going to survive the next passage.

When I first arrived, if I spoke about the mystical things that happened while Lee and I were traveling, eyes would glaze over. Happily, I'm now meeting people who enjoy my stories. And I love theirs, as well. We storytellers always, sooner or later, find each other. I'm encouraging my friends to write down their stories before they forget them so they can share their stories with the world.

I'm exploring Austin's lovely neighborhoods on foot and admiring the pretty homes tucked away on tree-lined streets. I'm treating myself to lunches out. At Mother's Restaurant, under the watchful eyes of diners, I try to wrestle open a door (which goes to the trash cans in the back alley) thinking it is an exit door and I end up in a men's bathroom and then turn around quickly after seeing urinals along the wall.

As I'm heading into Alex and Tara's Spanish-style apartment building one afternoon, I slip on a wet patch from a recent rainfall and do a partial banana split just as my son's next-door neighbor walks by. Since I'm a klutz, it's a wonder I survived living on a boat for five and a half years without any injuries.

My son Thomas is now here in Austin with his wife and four children. We're all hoping that Markus and Jen will move here from Vermont. It would be a good fit, especially since he works in the aerospace industry.

I'm now living in a lovely suburb in the Hill Country, which is west of downtown. The topography there reminds me of my childhood in northeastern Alabama. On weekends, Don (a new friend) and I explore old cowboy towns and the Texas countryside with its numerous wineries. We wear our cowboy boots and our cowboy hats as often as we can.

I'd love to take off and explore other parts of the world, but in the meantime, there's just way too much to explore right here.

Acknowledgments

M any heartfelt thanks to my sons, Thomas, Markus, and Alexander Fredell for their steadfast, loving support and acceptance of my five-and-a-half year nomadic, at times dangerous, lifestyle.

Alex, my youngest son, was still in college when I left on this wild voyage and he never once complained. He had to fend for himself and figure things out on his own. I'm sure it wasn't easy. He is a true gentleman and I appreciate him very much.

Many thanks to my partner Don Buchanan for his patience and unwavering support as I put the finishing touches on my book.

Thank you Sara Kocek at Yellowbird Editors and Sally Garland and Anne Sanow at Greenleaf Book Group for your excellent editing work. Thank you also to Greenleaf's Adrianna Hernandez, my project manager and Neil Gonzalez, my cover designer.

I also want to thank Roosevelt Weeks, the former director of the central library in Austin, for his warm hugs and his encouragement as I finished the last chapters of my book. I was usually the first person in line when the library opened at 9:00 a.m. and he always made me feel welcome there.

Additional thanks go to the Laura Bush Library in Westlake and the Lake Travis Community Library in Lakeway, where I spent many hours.

And finally, I would like to thank Sally Adamson Taylor, an accomplished sailor, for being a wonderful role model. While I was cringing in fear during our grueling passage through the Strait of Gibraltar between the Atlantic Ocean and the Mediterranean Sea, she remained calm and collected.

———

I'm sad that Lee isn't here to read my book. He would have enjoyed looking back on our thrilling adventures together.

About the Author

I grew up in Anniston, Alabama, and come from a large, loving, close-knit family with great parents, two brothers, two sisters, loving grandparents, and lots of aunts, uncles, and cousins.

I left home at age eighteen to attend a junior college in Massachusetts. After watching several Swedish movies directed by Ingmar Bergman at Harvard Square, near the center of Cambridge, I decided to spend my third year of college at the University of Stockholm in Sweden. Choosing to ignore my parents' resounding "No!" I applied and was accepted to the university. My parents finally gave in.

On the flight from Atlanta to Kennedy Airport in New York I sat next to a guy named Rodrigo, the son of the president of the General Assembly of the United Nations, Emilio Arenales Catalan. When we disembarked from the plane in New York City he introduced me to his dad who was waiting for him on the tarmac with an entourage of security personnel. Rodrigo called me in Sweden many times and wanted to bring me to his home country, Guatemala, in his father's private plane. By then, however, I had fallen in love with Lars, who was from Stockholm. Lars came from notable families on his mother's side and his father's side. Both of their families owned large lumber mills in northern Sweden.

We were married in my hometown. Soon after our marriage, Lars was hired by an international cosmetic company in New York City, where he trained for an executive position with the company's new subsidiary in Gothenburg, Sweden. Bored with being at home in our tiny rental in Queens on Long Island, I worked at FAO Schwarz on Fifth Avenue and sold toys to famous actors, actresses, and singers. During my childhood, my mother had let us choose Christmas toys from the FAO Schwarz catalogue, so it was a lark to have a short-term job there.

When we moved to Gothenberg, I couldn't obtain a work permit so I took care of two preschool girls for a year while their mother worked. Thanks to them I became fluent in the Swedish language. During our four years on Sweden's west coast my first son, Thomas, was born. He was two years old when we were transferred to England, where Lars worked at the company's European headquarters in London. We settled down in Northwood, Middlesex, a London suburb, where our second son, Markus, was born.

Five years later, Lars was offered a job in White Plains, New York. We moved to southern Connecticut where our third son, Alex, was born. While he was in preschool I took courses in graphic art and became a graphic designer for a chain of newspapers. Since my job was flexible, I worked on the side as a commercial model in Connecticut and New York City for a well-known modeling agency in Greenwich, CT. I was depicted in magazine and newspaper ads as a housewife, a mother, a doctor, a scientist, a high-powered business executive, and a marathon runner. A section of Central Park was shut down for that thrilling photo shoot.

In my spare time, I wrote humorous essays for a newspaper chain in Connecticut about my life experiences. The lead editor published everything I turned in. Meanwhile other writers encouraged me to send my stories to national magazines and I listened to their advice. To help launch that new career direction, I took a writing course at The New School in New York City where my professor invited me to join what was a prestigious group for writers. Through that group I met a woman who worked for O, *The Oprah Magazine* and she encouraged me to send her an essay. Oprah picked my essay to be included in her upcoming book of her favorite essays. Before it came out in print, however, I endured another major life change. And this is where my book begins.

www.ingramcontent.com/pod-product-compliance
Lightning Source LLC
Chambersburg PA
CBHW021210130626
46554CB00004B/1162